IRELAND AND
IRISH-AUSTRALIA

THE STATUE OF FATHER THEOBALD MATHEW
ERECTED IN CORK IN 1864
(See page 123)

IRELAND and IRISH-AUSTRALIA:
STUDIES IN CULTURAL AND POLITICAL HISTORY

Edited by
Oliver MacDonagh
and W.F. Mandle

CROOM HELM
London • Sydney •
Wolfeboro, New Hampshire

© 1986 Oliver MacDonagh & W.F. Mandle
Croom Helm Ltd, Provident House, Burrell Row,
Beckenham, Kent BR3 1AT
Croom Helm Australia Pty Ltd, Suite 4, 6th Floor,
64-76 Kippax Street, Surry Hills, NSW 2010, Australia

British Library Cataloguing in Publication Data
Ireland and Irish-Australia: studies in
    cultural and political history.
    1. Ireland — History
    I. MacDonagh, Oliver   II. Mandle, W.F.
    941.5   DA910

    ISBN 0–7099–4617–1

Croom Helm US, 27 South Main Street,
Wolfeboro, New Hampshire 03894–2069

Library of Congress Cataloging-in-Publication Data

Ireland and Irish-Australia.

    1. Ireland — Civilization. 2. Ireland — Politics
and government. 3. Irish — Australia — History.
I. MacDonagh, Oliver. II. Mandle, W.F.
DA925.17 1986   941.5   86-13485
ISBN 0-7099-4617-1

Printed and bound in Great Britain
by Billing & Sons Limited, Worcester.

Contents

Preface

All the essays in this book originated as papers delivered to a Conference on Ireland and Irish-Australia held at the Australian National University in Canberra, 27–30 August 1985. This Conference was a successor to that on Irish Culture and Nationalism, also held in Canberra, in 1980. It is hoped that the series will continue, at shorter intervals, and that, as with the 1980 and 1985 Conferences, the majority of the proceedings will be published later. One important feature of the past — and we trust, future — Conferences is that attendance and participation were not confined to professional scholars. We aim not only to disseminate the fruits of new research and fresh reflections but also to enlist public support for the causes of Irish-Australian studies and the study of Irish history, literature and culture in Australia.

We are very grateful to our sponsoring institutions, the Department of History in the Research School of Social Sciences at the ANU and the School of Liberal Studies at the Canberra College of Advanced Education. To these we must add the Humanities Research Centre at the ANU which provided us with a venue and bore our intrusion most patiently and kindly. We are also deeply grateful to the Irish Cultural Relations Committee for its generous support of the enterprise, and in particular to the Irish Ambassador to Australia, His Excellency Mr Joseph Small, for his unceasing encouragement and help and his unstinting hospitality.

The greatest contribution of all to the Conference's success was the work of its Secretary, Mrs Pamela Crichton, and she was most ably assisted by the Secretary of the Department of History, Mrs Beverly Gallina. It would be hard to find a formula of gratitude which would adequately convey how much we owe to them.

O. MacD.
W.F.M.

Notes on Contributors

Donald H. Akenson is Professor of History at Queen's University, Kingston, Canada. His publications include *The United States and Ireland* (1973), *Between Two Revolutions: Island Magee, Co. Antrim, 1798–1920* (1979) and *A Protestant in Purgatory; Richard Whately: Archbishop of Dublin* (1981).

Gerard Brennan is a Justice of the High Court of Australia.

Vincent Buckley has a personal Chair in the Department of English at the University of Melbourne. Among his recent publications are *The Pattern* and *Late Winter Child* (1979), *Cutting Green Hay — Friendships, Movements and Cultural Conflicts in Australia's Greatest Decades* (1983) and *Memory Ireland: Insights into the Contemporary Irish Condition* (1985).

Philip Bull lectures in History at La Trobe University. He was Assistant Keeper of Western Manuscripts at the Bodleian Library, Oxford, before he took up his present position.

Tom Dunne lectures in History at University College, Cork. He published *Theobald Wolfe Tone: Colonial Outsider — An Analysis of his Political Philosophy* in 1982, and is at present preparing *Nationalism: the Irish Experience* and *England, Ireland and the Empire 1868–86* for publication.

David Fitzpatrick lectures at Trinity College, Dublin and is the author of *Politics and Irish Life, 1913–21* (1977) and *Irish Emigration 1801–1921* (1984).

James Griffin is a Senior Research Fellow in the Department of Pacific and South-East Asian History in the Research School of Pacific Studies, Australian National University. He is the co-author of *Papua-New Guinea: A Political History* (1979).

Ken Inglis is a Professor of History in the Research School of Social Sciences, Australian National University. His works include *Churches and the Working Classes in Victorian England* (1963), *The Australian Colonists: an Exploration of Social History 1788–1870* (1974) and *The Rehearsal: Australians at War in the Sudan 1885* (1985).

Edith Mary Johnston is Professor of History at Macquarie University. Her publications include *Great Britain and Ireland 1760–1800* (1963) and *Ireland in the Eighteenth Century* (1974).

Oliver MacDonagh is W.K. Hancock Professor of History in the Research School of Social Sciences at the Australian National University, and Chairman of the Management Committee of the Australian Bicentennial History Project. His publications include *Ireland: the Union and its Aftermath* (1968; rev. edn, 1977), *Early Victorian Government* (1977) and *States of Mind* (1983; rev. edn, 1985).

W.F. Mandle is Head of the School of Liberal Studies at the Canberra College of Advanced Education. He is the author of numerous articles on sports history and of *Going it Alone: Australia's National Identity in the Twentieth Century* (1978).

F.X. Martin is Professor of Medieval History at University College, Dublin and a General Editor of the *New History of Ireland*.

Patrick O'Farrell holds a personal Chair in History at the University of New South Wales. His books include *Ireland's English Question* (1971), *England and Ireland since 1800* (1975), *The Catholic Church and Community in Australia* (1977) and *Letters from Irish-Australia 1825–1929* (1984).

Portia Robinson lectures in History at Macquarie University. She is the author of *The Hatch and Brood of Time, a Study of the First Generation of Native-Born White Australians c.1788–1828* (1985).

Peter Steele lectures in the English Department at the University of Melbourne and is Provincial of the Australian Province of the Society of Jesus. He is the author of *Word from Lilliput* (1973) and *Jonathan Swift, Preacher and Jester* (1978).

A.T.Q. Stewart lectures in the Department of Modern History at the Queen's University of Belfast. His publications include *The Ulster Crisis* (1967), *The Narrow Ground: Aspects of Ulster, 1609–1969* (1977) and *Edward Carson* (1981).

Iain Topliss lectures in the English Department at La Trobe University, where he helps edit *Meridian: the La Trobe University English Review*. He received his doctorate from Cambridge for a thesis on Maria Edgeworth. He is planning a study of the writing of history in eighteenth-century Ireland.

1   Data: What is Known about the Irish in North America?

Donald H. Akenson

I

The great era for the Irish in North America, the period in which they made up the great proportion of the population and had the greatest impact as an ethnic group, was the nineteenth century.[1]

This is not to gainsay their considerable importance and interest since then, but merely to suggest that as historians we must maintain a perspective and remember that more recent events, like objects held close to our eyes, are not necessarily larger or more important than those at a distance.

The case of the Irish in North America obviously is relevant for students of the Irish in Australia and New Zealand. Not only is there a comparative dimension involved, but there is the matter of the 'portability' of the scholarly literature. There is a vast body of writing on the Irish in North America (particularly in the United States) and to the extent that it is based on accurate data and on sensible interpretations of those data, the literature will provide useful suggestions for Australasian scholars. But, fair warning: if the data-base of the North American literature is inadequate, or the reading of the data biased, then valid comparisons to the Australian and New Zealand cases will be impossible and the inspirations provided by the North American writings will be no more useful than opium dreams.

What is meant in this paper by the term 'Irish'? For our purposes, 'Irish' includes all persons who make or made their permanent home in the geographic island of Ireland; this includes Protestants as well as Catholics, Ulstermen as well as Kerrymen, descendants of Norman lords and of Scottish planters as well as of earlier Celtic invaders, speakers of English as well as of Irish Gaelic. And, when they settled in several New Worlds, it includes all those individuals and their descendants.

1

This non-sectarian definition has three advantages: it avoids what James Joyce called 'the old pap of racial hatred'. Of course, one must pay attention to the various Irish sub-groups, but only while remembering that each of them stemmed from a larger, common Irish socio-political system. Further, this definition has the virtue of being easily operational: one does not need to make complex decisions about who 'really' was Irish. Granted, someone in North America who belonged to the Ancient Order of Hibernians or to the Orange Order probably had a stronger sense of ethnic identity — was 'more Irish' — than someone whose sole act of ethnic affiliation was to fill in a census form every ten years, but so meagre is our knowledge at present that it would be hubris to try to become too subtle in our shading. Finally, this simple definition has the advantage of inclusiveness. For scholars who wish to use the behaviour of the Irish in various New Worlds to cast light on the home culture, this is particularly important, as one needs to know not only what the most frequent modes of behaviour were, but what were the ranges of behaviour.

In collecting data, particularly demographic material, on the Irish in the New World, one must carefully distinguish between the immigrants from Ireland and their descendants. This seems a simple-minded point, but, alas, Canadian and American historians, as well as contemporary nineteenth-century observers, have been very muddy about what they mean. Often 'Irish' is employed to mean immigrants from Ireland, but, equally often, it is used to refer to all their descendants as well. Obviously, if an historian collects data only on the immigrant generation and then writes that 'the Irish' in North America behaved in a certain way his work will be terribly misleading. Thus, let me suggest that we agree to denominate the migrant generation as the 'Irish-born' (the term most often used in census materials) or as 'first-generation' North Americans (the most common label employed by sociologists). When 'the Irish' in North America are discussed, the reference is to the multigenerational collective experience of the migrants *and* their descendants. In underscoring this distinction one is implicitly emphasising the point that the chronicle of the immigrant generation is only a part of the story of any ethnic group.

II

The accepted scholarly interpretation of the Irish in the United States is encapsulated in William V. Shannon's oft-quoted phrase, 'The history of the Irish in America is founded on a paradox. The Irish were a rural people in Ireland and became a city people in the United States.' Thus, the central question for historians of the Irish in America has been: Why did they become an urban people?

In response to this question, a general, if not quite universal, consensus has emerged among American social historians. First, it is generally accepted that the Irish landed in America so poor that they could not immediately move inland, but had to stay in the Atlantic seaboard cities. Secondly, it is believed that even when the Irish had accumulated enough cash to move inland to farm they did not do so, largely because the former Irish peasants did not have the necessary skills to farm in the New World. Or, to put it less obliquely: they were too technologically backward to be good farmers. Thirdly, it is generally accepted that even had the Irishman possessed both the money and skills to farm, he would not have chosen to do so, because the Famine had so terribly traumatised him. 'The Irish rejected the land for the land rejected him,' is William Shannon's summation. And, fourthly, it is generally agreed that the Irish were culturally unadapted to rural American social life. The Irish, it is claimed, needed close and compatible neighbours. The loneliness of a farm, or even of the rural hamlet, was not for them. Professor Lawrence McCaffrey has suggested that 'when the Irish finally did begin to move west, most of them preferred places like Chicago, St Louis, St Paul, and San Francisco to farms'.

In their writings, historians of the Irish in the United States often use the term 'Irish-American' to denote the Irish immigrants and their descendants in the United States. That term is a code-word. It actually means 'Irish Roman Catholic'. Excluded from it are all Protestants whether they be of Ulster-Scots origin (often called the 'Scotch-Irish' in American historical writing) or of Anglo-Irish background. In other words, there is an equation in American historical writing of the terms 'Irish', 'Irish-American,' and 'Irish Catholic'.

The validity of this equation is central to most studies of the Irish in the United States. In order for the equation to be valid, it is virtually universally presumed: (1) that the really important events in the story of the Irish in America did not begin until the Great

Famine of the mid-nineteenth century; (2) that after mid-century, migration by Irish Protestants to the United States was virtually nil; usually it is held that the only significant Protestant migration was that of the Ulster-Scots and this movement is said to have been completed by the end of the eighteenth century.

These, then, are the main components of the agreed explanation of why the Irish in the United States became a city people. What has been the interpretation of the Irish in Canada put forward by Canadian historians? That is hard to say. The only serious attempt at a general history of the Irish in Canada was Nicholas Flood Davin's work of 1878, a goldmine of anecdote, but hardly a scholarly depiction. There has been no attempt at a modern synthesis. Instead, there are a few truly awful works of ethnic piety, and numerous incidental references in regional histories that indicate that the Irish in Canada seem to have scattered themselves all over the country, both city and countryside. Until recently there were only three analytic attempts at dealing with the process of assimilation of the Irish into Canadian society (by John Mannion, H. Clare Pentland, and Kenneth Duncan) and two of these (Pentland and Duncan) began with the fundamental assumption that the Irish in Canada in the last century were a city people. These two studies were widely circulated and highly influential.

Two recent studies, however, have established that the Irish in nineteenth-century Canada were *not* a city people. In the more important of these two, Professors A. Gordon Darroch and Michael D. Ornstein drew a large nationwide random sample from the heads of households recorded in the 1871 census (approximately 10,000 cases) and they found that the Irish were more likely to support themselves by farming than by any other occupation: 58.3 per cent of Protestants of Irish ethnicity and 44.3 per cent for Catholics.[2] When one takes into account the fact that farmers were only part of the rural economic structure, it is clear that most persons of Irish ethnicity in Canada lived in small towns and in the countryside and that both Irish Catholics and Irish Protestants could successfully adapt to non-urban life. The second study, my own on the Irish in Ontario, showed that both Irish Catholics and Irish Protestants, both immigrants and their descendants, settled overwhelmingly in the countryside. For example, in 1871, approximately 66.3 per cent of Irish-descended Catholics and 83.2 per cent of Irish-descended Protestants were living in rural areas. Both Protestants and Catholics were able to stand the loneliness and isolation of pioneering life and both were able to meet the technological requirements of Canadian farming.

III

Thus, we have a historical problem: the accepted view is that in the nineteenth century the Irish in the United States were a city people, and the numerically established fact is that in Canada they were a rural people. Faced with this seeming conundrum there is a temptation to be quintessentially Canadian, that is, to be deferential and polite. One could murmur a suggestion that the American pattern is the norm and that the Canadian is something of a deviation, a regional deviation, our own to be sure, but a deviation none the less. Or, one could avoid the possibility of confrontation with the American historians simply by hoisting the national flag and sailing away: Canada is a different country, after all, and that the Irish in Canada behaved differently from the Irish in the United States requires no explanation, just acceptance.

That will not do.

I will argue below that there is here a genuine clash of-historical interpretations whose mutual incompatibility cannot be obviated, and, that the Canadian version has a much higher probability of being accurate than does the American.

Of course, the American and Canadian cases are not identical, but one should not throw up unnecessary roadblocks to their comparison. By roadblocks, I mean facile suggestions such as: that the US and the Canadian cases are not comparable because there was a higher proportion of Protestants among the Irish migrants to Canada than to the US; that those Irish Catholics who came to Canada were 'loyalist' in politics, as compared to those who went to the republic to the south; and that the Irish Catholics who moved to Canada were in some ways culturally advantaged in comparison to those who went to the United States.

Concerning the first of these objections, it is true that there were proportionately fewer Catholics than Protestants among the Irish in Canada — in the case of Ontario, roughly one-third of the Irish cohort was Catholic — but the size of the total Irish Catholic group in Canada certainly is large enough to permit it to be studied as a separate sub-group. Over the run of nineteenth-century Canadian census data one has an aggregate of several million data points on persons of Irish Catholic background. In its main features this group can legitimately be compared and contrasted with the Irish Catholics in the United States.

The objection that the Irish Catholics who came to Canada were in some ways not real Irishmen, because they settled under the Crown, is doubly spurious. In the first place, no one has yet shown that the political outlook of the bulk of the Irish Catholic migrants to America was any different from the attitudes of those who sailed to Canada. (Remember: we are here trying to explain the apparently contrasting behaviours of large bodies of people, and are not concerned with highly-politicised minorities.) Indeed, the standard study of nineteenth-century Irish Catholic activism, Thomas N. Brown's *Irish-American Nationalism: 1870–1890* (J.B. Lippincott, Philadelphia, 1966), argues that the Irish nationalism of most Irish Catholics in the US was a response to their problems in American society, not the result of a set of strong beliefs brought from the homeland. Thus, one cannot use political attitudes in the New World as an independent explanatory variable. Second, and more important, *even if* Irish Catholic migrants to America tended to be 'republican' in political outlook and those who arrived in Canada tended to be 'loyalist', that point would be irrelevant to the question at hand, unless one could specify the causal linkage whereby loyalism to the British Crown made a person a more effective rural pioneer than did distaste for the imperial throne. Certainly the idea that republicanism is not compatible with success in a rural environment would have come as a great shock to the more radical members of the Irish Land League and to successive governments of the Irish Free State and of the Republic of Ireland.

As for the third suggestion, that the Irish Catholics who migrated to the United States were in some way culturally and technologically disadvantaged as compared to those who migrated to Canada, I can find no evidence that the abilities and acumen of the Irish Catholics in America were any less than those of the Irish Catholics in Canada (or, for that matter, of the Irish Protestants in either country). At heart, any such argument that the Canadian experience is an inappropriate comparison to the American one, must come down to an assertion (suitably disguised to make it palatable to American social historians) that among the Catholic migrants to North America, Canada received the winners and the United States the losers. That is: that Canada received those who were able to adapt to forms of agricultural technology unknown in the home country, who had the character to cope with the isolation of life in the countryside, in addition to having the tenacity to amass enough resources to enter commercial farming. Manifestly, this is hard to accept. Yet, unless one is willing to argue that the difference between Canada and the United States with regard to Irish Catholics was simply the difference between winners and losers, and unless one can specify the set of mechanisms that resulted in such an efficient social sorting as between these two countries in the New World, then one must conclude that the two groups are legitimately comparable and look for specific mechanisms in the New World to explain their apparent divergence.

IV

At this point a fundamental question of the historian's craft arises. Historians must continually check the ground on which they stand. Before attempting to explain any phenomenon, a good historian asks: Did that really happen, or is it merely my own perception that it occurred? Assuming that one accepts the evidentiary canons of our profession, there are myriad practical techniques for distinguishing historical reality from historians' fancies. In terms of the present discussion, the reality–perception problem may be formulated as follows: given that the Canadian data prove beyond dispute that in the nineteenth century the Irish in Canada were not a city people, what is the evidence that the Irish in America were?

In order to generalise about the occupational and residential patterns of the Irish migrants to the New World and of their descendants, one needs to have information on every individual or a representative sample of those individuals. The only potential source of such data are government-sponsored censuses. Local studies, such as those of one city or county, are of great intrinsic interest, but will cast no light on general, nationwide patterns and, indeed, can be very misleading. Thus the matter at hand can be further refined into a single operational question: Are the nineteenth-century American census data as good as the Canadian? For convenience the character of the available census data is summarised in Table 1.1.

A primary rule of historical scholarship is that in the usual case the grounds of presumption are negative. That is, an event or phenomenon is assumed not to have occurred unless there is positive

Table 1.1: North American Census Data in the Nineteenth Century

	Canada	United States
First national census	1871. Various provincial censuses before that.	1790. Revised in late 1920s by ACLS to give ethnicity data. This and subsequent ethnic revisions unacceptable. (See Akenson, 'Estimates of Ethnicity', *passim*.)
Pre-Famine enumeration of the Irish-born	In various provincial censuses. 1841–42 for Ontario.	None.
Post-Famine enumeration of the Irish-born	In various provincial censuses, and in dominion censuses of 1871, 1881, 1891, 1901.	1850, 1860, 1870, 1880, 1890, 1900.
Enumeration of entire multi-generational ethnic group by primary affiliation	1871, 1881, 1901.	Never done. However (a) 1870 'yes/no' question *re* foreign-born parents; (b) 1880, 1890, 1900, nationality of foreign-born parents tallied; (c) 1970 and 1980 ethnicity question asked, but multiple ethnicities permitted.
Enumeration of Irish-born by religion	Done at major censuses; historian must do own cross-tabulations.	Religious persuasion never asked. One experiment done in 1957; results suppressed.
Enumeration of persons of Irish ethnicity by religion	1871, 1881, 1901; historian must do own cross-tabulations.	Data never collected.
City/non-city enumeration of the Irish-born	Done in most provincial censuses and in all dominion censuses; historian must do own cross-tabulations.	Published data available for 1850, 1860, 1870, 1880, 1890, 1900. Require some processing by the historian.
City/non-city enumeration of the Irish-born by religion	Ditto.	Impossible to do.

City/non-city enumeration of persons of Irish ethnicity	1871, 1881, 1901; historian must do own cross-tabulations.	Impossible to do but data on residence of first and second generation may be inferred 1880, 1890, 1900.
City/non-city enumeration of persons of Irish ethnicity by religion	Ditto.	Impossible to do.
Occupational enumeration of the Irish-born	Done for heads of household at most provincial censuses and in all dominion censuses. Historian must do own cross-tabulations.	Published data available for 1870, 1880, 1890, 1900. Require some processing by the historian.
Occupational enumeration of the Irish-born, by religion	Ditto.	Impossible to do.
Occupational enumeration of persons of Irish ethnicity	1871, 1881, 1901. Historian must do own cross-tabulations.	Impossible to do, but information on first and second generation may be inferred 1880, 1890, 1900.
Occupational enumeration of persons of Irish ethnicity by religion	Ditto.	Ditto.

evidence that it indeed did happen. (An exception is made for certain occurrences, mostly in the physical world — such as the rise of the sun in the east — wherein the event occurs at regular and predictable intervals and is presumed to have occurred unless negative proof to the contrary exists.) Table 1.1 suggests that there is no positive evidence available either for the existence of the fundamental 'fact' of the history of the Irish as an ethnic group in America — that they were a city people — or of the secondary 'facts': that the Irish in America became an important phenomenon only after the Famine and that Protestants migrated to the US in such small numbers in the nineteenth century as to be virtually negligible. Notice that there are no demographic data whatsoever on the religion of the Irish in America, that there never has been a satisfactory enumeration of the Irish as a multi-generational ethnic group, and that it is not the story of the Irish that begins in 1850, but merely the run of data on Irish immigrants in the United States!

Some of you may be reminded of the story, perhaps apocryphal, of King Charles II and the *savants* of the Royal Society. The monarch set the sages a pretty exercise, namely to explain why, if one added a live fish to a bowl of water the vessel did not overflow, but if one introduced a dead fish, water spilled down the sides of the bowl. The professors explained why this 'fact' occurred. Similarly, an extraordinary amount of ingenuity, not to say guile and creativity, has been expended by historians of the Irish in America in explaining a set of demographic 'facts' for whose existence there is no affirmative evidence. King Charles would have been amused.

V

Strictly speaking, the discussion could end here, and if this were a formal debate, one would sit down: having shown that in a situation where the grounds of presumption are negative, there is no affirmative proof, one has won the day. Let me go further, however, and indicate that within the unfortunately rudimentary US demographic data there are pieces of positive evidence which suggest that the Irish in America were *not* a city people.

Consider the 1870 US census, the first one for which cross-tabulations of Irish birth and place of residence are easily done. A standard definition of a city employed by urban historians of the period is that it has a concentration of 25,000 or more persons. In

1870 44.5 per cent of the Irish-born in the US lived in the 50 largest cities, the smallest of which had a population of 26,766. Certainly that is a significant degree of concentration amongst Irish immigrants. However, it is also a statement that well over half of the Irish immigrants to the US did *not* live in cities.

Actually, though, even the statistic that, roughly, 55 per cent of Irish immigrants did not live in cities in 1870 considerably overstates the degree of city residence among the Irish. Why? First, because 1870 is a relatively late date on the curve of urbanisation of the US. The nation was roughly 75 per cent rural in 1870, but had been 85 per cent so in 1850 and 91 per cent in 1830. Second, and more important, because the 1870 residence data are only for the immigrant generation and not for the entire ethnic group. The children and grandchildren of Irish immigrants who had arrived earlier in the century are excluded from these figures, and they would have had a much higher propensity to live outside of cities than would the immigrant generation of 1870. This holds in part because the second and third generations' parents and grandparents had arrived at a time when the US was more rural, and thus had been more likely to feed originally into a non-city economy, and in part because by the second and third generation, resources would have been accumulated that permitted the children and grandchildren of Irish immigrants to participate fully in the high degree of geographic mobility that characterised nineteenth-century American society.

Mention of the second, third and subsequent generations calls attention to the existence in American census data of a *demographically invisible majority* among the nineteenth-century Irish in America. One can obtain occupational and residential tabulation of the Irish-born only beginning in 1870, a time when there were approximately 1.85 million Irish-born in the US. However, between 1820 and 1850 there had been very roughly a minimum of 1.04 million Irish immigrants into the US. (The sources are very murky about the precise number.) Of course immigrants have children and for each Irish-immigrant of, say, 1830, one can expect there to have been second-generation offspring by 1850 and third-generation by 1870. And even the Famine migrants would have had children, and in some cases, grandchildren, by 1870. Precisely what the 'multiplier' was cannot be determined, but strong indirect evidence suggests that by 1870 there were considerably more second and later generation individuals in the Irish ethnic cohort than there were immigrants. Yet there are no residential or occupational data on this, the larger portion, of the Irish ethnic cohort, and these are the very people in the cohort who were least apt to be trapped in large urban ghettos.

Having suggested that an unprejudiced look at the US demographic data provides positive evidence that the Irish in America were not a city people and also that their collective history began before mid-century, one must confess that there is no American census data indication that there was a large number of Protestants in the US-Irish ethnic cohort — nor can there be, given the American government's refusal to ask people what their religion is. However, Irish population, both Presbyterian and Anglican, declined significantly in absolute numbers, although proportionately less than did the Catholic. Moreover, given that, in all probability, the Protestants, being better-off than the Catholics, did not suffer as high a mortality rate as did the Catholics, it follows that the Protestants probably had an emigration rate equal to that of the Irish Catholics.

This point forces the traditional historian of the Irish in the US onto an uncomfortable cleft-stick. He can agree that, yes, the Protestants did have as high a propensity to emigrate from Ireland as did the Catholics, but that this has nothing to do with American history, for all the Protestants went to Canada. This is highly unlikely, for a number of reasons that I do not have the time to develop in the present context, but even if it were true, a central part of the traditional interpretation would have been surrendered: that is, it would mean that the data which show that the Irish in the US were not a city people would mean necessarily that Irish Catholics in the US were not a city people. Alternatively, a defender of the traditional view could admit, yes, there was a significant Irish Protestant migration into America, but that the Protestants were the ones who settled in non-city areas and, thus, the idea of the Irish Catholics as a city people is saved. There are statistical reasons why this suggestion is inherently improbable. Even were it true, its acceptance would force the abandonment of another segment of the traditional interpretation: in this case the idea that in the US one can equate 'Irish-American' with Irish Catholic.

In sum, not only is there no affirmative demographic evidence for the traditional view of the Irish in nineteenth-century America, there is some, admittedly indirect, positive evidence that the traditional ideas are not merely not-proved, but are directly opposite to the truth.

VI

No one who has spent any significant time in Irish studies will deny that there are some highly impressive studies of the Irish in specific localities in the United States, and some compelling biographies of individual Irishmen. Yet, one nevertheless is left with the puzzling facts that the widely accepted generalisations made about the Irish as a nationwide ethnic group are without evidentiary support; that there is some demographic evidence which suggests that the traditional ideas are not proven, but are most certainly wrong; further the Canadian case strongly suggests that the common cultural assumptions about nineteenth-century Irish immigrants are wildly inaccurate and indeed are virtually racist in their assumptions of Irish cultural backwardness.

Two questions then remain: by what means have the historians of the Irish in the United States misled themselves? And why?

The mechanisms of self-delusion are not complex. Elementary logical fallacies — that is, ways of falling into error — have permeated historians of the Irish in America to ignore the lack of a satisfactory data-base. Time allows mention of only three of these but these are endemic. First, that the fallacy of viewing a subset as if it were a whole, is very common. One should not discuss a subset or any body of data until one places it in the context of the entire body from which it is drawn. Sometimes a subset will be almost perfectly representative of the larger body from which it is taken. This is the case of a well-designed random sample and in such instances, after one has established the validity of one's sampling procedures, one can then discuss the sample as revealing characteristics of the whole body of data. In the case of the non-random subset, however, one cannot do so. In practical terms, this fallacy of misusing subsets is most frequent in studies of Irish-Catholic urban communities. These studies virtually never place the particular data being presented in their proper demographic context, the Irish throughout the United States. At their worst such studies lead to a dizzyingly tautological spiral: a scholar studies only urban Irish Catholics and then concludes that the Irish in America were urban Irish Catholics.

Secondly, the fallacy of false relativism has been often embraced by historians of the Irish in the United States. A neutral example will indicate how this works:

1. Take the case of Scandinavians and multiple sclerosis. It is well established that they have a higher incidence of the disease than do most other European groups.

2. The Scandinavians, therefore, can be said to be relatively prone to multiple sclerosis.

3. It would be absurd, however, to describe most of the Scandinavian population as suffering from the disease, because actually only a very small minority of the population experience it.

Absurd, yes, but in Irish-American studies it prevails, in the following form:

1. It is a well-established fact that the Irish in nineteenth-century America had a higher incidence of city residence than did most other European immigrants.

2. The Irish, therefore, can be said to have a relatively high propensity for city living.

3. Therefore, it is concluded the Irish were a city people.

Absurd, yes, again, but it is through this elementary fallacy that the compelling evidence that the Irish were not a city people is wished away.

Thirdly, nominalism as a fallacious way of thinking is rampant. At its simplest this takes the crude form of renaming things that do not agree with one's preconceptions, and thus they are expected to disappear. It sometimes is argued that the only real Irish in America were those who kept a sharp sense of ethnic identity, lived in large Irish ghettos, went to Mass, and supported the *Clan na Gael*. A fascinating mode of thought to be sure: one conjectures what the reaction might be if these scholars employed a similar technique in dealing with, say, American blacks, suggesting that the only real blacks were those who lived in large cities, played basketball, and attended Pentecostal churches.

One could go on. The point is that historians of the Irish in the United States, having decided on grounds external to the evidence and prior to assessment of its fundamental character, what it should reveal, have produced studies whose aim is to demonstrate the centrality of those assumed features. That this is done unconsciously makes the errors no less misleading. What is called for in reaction to these pervasive shortcomings is a discussion of the Irish in North America within the canons of responsible historical method.

One of the chief, and unsung, roles of the historian is to protect the dead from the living. My brief concerning the Irish in the United States is that they were a much more adaptable, less culturally backward group than is usually believed.

The history of the Irish in America (and much of the history of the Irish homeland) has been written with a rigid cultural determinism, wherein virtually all matters of economic and social status are seen as being set primarily by cultural factors, particularly by religion and by linguistics. For example, in a widely-read recent study, Dr Kerby Miller suggested that in the

age of migration, 1790–1922, many Catholic Irish were more communal, dependent, fatalistic and prone to accept conditions passively than were the Protestants they encountered in either Ireland or America, and less individualistic, independent, optimistic and given to initiative than were these Protestants . . . . Indeed their perspectives were so pre-modern that to observers from modern business cultures, they often seemed 'irresponsible', even 'feckless' or adolescent.[3]

And, as the argument goes, they could not do well in America, particularly in frontier farming or in small-town commercial life. There is no profit in belabouring the obvious fact that such cultural determinism is insupportable, given the massive Canadian empirical evidence to the contrary. The Canadian case lays to rest forever the notions that the Irish Catholics were too impoverished, too technologically backward, too burned by the Famine to enter farming in the New World and too afraid of frontier loneliness to adapt to rural life in North America. They could adapt and in myriad cases they did.

The curious and unsettling point that remains is why has a set of stereotypes of the Irish in the United States developed and been propagated? Had an outsider said such things about the cultural backwardness of the Irish, he immediately (and with good reason) would have been attacked for harbouring ethnic prejudices so strong as to border on racialism. These charges are never raised, however, because, first, the majority of people who have written the history of the Irish in the United States as an urban Catholic cohort are themselves of Irish-Catholic background, and secondly, it is almost equally certain that the majority of professional historians who are serious consumers of this history are of urban Catholic backgrounds as well.

What we have in the generally accepted story of the Irish in the United States is a set of constructs that are mythological, and their function can be analysed like those of any myth. I would speculate that the mythology produced by the historians of the Irish in the United States not only has been acceptable to the Irish-Americans as a group, but has served a vital social function. In fact, I suspect that what historians have propounded as the social history of the Irish in America is merely the articulation and codification at a relatively high intellectual level of a set of useful and protective folk-beliefs that the Irish-American community has evolved concerning itself.

How could it be of any benefit for a group to have its agreed history so out of kilter with the actual evidence? For the Irish-Americans, the historical mythology seems to have served two functions. The first of these has been to make the past less of an alien time, less of a strange and foreign land, than actually is the case. The patently unjustified belief that the Irish were a city people from the very beginning of their history in the United States has grafted a false sense of collective continuity into the accepted historical mythology of the Irish-Americans. The migration of the children and grandchildren of rural and small-town Irish persons into the cities during the later years of the nineteenth and during the twentieth centuries must have been as important and traumatic a break with the past for the Irish as for any other group. Yet, by covering over this disjuncture in the historical experience of the Irish-Americans as a group, the accepted historical mythology has allowed members of the group more easily to appropriate relevant meanings (true or false, it matters not) from what they hear of events of the middle of the last century, particularly the Famine era.

The second major attribute of the myths of Irish-American history is that they have created a false, but highly useful, collective baseline against which to measure the performance of members of the ethnic group in the twentieth century. Almost perversely, from the early years of the present century onwards, Irish-Americans have had a vested interest in 'bad-mouthing' their forebears. Specifically, by propagating the myth that the Irish-Catholic migrants to America were too technologically backward and too financially incontinent to save enough money even to get into frontier farming, historians implicitly have made the twentieth-century Irish look good. After all, look at how far back their great-grandparents were.

Within the accepted mythology of Irish-American history, lies embedded a demonology. The historical myth holds that the reason that the Irish-Americans were stuck in cities and were not able therefore to reap the bounties of the American heartland, was that the bastard British forged shackles in the form of cultural and economic limitations that could not be shaken off, even in the New World. To an individual who was not making much of an economic success of his life in late nineteenth or early twentieth-century America, it must have been a great comfort to have been able to blame the old enemy rather than either the discriminatory structure of the American republic or one's own self.

The real test of any mythology is not its accuracy — that is irrelevant — but whether or not it works. To work, its components must fit together smoothly and without gross and unsettling internal contradictions, and the myth must serve a need, a function, in the community wherein it is believed. Considered as a system of myth, the accepted view of the Irish in America has served well. It has worked.

Historians, though, should not so easily be led to confuse myth and history.

Notes and References

1. Amplification of the views given in this paper and detailed discussion of the evidence on which they are based are to be found in Donald H. Akenson, *Being Had: Historians, Evidence and the Irish in North America* (P.D. Meany Co., Toronto, 1985); *The Irish in Ontario: A Study in Rural History* (McGill Queen's University Press, Kingston and Montreal, 1984); 'Why the Accepted Estimates of the Ethnicity of the American People, 1790, are Unacceptable', *William and Mary Quarterly*, vol.41 (1984), pp.102–19, 125–9; 'An Agnostic View of the Historiography of the Irish Americans', *Labour/Le Travailleur* (Fall 1984), pp.123–59.

2. Darroch and Ornstein's project is ongoing, and has the largest data-base of any work yet assayed in nineteenth-century ethnic history in North America. Two of their articles are seminal: 'Ethnicity and Occupational Structure in 1871: The Vertical Mosaic in Historical Perspective', *Canadian Historical Review*, vol.61 (September 1980), pp.305–33; and 'Ethnicity and Class, Transitions over a Decade: Ontario, 1861–1871', in Canadian Historical Association, *Historical Papers 1984*, pp.111–37.

3. 'Emigrants and Exiles: Irish Cultures and Irish Emigration to North America, 1790–1922', *Irish Historical Studies*, vol.22, no.86 (1980), p.105.

2 The Irish and Law in Australia

Gerard Brennan

Let me start with an Irish statement: the subject is too big for me to talk on. I am not an expert on the Irish people and I do not know all the law in Australia. Well, you may ask, if the subject is too big, why did you agree to speak on it? The primary answer is simple: a request by Oliver MacDonagh is not easy to refuse. The secondary answer is more complex. I and many other lawyers in Australia are indebted to the Irish, not only for our biological heritage, but for such gifts of compassion, generosity, humour and irreverence as we have ourselves inherited or have enjoyed in our colleagues. I and other lawyers in this nation are indebted to the law in Australia. It is the emanation of our people's culture, a reference point of principle in an increasingly turbulent sea of pragmatism, a system which we help to mould and by which we in turn are moulded. It is our hearth and our home. And so I undertake this task as a kind of penitential work — perhaps an expiation for sins of ingratitude to those who, in myriad ways, have given to my generation a legal system which, if kept in good repair, can serve the needs of a free and confident nation.

The Irish contribution to this system is at once significant and indefinable. Its significance can be charted in part by reference to some of the great lawyers who came from Ireland to this country, and who were distinguished practitioners, judges and legislators in the infant colonies. Their contribution, though of the highest importance, does not exhaust the Irish influence on law in this country. For my part, I think more of some of the counsel of Irish origin with whom I practised at the Bar in Queensland and whose facility with language and whose refusal to regard life too seriously made them powerful advocates before the jury. They belonged, so it was said — and not always in laudatory tones — to the Irish school of advocacy. When they would address themselves, usually after a dramatic pause, to the gentlemen of the jury — for 30 years ago sex discrimination was the norm in jury panels — the turning-point in the case was reached and the *cognoscenti* would wander in

18

to listen to the flowing oratory. The Old Munster Circuit had no better stories to tell, no more pungent witticisms to recall. There was, of course, an earnestness of purpose to it all. Justice was not an abstract virtue; it was something to strive for day by day. And if, at the end of the day, a sense of failure or injustice lingered, you might find counsel being consoled and refreshed by listening to Emmet's Speech from the Dock or Padraigh Pearse's Oration at the grave of O'Donovan Rossa. (A record of the same was frequently played to the faithful in a set of Chambers renowned for good conversation, unshakable views and some humour.)

I must not get lost in reminiscence. I must go back to the beginning and recall some of the eminent few and the contributions which they made to the establishment of a legal system in this country. Of course, legislators and administrators played critical parts in the establishment of Australia's legal system, but I have put most of them aside to focus on the professional lawyer. To try to keep these remarks within tolerable limits, I have largely passed by the mass of Australian lawyers born of Irish parents, although they were the chief means by which Irish traditions and values influenced Australian legal institutions. I shall mention those of Irish birth who played a significant role in establishing the Australian legal system, though I must caution that the list is not exhaustive and emphases may be misplaced.

The British settlements which were established in various parts of what is now Australia were governed by and under English law. Colonial modification of, or abrogation of, English laws that were applicable to the colonies were valid only to the extent authorised by English law. Until recent times, that has been the underlying theory and the practical reality of legal development in this country. The laws of the Aboriginal peoples were largely unknown by the colonial governments and have received little recognition by the Anglo-Australian legal system,[1] although the practices of some Aboriginal peoples have sometimes been taken into account in imposing criminal punishment. The application of English law — imperial legislation, common law and equity — was administered by courts from which appeal lay to the Privy Council. The Privy Council, whose remaining jurisdiction has become anachronistic and a source of inconsistency in Australian legal principle, was in earlier times the tribunal which kept Australian law uniform and in conformity with the law of England.

It follows, of course, that Irish lawyers in the Australian colonies had but a limited opportunity to contribute to the development of a peculiarly Australian legal system. They were necessarily priests of an established oracle, and it was an oracle with which they were familiar.

Prior to the Federation of the Australian colonies on 1 January 1901, each colony had its own legal system connected with the other colonial systems by their common stock of English law, including English legislation, and by their common subjection to Privy Council appeals. The history of Irish participation in these systems must therefore be approached colony by colony.

New South Wales

Roger Therry was a Dublin man, whose father was one of the early Catholic barristers admitted to that profession when the penal laws were relaxed at the end of the eighteenth century. Roger was born in 1800 and though he went to Trinity College, Dublin (TCD) he did not take a degree. He was called to the English and Irish Bars and, having been private secretary to Canning, the Prime Minister, he was appointed Commissioner of the Court of Requests in New South Wales. With his wife, Anne, he arrived in Sydney[2] on 4 November 1829, a town in which he found a 'variety of strange sounds and divers tongues that met the ear . . . a City of Babel on a small scale'.[3] His was the tenth name on the roll of NSW barristers and he conducted a successful practice while discharging his duties in the humble jurisdiction of the Court of Requests.

Therry was joined in Sydney by a fellow student whom he had met at TCD. John Hubert Plunkett, born in 1802, had been a successful barrister on the Connacht Circuit. Daniel O'Connell gave him the credit for the success of his candidates in Connacht in 1830. Plunkett was appointed Solicitor-General of New South Wales. He arrived in Sydney in 1832. In 1836 he became Attorney-General.

Plunkett and Therry were men of ability and integrity. In 1838, they prosecuted to conviction the perpetrators of the infamous Myall Creek massacre in which a large number of Aboriginals — men, women and children — were slaughtered. The rigorous enforcement of the law in protection of the Aboriginal people excited a great deal of comment, but the Attorney-General and his junior counsel earned public respect for their impartial enforcement of the law.

In 1839, Plunkett and Therry each declined appointment as an acting Judge of the Supreme Court of New South Wales. At that time they were regarded by Governor Gipps as 'the two most distinguished barristers of New South Wales'.[4]

Plunkett's contribution to the law in New South Wales was made chiefly in the political forum. He secured the passage of the Church Act in 1836, which established legal equality between Anglicans, Catholics and Presbyterians, and was later extended to Methodists. He became President of the Legislative Council and he was elected to the Legislative Assembly for a term. He was a noted leader of Catholic opinion, a firm supporter of Caroline Chisholm, a force in the establishment of St Vincent's Hospital and a protector of the hospital against ecclesiastical administrators. He sat on the Wentworth Committee for the establishment of the University of Sydney and became its Vice-Chancellor. He was a founding fellow of St John's College within the University. He died in East Melbourne just short of his 67th birthday and was buried in Sydney near Archpriest Therry.

Therry's career followed a different course. For a time he was Attorney-General during Plunkett's absence in England, then he applied to be, and was, appointed as Resident Judge at Port Phillip. That appointment was not well received by the Port Phillip community at first, but during the year he spent in Melbourne (1845) he earned their respect. From 1846 to 1859 he was a judge of the Supreme Court of New South Wales. During most of that time he was the Primary Judge in Equity. In May 1850 he held the first Circuit Court for the district of Moreton Bay. He pleased the Circuit dinner held in his honour in Brisbane when he told them: 'I feel that I am in the presence of a scene that cannot be exceeded in the loveliness of its landscape.'[5] After Therry retired, he lived in Paris and London before returning to his native Dublin. He wrote his *Reminiscences* which received a more enthusiastic reception in London that in the Antipodes. In 1869 he was knighted and five years later he died.

Both Plunkett and Therry were champions of the Irish community in Sydney and proud defenders of the interests of their Catholic co-religionists. They were not the only Irish lawyers in the early days of the colony. Thomas Callaghan, another Dublin man, came to New South Wales as an immigrant in 1839 shortly after graduating from TCD. He earned an income as a barrister, supplemented by legal reporting for the Sydney *Herald*. In 1844 he published in two volumes the Imperial and colonial legislation in force in the Colony — *Callaghan's Acts*. He became Chairman of Quarter Sessions and one of the first three District Court Judges. In 1863, he died in a riding accident at Braidwood where, in St Bede's Church, an obelisk was erected in memory of his impartiality and ability.

Sir James Martin and Sir Frederick Darley were Chief Justices of New South Wales in virtual succession. Both were born in Ireland. Martin arrived in Sydney in 1821 as a child aged 18 months. His parents were poor but they made great sacrifices to secure an education for their brilliant son. He became a solicitor and a passionate if conservative patriot. He became a barrister and Attorney-General. On two occasions, he was Premier of the state. Sir Henry Parkes thought him to be an imperious man who 'loved power for power's sake', but when he became Chief Justice in 1873 he discharged the duties of his office to the satisfaction of profession and public alike. He died in 1886 and was succeeded, after a brief interregnum, by Darley.

Darley was ten years younger, educated in Ireland, a graduate of TCD and a member of the Munster Circuit. He came to Sydney to practise as a barrister in 1862 and became Queen's Counsel in 1878. He was prevailed upon to accept appointment as Chief Justice in the public interest and at considerable financial sacrifice. He was a sound judge, especially in equity and company law. He was jealous of judicial independence. He sought no public recognition though he was laden with honours. Desiring to be remembered only as 'an old Irish gentleman' he died while in London in 1910 and was buried in the family vault at Dublin.

In turn, he was succeeded by a noted Irish-Australian, Sir William Portus Cullen, born near Kiama in New South Wales in 1855. He graduated with first class honours in classics from Sydney University and later took a degree in law. He favoured Federation, was a member of the Legislative Council, and — almost alone among the conservative lawyers of his time — he favoured the abolition of Privy Council appeals.[6] He became Chief Justice of New South Wales in 1910, an office which he held until 1925. He continued for some years as Lieutenant Governor and Chancellor of Sydney University. He died in 1935.

Another Australian-born lawyer of Irish parentage who should be mentioned was Daniel Deniehy, the son of two transportees from

Ireland, whom W.B. Dalley described as 'the most gifted Irish-Australian of our history'. Born in 1828, he was taken on a visit to Europe, England and Ireland before he was 16, returning to study law in Sydney. Admitted as a solicitor in 1851, and elected to the Legislative Assembly in 1856, he was a man of letters and a gifted orator. But his capacities for liquor and satire lost him the influence which his genius would otherwise have commanded. He left a touching indication of his spirit in a letter he wrote to his wife a few hours before his death in 1865:

> Brave things have been written on the love, and truth, and goodness, and heroism, and courage, and suffering, and faith of women, but one year's history of your life would be sufficient for all that has entitled them to the honour and veneration and gratitude of mankind.[7]

Victoria

The first barrister to arrive in Victoria was E.J. Brewster, a nephew of the Lord Chancellor of Ireland. The second was James Croke, the third was Redmond Barry. All three were graduates of TCD and members of the Irish Bar. Brewster left the Bar to engage in land dealing and later, to become a clergyman in the Church of England. Croke became Crown Prosecutor, renowned for his ability and independence. Barry became not only a distinguished judge but a leading figure in the colony.

In 1841, a resident judge was appointed for the Port Phillip district, but the appointee had to be replaced after a short time. William Jeffcott of Tralee took his place briefly, followed by Judge Therry from Sydney for 18 months. After separation from New South Wales in 1851, a'Beckett was Chief Justice until 1857 when the long reign of Irish Chief Justices began. Stawell, Higinbotham, Madden and Irvine successively filled the office until 1935. All were Irish-born; all save Madden a graduate of TCD. They were joined on the Supreme Court by other Irish lawyers of great distinction, notably Sir Redmond Barry and Sir Robert Molesworth. They too were TCD graduates. Barry was a leading barrister at the time of separation and was the first Victorian Solicitor-General. He was appointed to the Supreme Court in 1852 but, despite his application to be appointed Chief Justice when a'Beckett retired, he was never appointed to that office. He was active in the foundation of the Philosophical Institute, the Philharmonic Society, the Horticultural Society, the Melbourne Hospital, the Melbourne Library, the Victorian National Gallery, the Melbourne Club[8] and Melbourne University of which he was the first Chancellor: an office which he held until his death in 1880. He presided over the trial of the now legendary bushranger Ned Kelly whose response to the sentence of death was: 'I will see you there where I go.' Sir Arthur Dean comments: 'Much has been made by the superstitious of the fact that Barry died unexpectedly twelve days after Kelly was hanged.'[9]

Molesworth served as a Supreme Court Judge for 30 years (1856–86) with great distinction. He was appointed also to be Chairman of the Court of Mines over which he presided during years of feverish mining activity and in which he developed the basic principles of mining law that were adopted in other Australian colonies.[10]

Charles Gavan Duffy declared himself to be the first emancipated Catholic in Ireland, but his conflict with ecclesiastical power as much as his conflict with the power of government decided him to leave Ireland. 'An Ireland where Mr Keogh typified patriotism and Dr Cullen the Church was an Ireland in which I could not live.'[11] He arrived in Melbourne with his wife Susan and three of their children including Frank in January 1856. There he was greeted by a welcoming committee. He hung up his barrister's shingle but he was soon constrained to enter Parliament and in time became Premier of Victoria. After Susan, who was his second wife, died in 1878, he returned to Europe. In France he married Louise who bore him four children including George. Frank became Chief Justice of the High Court of Australia. George became the President of the High Court of Ireland.

Of the Victorian Chief Justices, George Higinbotham should be especially mentioned. He arrived in Melbourne in 1854 as one of the 300,000 immigrants who swept into Victoria in the nine years up to 1860.[12] He became editor of the *Argus* newspaper in the columns of which he espoused radical views that he later carried into politics as Attorney-General. Professor Manning Clark says that he

> was a man with Christ-like qualities who spent much of his time with lawyers and accountants, a gentle spirit who found himself with the measurers, an enlarger surrounded by straiteners. He had a face of such delicacy, mildness and sweetness that those in

his company felt they were in the presence of a cherub, an angel who had been vouchsafed a vision of God's throne. He was kind to drunks, whom he sheltered from the abuse of the self-righteous, tender with women and very gentle with little children.[13]

He was elected on a platform of 'manhood suffrage, total separation of Church from state, state aid to denominational education, reform of land tenures and an abhorrence of faction and cabal.'[14] Whether as politician or, later, as judge, he held strongly, indeed idiosyncratically, to the view that the Victorian Constitution conferred on the colonial government 'very large and, in my opinion, almost plenary powers of internal self government'.[15] As Chief Justice in 1887, he made it clear that, if he were appointed Acting Governor, or Lieutenant Governor while the Governor was on leave he would refuse to communicate with the Colonial Office.[16] He refused the customary knighthood. During the maritime strike of 1891, he publicly sent £50 and a further £10 per week towards the relief of the strikers' families. Alfred Deakin held him to be a man of magnetic influence, radical thought and dominating will. 'Such a man', wrote Deakin, 'rare in the world, seemed rarer still in Australia where his inflexible purity of life and aim, his irresistible charm and grace, and his transcendent power of convincing and being convinced, left an indelible impression upon so many minds and characters.'[17]

Tasmania

Sir Valentine Fleming was born in England though his family hailed from Tuam. He graduated from TCD, became Solicitor-General in Hobart in 1844 and Chief Justice in 1854. He held that office until 1869 and again he acted as Chief Justice from 1872 to 1874. The Bar presented him with a testimonial which spoke of his ability, care, courtesy and constant impartiality.

Queensland

The second barrister to sign the roll in Queensland was Charles William Blakeney. Born in County Roscommon in 1802 he was the grandson of Archbishop Newcome, Primate of Ireland. He entered but did not graduate from Trinity College, was called to the Bar in England and Ireland, gambled away an inheritance and settled in Brisbane in 1859 and became the Member for Brisbane in the first Legislative Assembly in the following year. In 1865 he became the first Judge of the Western District Court. He stimulated a controversy over the competence of the juries in Roma, prompting a juror to write to the press complaining of Blakeney's severity. He resigned in 1875 and died in the following year.

Patrick Real was from Limerick. He arrived in Brisbane as a child with his recently widowed mother in 1851. He left school at 12 and worked as a carpenter and in railway workshops. In those days, entry to the Bar was reserved to those who could be supported or who could support themselves for the three-year period before a student at law submitted himself to his examinations. During this period, a student at law could not be engaged in any trade, business or employment other than that of judge's associate or principal secretary or minister of the Crown. Real was therefore obliged to save enough from his trade to support himself and his mother for the three years during which he completed his legal studies. He did so. In 1874, he was admitted to the Bar. He soon entered the front rank of the profession.[18] He was appointed a Judge of the Supreme Court in 1890, retired in 1922 and died in 1928. Real was a member of the Commission for the establishment of the University of Queensland. One of Real's pupils was a young and brilliant barrister of Irish parentage, T.J. Byrnes, whom Sir Samuel Griffith was to appoint Solicitor-General and who became Premier of the State and one of its legendary heroes.

Virgil Power, though born in Queensland, received his secondary education in Ireland and graduated BA from Dublin University. He returned to the Queensland Bar where he was an outstanding advocate. He was a Crown Prosecutor and was appointed a judge of the Supreme Court when the first appointment was made to Rockhampton.

Although the Irish Bar did not staff the Queensland profession, the Irish influence in Queensland has been extensive and enduring. Among the Chief Justices of the State there have been several of Irish lineage: Hugh Macrossan, Neil Macrossan, T.W. McCawley and Sir William Webb, later a Justice of the High Court.

South Australia

Irish immigration to South Australia was limited, but an Irishman, Sir Robert Torrens, Premier of the state for a time, made a lasting contribution to the Australian legal system and, indeed, to legal systems in other parts of the common law world. He graduated MA from TCD but he was not a lawyer. In South Australia he became Treasurer and Registrar-General in 1852 and five years later he introduced a Real Property Act which created a workable system of land title by registration. The Torrens System which radically altered conveyancing procedures, was quickly adopted throughout the Australian colonies.

The first Chief Justice was Sir John Jeffcott, whose brother William served for a time as the second resident judge at Port Phillip. Born in Tralee in 1796 and a graduate of TCD, John had been Chief Justice of Sierra Leone, a post not coveted by many. During a visit to England, when he was knighted, he engaged in a duel. His opponent was wounded but lingered for a time. The judge left for Africa but returned to England to face a charge of murder after his opponent died. In the meantime, his seconds had been indicted and tried. Despite a strong Crown case against them and an adverse summing-up by the trial judge, the jury acquitted.[19] When the judge was ultimately brought to trial, the prosecution offered no evidence and he was acquitted. Then he was unemployed for a time, but successfully pressed his application for appointment as Chief Justice of South Australia. He arrived in Adelaide via van Diemen's Land in April 1837 but his term of office was brief. He drowned in a boating accident at the mouth of the Murray River in December of that year.

A more conventional figure was Mr Justice Crawford born in County Longford, son of the Vicar-General of the diocese of Armagh. A barrister and a Trinity College man, he served as the puisne judge of the Supreme Court between 1850 and his death in 1852 at the age of 40. In his short career, he had a powerful influence in establishing the authority of the court and setting higher professional standards.

Western Australia

Sir Walter Dwyer, born 1875, was a Tipperary man who, like Patrick

Real, came to Australia at a young age. He was admitted as a legal practitioner in Western Australia in 1907, was a noted advocate and the founder of the firm Dwyer, Durack and Dunphy. In 1926 he became the first President of the WA Court of Arbitration. He was one of the first trustees of the Public Library, Museum and Art Gallery of WA. He retired from office in 1945 and died in 1950.

Federation and the High Court

The creation of the Commonwealth of Australia was achieved after much debate both in the Colonies and in London. This is not the occasion to note the parts played by Irishmen in the federal movement. One of them was Cardinal Moran, the Archbishop of Sydney, whose candidature for election to a Federal Convention was both unsuccessful and the occasion of a resurgence of sectarian bitterness.[20] When the High Court was established in 1903, three justices were appointed. Sir Samuel Griffith, Chief Justice of Queensland, was appointed Chief Justice of the High Court. Barton, the first Prime Minister, was the second Justice. Richard O'Connor, Sydney-born of Irish parents, was the third. O'Connor had been a protagonist of Federation with Barton and a member of Barton's federal ministry. The three foundation justices were judges of great ability. They established the authority of this Court in the Australian judicial hierarchy, and confirmed it in its role as the keystone of the federal arch.

They were joined by two other justices when the membership of the court was expanded to five in 1906 — Isaac Isaacs and Henry Bournes Higgins. Higgins, one of the greatest jurists that this court has known and one of the greatest patriots and reformers that this nation has known, was born on 30 June 1851 in Co. Down, the second of the nine children of John and Anne Higgins. John was a Wesleyan preacher who decided to emigrate sending his family ahead of him to Melbourne in 1870. Henry went to work and later, aided by a university exhibition, he completed degrees in Arts and Law at Melbourne University. One of the professors who influenced him was W.E. Hearn, a Trinity College man and a constitutional lawyer of distinction. In 1876 Higgins was called to the Bar, where his practice brought him financial security that he had not earlier known. He was an ardent federalist, a champion of religious tolerance and devoted to the interests of working men and women. He secured the insertion of the industrial conciliation and arbitration clause in the Constitution and became, in succession to O'Connor, the President of the Arbitration Court. He proclaimed the new jurisdiction to be 'A New Province for Law and Order'.[21] In the Harvester judgment, he propounded a test for fixing a basic wage, sufficient to provide food and water, shelter and rest for employees and their families 'and a condition of frugal comfort estimated by current human standards'. A recent biographer[22] says that Higgins adopted the phrase 'reasonable and frugal comfort' from Pope Leo XIII's encyclical letter, *Rerum Novarum*. He was instrumental in effecting the High Court's reversal of its original approach to constitutional interpretation. In the *Engineers Case*,[23] when principles favourable to the growth of the Commonwealth's power were espoused, he wrote a separate and perhaps a more closely reasoned judgment than the majority. Higgins was an industrious and successful equity lawyer who became a champion of the labour movement; a non-Labour man who accepted appointment as Attorney-General in the first federal Labour government under Prime Minister Watson in 1904; a man of great personal reserve and dignity who engaged in public controversy with Prime Minister Hughes in defence of the Arbitration Court. He was a rebel for causes which were identified with the aspirations of the young Commonwealth. He was held in universal esteem and when he died in early 1929 he was described by Sir Frank Gavan Duffy as 'a man of the most sterling integrity and kindliest nature'. His name can be seen in the Australian National University, Canberra without the title of the customary knighthood which has hitherto been accepted by most Justices of the Court.

Sir Frank Gavan Duffy, son of Sir Charles Gavan Duffy, was educated at Stonyhurst and the University of Melbourne. In 1874 he was admitted to the Bar. He was a powerful advocate, 'quick-witted and of sparkling vitality'.[24] He founded the *Australian Law Times*. One of the leaders of the Victorian Bar, he was appointed a Justice of the High Court in 1913 to succeed Sir Richard O'Connor and Chief Justice in 1931. He retired in 1935.

Of course, this selection of Australian lawyers who were born in Ireland does not give us a full or balanced picture of the contribution which the Irish have made to the Australian legal system. But some themes emerge. It is clear that Trinity College and the King's Inn in Dublin imparted much of the learning which was essential to establish a working legal system in Australia — learning which colonial training might not have imparted adequately in the early days. It is clear also that many of the eminent Irish lawyers who made such a significant contribution to the colonial courts were drawn from the ranks of the Protestant Ascendancy. It is not surprising that few of the emigrant Irish lawyers were Catholics, for it was only in 1791 that the penal laws prohibiting Catholics from the practice of the law in Ireland were withdrawn.[25] Though nineteenth-century Australia was the scene of several bitter sectarian conflicts, the Irish lawyers — both Protestant and Catholic — were generally and genuinely tolerant and open men.

Two Irishmen of the Protestant tradition were among Australia's greatest judges: Higinbotham and Higgins. Dr H.V. Evatt, when a Justice of this Court, writing in the *Harvard Law Review*,[26] nominated four great Australian judges: Griffith, Isaacs, Higinbotham and Higgins. He summarised their contributions thus:

> whereas Griffith emphasized State rights as against those of the Commonwealth, and Isaacs emphasized Commonwealth rights as against those of the States, and Higinbotham emphasized the rights of colonial self-government as against the claims of British imperialism, Higgins' principal concern was that, wherever possible, the law should lay its protecting shield over the poor, the weak and the oppressed.

It is no accident that independence and compassion were the qualities that shone through the judicial work of these Irish-Australians.

A theme which emerges from the lives of Martin, Higgins and Real is the opportunity which legal practice offered for the children of poor Irish immigrants to achieve eminence and financial security in one generation. The Irish love of language and sense of independence were natural endowments which carried many Irish-Australians to success in the profession. It needed the addition of great intellect and industry to produce such jurists as Sir Richard O'Connor and Sir Leo Cussen, of the Victorian Supreme Court, but there have been many other distinguished Irish-Australian lawyers. And that consideration raises two questions which would prove fascinating to pursue. To what extent has the legal profession been the means of securing the social and intellectual advancement of the children of immigrants, and particularly Irish immigrants, to Australia? And in what respects have Australian laws and legal institutions been formed by the ideas and values which are characteristic of immigrant families? I must leave to others the pursuit of these questions, but I hazard two opinions. The first is that a legal profession which is easy of entry but demanding in its standards is essential to a free and confident nation and conducive to social mobility within it. The second is that the ideals and values which the Irish contributed to Australian life — sometimes vital, sometimes diluted — have been reflected in those laws and institutions which were established before the Second World War.

If these opinions be valid, the true Irish influence on Australian laws and institutions is no less than, and no different from, the Irish influence on Australia as a whole. And that has been enormous.

Notes and References

1. Other than in some land rights legislation, e.g. section 71(1) of Aboriginal Land Rights (Northern Territory) Act 1976, which provides

> Subject to this section, an Aboriginal or a group of Aboriginals is entitled to enter upon Aboriginal land and use or occupy that land to the extent that that entry, occupation or use is in accordance with Aboriginal tradition governing the rights of that Aboriginal or group of Aboriginals with respect to that land, whether or not those rights are qualified as to place, time, circumstances, purpose, permission or any other factor.

2. R. Therry, *Reminiscences of Thirty Years Residence in New South Wales* (facsimile edn, Sydney UP, Sydney, 1974), p.13.

3. Ibid., p.40.

4. Ibid., p.19; *Historical Records of Australia* (Canberra, 1914–25), series I, vol.20, p.59.

5. Therry, *Reminiscences*, p.29.

6. J.M. Bennett, 'Sir William Portus Cullen', *Canberra Historical Journal* (1977), p.83.

7. Cited in B.T. Dowd, 'Daniel Henry Deniehy', *Journal of Royal Australian Historical Society*, vol.23, no.2, (1974), p.91.

8. P. Ryan, *Redmond Barry* (Oxford UP, Melbourne, 1972), p.20.

9. A. Dean, *A Multitude of Cousellors* (Cheshire, Melbourne, 1968), p.71.

10. Ibid., p.66.

11. C. Pearl, *The Three Lives of Gavan Duffy* (New South Wales UP, Kensington, 1979), p.155.

12. N. Stephen, 'George Higinbotham', 1983 Daniel Mannix Memorial Lecture (Melbourne UP, 1983), p.11.

13. C.M.H. Clark, *A History of Australia* (Melbourne UP, Melbourne, 1978), vol.4, p.109.

14. Stephen, 'George Higinbotham', pp.16–17.

15. *Toy v. Musgrove*: see Z. Cowen, 'Sir John Latham and Other Papers', referred to in Stephen, 'George Higinbotham', p.27.

16. Dean, *Counsellors*, p.77.

17. A. Deakin, *The Federal Story*, 2nd edn (Melbourne UP, Melbourne, 1963), p.8.

18. H. Gibbs, 'Some Aspects of the History of the Queensland Bar', *Australian Law Journal*, vol.53 (1982), p.66.

19. R.M. Hague, *Sir John Jeffcott* (Melbourne UP, Melbourne, 1963), pp.46–7.

20. R. Ely, *Unto God and Caesar* (Melbourne UP, Melbourne, 1976), Ch.3.

21. The title of the book which was published by Constable, London in 1922, following a series of earlier articles in the *Harvard Law Review*.

22. J. Rickard, *H.B. Higgins, the Rebel as Judge* (Allen and Unwin, Sydney, 1984), pp.173–4.

23. Amalgamated Society of Engineers *v.* The Adelaide Steamship Co Ltd (the 'Engineers case'), *Commonwealth Law Review*, vol.28 (1920), p.129.

24. Dean, *Counsellors*, p.151.

25. R.W. Bentham, 'The Bench and Bar in Ireland', 1 *Tasmania University Law Journal*, vol.209 (1959), p.217.

26. H.V. Evatt, 'Mr Justice Cardozo', 52 *Harvard Law Review*, vol.357, p.359.

3   W.B. Yeats: Political Poetry or Poems to the Editor

Vincent Buckley

I hope you will take this paper as an interim report on the first stage of investigating some questions about Yeats' poetry. As I have looked further into the matters I raise, I see that, without certain answers, one can't be sure what questions need asking; and even with this first stage I am not yet in a position to give these answers. I should therefore prefer to discuss only the period and the poems on which I can speak today. It is very tempting to improvise some guesses about the next phase, that of 1916, but I have to resist the temptation, for I have worked intermittently on these poems for 20 years, but not in precisely the terms I am using of the poems of 1913, and it is clear to me that the questions about them need to be formulated in slightly different terms.

The problem of W.B. Yeats as a politician and political poet is no closer to a solution than it was 30 years ago. At that time, of course, or at any time before Conor Cruise O'Brien's famous article, 'Passion and Cunning: Politics in the Poetry of W.B. Yeats' (BCC),[1] few would have agreed that a problem existed: there was an orthodox reading of his *oeuvre* (including life, works and explication), and it saw no splits or contradictions anywhere in that *oeuvre*. This orthodox reading had become institutional, because it was central to the notes and later to the Commentary by A.N. Jeffares,[2] and to the *Reader's Guide* by John Unterecker,[3] although Unterecker's exposition, which is slightly vague, does not have all the ingredients of the reading. It is spread throughout these and other readings, throughout scores of the papers at the Sligo Summer School, through yearly lectures in a thousand places of instruction: it is the Ur-Reading and it is not clear *where* it started.

It goes like this: Prepared by his contacts with the myth-livened peasantry (or, as it happened, servantry) of the west of Ireland, Yeats became in his youth an ardent, idealistic nationalist. This position was deepened when, under the influence of the old Fenian

33

John O'Leary and his disciple Maud Gonne, he became a 'republican of the school of John O'Leary' (non-violent) and was inducted into the Irish Republican Brotherhood. He became extremely active in nationalist literary ventures, and was also for periods an activist in mass demonstrations and other organised defiance of a sort involving 'direct action'. This was his 'political period', but it began to end in 1903, when he entered on a new phase of a creative career. The reasons were as follows: (a) He was shocked and disillusioned by Maud Gonne's sudden marriage to the Yahoo John MacBride, and in shock he forswore the politics of which she was the sacramental presence; (b) with his new friend Augusta Gregory, he became absorbed in setting up the Abbey Theatre; (c) Irish politics had become a dirty, trivial and unidealistic business; and (d) The Wyndham Land Act, latest in a long line of such enactments, and brought about by a Gregory connection, John Shaw-Taylor, gave such generous provisions for the Irish tenant farmers that land ownership was no longer a general source of inflammation in Irish politics. The presence of this last in the package of reasons is stressed by A.N. Jeffares, but also by several others; it is seen as reinforcing the view that, after 1903, a genius could have no need of 'politics' (a concept of very special meaning in this context).

However, the story continues, Yeats was fired out of his anti-political life by events which, ten years later, called for a new expression of his old O'Learyite idealism. He thus became involved in politics in another special sense, while remaining in other senses against and/or above politics. The events were (a) the failure of the new Catholic millionaire class and its politicians to build a gallery to house the paintings donated by Hugh Lane, another Gregory connection; (b) the brutality shown by the chief millionaire of this group, William Martin Murphy, in locking out his workers and causing the great lock-out (and strike) of 1913; (c) the Easter Rising of 1916 which transformed banal people and activities into the stuff of myth, 'a terrible beauty'. In all these matters Yeats arose from overwork to challenge the hegemonic power of the new sub-aristocratic, native, gross, Catholic philistinism. While he intervened in politics, his challenge was, in an important sense, anti-political.

In 1965 Cruise O'Brien produced an essay which denied the whole of this account and insisted that it was based on a false consciousness about the concept 'politics', reinforced by carefully planted misreadings and selected quotations. Instead of being against or above politics, Yeats was always political, in the most important sense of that word; he was not against sectional or class interests as such, he represented one set of these against others. His chosen group was élitist, authoritarian, paternalist, and incipiently Fascist; his flirtation with General O'Duffy's Blueshirts in 1933 was no mere impulse of the moment, but a logical implication of his lifelong political self-identification.

For O'Brien, Yeats was always an automatic and instinctive politician, at times an openly calculating one:

> I no longer believe Yeats's political activities to have been foolish or fundamentally inconsistent or his political attitudes to be detachable from the rest of his personality, disconnected from action, or irrelevant to his poetry. His politics were, it now seems to me, marked by a considerable degree of inner consistency between thought and action, by a powerful emotional drive, cautious experimentation in action, and, in expression, extravagances and disengagements which succeeded one another not without calculation and not without reference to the given political conjuncture of the moment.[4]

Nor had he been drawn into politics by Maud Gonne; he had been recruited by O'Leary before he met her, and 'the most active phases of his political life were to come after he had quarrelled with Maud Gonne';[5] what she did was to prolong his commitment beyond its likely end. Further, the 'school of John O'Leary' was Fenian, a tradition of violence if a discriminating one, which when Yeats joined it was between engagements as it were; it was 'extreme but not dangerous'. This combination has a natural appeal to two of Yeats' most enduring characteristics: his pride and his prudence![6] These meshed with his opportunism, which emerged in his poem, to be published in *United Ireland*, on the death of Parnell. 'It has been a success', he reported to his sister immediately after its publication. 'He has an eye for an opportunity', O'Brien comments, 'a politician's eye, and a politician's sense of timing.'[7]

When he 'turned aside' from Irish politics, 'he did not cease — he never ceased — to be an Irish nationalist, but his nationalism now became aristocratic and archaising instead of being popular and active';[8] yet, now, 'politics become explicit in his poetry', and, with his poem 'No Second Troy', 'his bitterness about Maud Gonne's marriage took a political form'.[9]

Similarly, his attack on Murphy over his brutal lock-out was not actuated solely by 'humanitarian zeal' but by competitive dislike for the middle class (Catholic) which had taken or was taking the social positions once occupied by Yeats' own middle class (Protestant).[10] The lock-out began in August, but Yeats did not protest until after 21 October when a letter from the Catholic Archbishop of Dublin added a new dimension to the conflict.[11] And, if we may jump some 20 years, his support of, irony towards and disengagement from General O'Duffy and his Blueshirts are all traced in a chronology which makes it quite clear that Yeats' excitement is greatest when they look like winning, and his sense of their comedy most acute when it is obvious they have lost.[12]

It is not 'force and marching men' that he disbelieves in, but a failure to use them. He was in fact a Fascist, but an intermittently active one; or, in O'Brien's words, he was 'as near to being a Fascist as his situation and the conditions of his country permitted'; he aligned O'Higgins with Mussolini, his Italian prototype, and worked hard 'to create a movement in Ireland which would be overtly Fascist in language, costume, behaviour and intent. He turned his back on this when it began to fail, not before.'[13] In this he was characteristic of the Irish Protestant middle class, though he lacked one loyalty which restrained their Fascist tendencies — loyalty to Britain.[14] He *was* restrained, in a sense, by his irony and caution, 'and his phases of detachment [were] not less real than his phases of political commitment.'[15] The hatred of England that flared up in his last three years of life was merely a new and violent expression of the syndrome, with all its emotional contradictions, which governed his life.

That is O'Brien's case. How did it affect the views of those against whose orthodox mystifying picture it was directed? In the case of Jeffares, it had the intriguing effect that, while he had been O'Brien's editor, and while he cited O'Brien several times in the *Commentary*, he did not once acknowledge that O'Brien's case stood as a refutation of his own. It is as though O'Brien were merely a stray contributor to *Notes and Queries*, drawing our attention to some arcane detail, rather than the most subversive text in the whole history of the debate. Elizabeth Cullingford now takes a different tack; for her, O'Brien is to be refuted rather than ignored; and she refutes him by repeating the old orthodoxy, but in a new form. Instead of abandoning politics in 1903, Yeats is seen as transforming them; instead of turning conservative and introspective, he remains idealist, romantic, populist and democratic. O'Brien has simply made a mistake — throughout.

I shall pause with this for a moment, because Cullingford's account is likely to be regarded as a total answer to O'Brien, and the Jeffares thesis restored under a different colour. I find Cullingford's book so simplistic that it is hard to deal with, and simplistic most of all in that she thinks it sufficient, in discussing Yeats' motives, to quote Yeats himself. This rules out by fiat all moves towards deconstruction and inhibits all radical investigation. It therefore leads persistently to half-truths and quarter-truths, as when she sees his 'withdrawal from politics' after 1903 as a return to populism and national responsibility, i.e. as the reverse of elitist. Similarly, he leaves the IRB for idealist reasons, because it 'was riddled with spies and informers'.[16] He deplored propaganda, but 'did not divorce art from politics. In Ireland, indeed, politics were the basis of art.'[17]

She also endorses Yeats' class-valuation: the Wyndham Land Act, she says cheerfully, 'finally solved the Irish land question'; Yeats' admiration for John Shaw-Taylor she sees as a spontaneous response to a magnificent initiative taken, as it were, from totally outside Yeats' circle of friends and acquaintances. Everything he does is disinterested in this sense, and so is everything done by his friends.

When she comes to the episode of the 1913 lock-out, and Yeats' indignant letter, Cullingford tackles O'Brien directly. He 'is naturally worried by this letter . . .'.[18] But to a non-partisan reader, O'Brien does not appear in the least worried; on the contrary, he fastens on the letter eagerly because its very paradoxes will advance his case.

My own interest is in the poetry chiefly, and I propose neither to interpret it through explications found in the prose nor to use it to support a view of the facts asserted in the prose, but to run certain groups of poems together with the groups of letters contemporary with them to see how each medium replicates, redirects or comments on, psychological manoeuvres found in the other, and then to detach the poetry from its deceptive twin. It could be an object lesson in *not* reading the poems through the letters, or, rather, in reading them together for the sake of separating them. Where O'Brien is asking, 'What are really Yeats' politics?', I am asking, 'What are the politics of his poetry?'.

I confine myself to the letters because the other documents are all too liable to compound mystifications by their very rhetoricality.

The letters frequently comment on poems contemporary with them, and often include drafts, sections, prose sketches or other manuscript versions. They also occasionally show Yeats shying away from the consequences which his bravado has had in the shocked or reproving response of his correspondent; I shall look at one such case later, though there are several.

Of the separate volumes of letters published, those to Sturge Moore have almost nothing positively germane to my question; those to Katharine Tynan and Lady Dorothy Wellesley are chiefly reprinted in Wade's *Letters*, although the Wellesley volume is a fascinating unit when read by itself. Wade divides his great volume[19] into six sections or volumes. Of these, the first, 1887–91, is dominated by Tynan and John O'Leary, the second, 1892–96, by those two plus, later, Olivia Shakespear; the third, 1897–1908, by Lady Gregory and George Russell (AE); the fourth, 1909–17, by Lady Gregory; the fifth, 1918–28, by Olivia Shakespear; the last, 1929–39, by Dorothy Wellesley.

His chief correspondents are thus women. No letters to Maud Gonne are left, but those to Shakespear and Wellesley are very revealing of Yeats' political attitudes partly because they are both Englishwomen to whom local detail has to be explained, and partly because he expresses those attitudes to them, and especially to Wellesley, in the course of commenting on actual poems. The addresses from which he wrote remind us forcefully how much of his life he spent out of Ireland, and out of firsthand touch with Irish life. For example, most of the letters we have from 1913 are written from England. He seems to have spent about ten months of that year out of Ireland.

One implication of these facts is the likelihood that he would change his tone, or his rhetoric, by a subliminal calculation based on where he was at a given time, how much closer to or further from a treasured correspondent, who might need to be instructed, or re-instructed, briefed or debriefed, alerted or reassured, about Yeats' attitude to events. We have one single example of this in his letters concerning the Blueshirt promise, threat, and passing; the recipient is Dorothy Wellesley; and we may be struck by the paucity of letters dating from the time of the Easter Rising; of those which exist, some were written while he was staying with Maud Gonne in Normandy.

Rearranging Wade's very serviceable scheme, I may perhaps divide Yeats' creative time into five periods: from the 1880s to 1903;

1903 to 1913; 1913 to the civil war; from 1922 to 1929 (basically the years of the Senatorship), and the final ten years, which may themselves be divided, at will or need, into two or more sections. I shall not deal with the early work, and shall try to say something about the second and the third periods, focusing in particular on the poems from 1913.

His volume of 1903, *In The Seven Woods*, shows the Gregory connection firming very strong. The venue of the poems, which date from 1901, is often Coole Park, and many have to do with Maud Gonne in a context of withering boughs. 'Old Memory' was written in December 1903. She had married in February.

The poetic result of that event is to be found chiefly in *The Green Helmet* (1910) and *Responsibilities* (1914). The first has more regretful poems; but the poems which show a *political* animus towards or analysis of his loss seem to date from late in this period: 'Words' and 'No Second Troy' are from 1908, five years after her marriage, and years too after its failure; while 'Peace' and 'Upon a House Shaken by the Land Agitation' are from 1910. If there is bitterness here, it is of a delayed sort; but it is certainly political in kind, and its kind is reactionary-conservative. The most memorable lines from 'No Second Troy' are those which deny the very basis and ethos of Fenianism:

Or hurled the little streets upon the great
Had they but courage equal to desire?[20]

And 'Upon a House . . .' really gives the lie, in a single poetic epiphany, to the repeated claim that the Wyndham Land Act had completely solved the land problem; in this poem, it is not that land-hungry peasants declare a problem, but that Yeats declares *them* to be one. What I think is remarkable about this volume is its shortage of substantial poems; poetically, it is not much for the labour of six years; and it is further significant that most of them are, in a sense, occasional poems, small and often sour commentaries in the margin of a life being lived elsewhere. The reason may be that Yeats has become engrossed in his labours for the Abbey Theatre, 'theatre business, management of men'. Whatever the reason, he has not so much deserted politics for poetry as deserted poetry for cultural politics. In a letter of 1908, Maud Gonne MacBride notices this and urges him to return to poetry.

'All things can tempt me from this craft of verse,'[21] he writes in the second last poem of the volume; but the rest of the poem is a high-sounding rationalisation of that fact.

Each volume after this is more substantial; and significantly *Responsibilities* opens with the famous 'Introductory Rhymes', with its new colloquial diction and its heraldic sequence of assertions about identity and *vertu* — creative purpose, in short. But these poems were written in years when the world was preparing for cataclysm, Ireland was preparing for civil war, and Britain was preparing to balance its books by mystifying most, if not all, its Irish subjects.

The matter which has caused most discussion since O'Brien's essay is that of Yeats' attitude towards William Martin Murphy and the anti-union lock-out of August 1913, an horrific social injustice which may have been a part cause of the Easter Rising. O'Brien holds that, in opposing Murphy, Yeats has a caste interest,[22] while Cullingford attributes only altruistic motives to him, and Jeffares does not think the question of his motives worth arguing about.

Some facts are pretty plain; there is a group of poems which practise a rather violent form of culture politics. The first is 'To a Wealthy Man . . .' (written December 1912–January 1913), and it is followed by 'September 1913' (written 7 September, and published next day in the *Irish Times*), 'To a Friend' and 'Paudeen' (both 16 September), and 'To a Shade' (29 September). Quite what calls out such spleen (whose nature can be seen clearly if we take Paudeen to be an equivalent to Paddy, instead of the 'diminutive of Padraig' which some commentators euphemistically insist on) has to be guessed at; for 1913 is a poor year for letters from Yeats. There are no letters printed in Wade between 5 August and November; there is therefore nothing contemporary with or directly on either the lock-out or the poem 'September 1913'.

There *is* the letter of 17 March to the *Irish Times* about the siting of the Municipal Art Gallery; by this time Yeats was finding himself in a quarrel based on a mistake; for his poem 'To a Wealthy Man . . .', published in the *Irish Times* on 13 January, had been resented and attacked by Murphy, who supposed it directed against him. The mistake is not altogether surprising, since, although Yeats identified his target as Lord Ardilaun, he did not make his identification public, and in a later letter, to Lady Gregory, he comments that his poem is 'not tactless and does not name Lord Ardilaun.'[23]

The aggression restrained by this tact is redirected a few months later against other targets; Paudeen is their generic name. He had in any case, asked Hugh Lane before publishing it, 'if it is not politic tell me so frankly. If you think it is politic I will try and see Hone to see if fitting publication and comment could be made in the *Irish Times*'.[24] This is the language and the tactical sense of politics.

The five poems are published together near the beginning of *Responsibilities*, introduced by and contrasted to the 'Introductory Rhymes' and 'The Grey Rock'. This placing is surely deliberate, since the five must be among the latest written of the poems in the volume; the effect gained is to contrast two opposed senses of value and style.

'To a Wealthy Man . . .' is a polemic full of self-validating cultural reference to the Italian Renaissance; Jeffares gives it six pages of notes — it is that sort of poem. It is also a poem that initiates an attack on not just an individual or a class, but a whole people; significantly, the sneer at Paudeen and Biddy is uttered here, *before* Murphy's offensive reply. In other words, it has racist overtones, and it is no wonder Murphy did not notice that Lord Ardilaun was its target:

Your open hand but shows our loss,
For he knew better how to live.
Let Paudeens play at pitch and toss,
Look up in the sun's eye and give
What the exultant heart calls good
That some new day may breed the best
Because you gave, not what they would,
But the right twigs for an eagle's nest![25]

Now, I don't usually read the poem in quite so defensive a light (or didn't, until I noticed the possibility that 'pitch and toss' also carried ethnic animus); I read it for its amusingly romantic picture of the Renaissance Italians at work and play. But it was published in the *Irish Times* as part of a controversy, and thus meets my description, a Poem to the Editor; it is a tactical poem, designed at once to assist a highbred unchallengeable norm and to drive wedges. But how is it tactical? Well, it is a manoeuvre executed to gain the advantage; it lines up Lord Ardilaun but does not identify him, so that Paudeen millionaires might draw the wrong conclusions; and is it possible that the whole of that lyrical run in the middle, what

I have called its amusingly romantic element, may be considered
tactically, in that such verbal bravura, while it may be mocked,
cannot be plausibly challenged, is beyond challenge? On this reading,
style would be a way of setting Yeats above the conflict, and so
would give him the victory in it, as commentators like Jeffares have
been happy to do, without question.

The world of this poem is extended in 'Paudeen', written several
months later. This is a vision poem, and it ends with a line which
suggests that in God's eye even Paudeen has value, but the title is
indicative, and the lines which everyone remembers and quotes are
those which refer to

> . . . the fumbling wits, the obscure spite
> Of our old Paudeen in his shop . . .[26]

This wording suggests that the class of Paudeens has now been
encapsulated in a particular individual in a particular shop: a
peculiar effect, but one designed evidently to suggest that the offensive millionaire who thinks himself so grand is really a village
shopkeeper: a huckster of whom it cannot be said;

> Merchant and scholar who have left me blood
> That has not passed through any huckster's loin.[27]

A double judgement is being made, an aesthetic one which disting-
uishes merchant from huckster and associates him with scholar
(pure as against grimy trade), and a social one, which sees the
Pollexfen merchant as filling out his appointed, honourable place,
while Paudeen is an upstart. It is a poem in praise of vision and
against upstarts.

The campaign continues, Yeats 2: Upstarts nil; he is now manoeu-
vring with great speed and confidence. 'To a Friend Whose Work
has come to Nothing' is dated the same day as 'Paudeen'. It is
ostensibly an elevated comforting of the creative friend, Lady Gregory, who thought it addressed to Hugh Lane. It probably refers to
the Lane controversy, and Jeffares says it 'probably relates to the
final decision of the Dublin Corporation about the Lane pictures'.[28]
In any case, the comfort, though splendid in its paradox, is set
against the caste enemy, again Murphy, who is beneath contempt:

> For how can you compete,

Being honour bred, with one
Who, were it proved he lies,
Were neither shamed in his own
Nor in his neighbours' eyes.[29]

This reminds me of Thomas Kinsella's remark about the Lord Mayor of Dublin, 'He is ignorant, and proud of it'. But Kinsella says nothing about breeding; Yeats bears down on the word with lovely force: Augusta Gregory is not 'honour born' or 'honour bound', but 'honour bred'; the upstart, however, is surrounded by neighbours in the same sad condition as himself, of not caring if he were proved a liar. That is the sort of people *they* are.

I would describe this and 'Paudeen' as poems to the editor, too, although they were first published in *Poems Written in Discouragement* (1913); in a way, they bypass the editor; they say things that letters to an editor could not afford to say; yet they will come to his attention by and bye. In fact, they were published very shortly after they were written. My guess is that they were written to be published in that semi-journalistic form.

'To A Shade', dated 13 days later, brings Parnell into the account; adducing an earlier victim of the Bantry Band to vindicate the later. The articulation of the rhetoric is now much more advanced, more experimental, so that the poem turns out a *tour de force*. The confidence has increased, too — a confidence if not to name, at least almost to name; and it seems connected with the fact that he has driven a conflict between castes or ethnic groups or interest groups or individuals back into its political chamber. Out of the frying-pan into the fire. What is at issue now is the split in the Irish Party 20 years before, that split and its very bitter consequent splits; Yeats is defending one political faction against its victorious enemies, a faction to which Murphy belongs:

A man
Of your own passionate serving kind . . .
. . . has been driven from the place,
And insult heaped upon him for his pains,
And for his open-handedness, disgrace;
Your enemy, an old foul mouth, had set
The pack upon him.[30]

The mode is that of the most elevated patriotic oratory, something above or beyond faction, set in Yeats' characteristically bounding free verse. It is often thought sufficient to call the effect 'mythologising', and so it is; but it is not beyond faction any more than it is beyond politics; it enlists mythologising in the interests of political advantage; for, if Parnell is mythologised here, his already potent mythic force is put to full use; in the interest of inflating others, Parnell is the biggest card to play. Yeats plays him in this, the fourth poem. In the process, he aligns Parnell with Hugh Lane 'A man/Of your own passionate serving kind . . .', and he brings a new element to his abuse of Murphy, 'an old foul mouth'.[31]

The political manoeuvres which are integral to the poetry may seem to have become cruder, but they are actually more subtle. They put Yeats into an excellent dialectical position: he can argue, if he chooses, that he is speaking only of one uncouth individual, or he can argue that he is attacking a new 'tendency' in Irish life. In hindsight, though, and PCC, it is clear that he is identifying an adversary group for those capable of decoding poems to the editor. This group is not just the Bantry Band, but all who are associated with them in fact and all who are implicated in the reader's mind by the immense suggestiveness of the rhetoric. Yeats is able to nail individuals, groups, tendencies and, if he wants to push it so far, the greater part of a nation. He does not want to push it so far.

In 'September 1913' it looked as if that was exactly what he wanted to do. A whole nation, or a whole aspect, or a whole side, or a whole potentiality, has gone:

> Romantic Ireland's dead and gone
> It's with O'Leary in the grave.[32]

It is no surprise that Yeats should invoke O'Leary in his polemic elegy; for O'Leary *was* his mentor, founder of his 'school', and is one of the few people who appear unmocked in *Autobiographies*. He has been in his grave, of course, six years, and Yeats did not go to his funeral, giving as the reason that he would not like the rest of the company; but, we recall, this was in the middle of his withdrawal from politics, so perhaps nationalist funerals were not on his agenda. He had left the IRB about 1900, and had very little real contact with O'Leary for some years before his death. What is deeply ironic, however, is that while he is invoking *this* grave to announce the death of romantic Ireland, Patrick Pearse is in training to stand by another grave, that of O'Donovan Rossa, to make one of the most famous speeches in all Irish history. That speech is romantic, and political, and purposeful, in a way Yeats is not for the moment conscious of, for the politics of culture have driven from his mind those of rebellion.

This is the key poem of the group, but it does not have quite the tone of the others, which of course follow it and elaborate different aspects of it. Further, it is returning to the concerns announced months before. Its mode is that of a ballad, with a two-line refrain, in stanzas composed of buoyant tetrameters. There are repeated notes of scorn, but not very much that I should call bitterness, and no personal self-reference at all.

The enemies are neither named nor otherwise identified: the vices of praying, saving, working a till and not believing in the delirium of the brave are treated as general ones. The scorn seems dismissive rather than obsessive. In effect, the poem is chiefly a hymn to Romantic Ireland, to an Ireland of the past, actual in that things happened in it, but potential in that those salvific ventures were always failures.

Romantic Ireland is evoked by synecdoche and naming; Yeats calls on O'Leary but, in seeking spiritual associates for him, leaps a long way into the past; he names no Parnellites, no Young Irelanders, and no Fenians besides O'Leary himself. All those he names are men of 1798–1803, all Protestants, one lord and two gentleman professionals. The others he evokes are Sarsfield (not named) and the Wild Geese, 100 years earlier. No Gaelic champion is mentioned: Romantic Ireland is not Gaelic Ireland, Yeats' eighteenth century is not that of O'Sullivan, O'Rathaille, Merriman or Eileen Dubh O'Connell, also an O'Leary, by marriage; they were before O'Leary in the grave.

It is a selective tradition, then; and it sounds grand. The names come out with such balanced rhythmic speed that they give the impression they were arrived at quickly. What is interesting is that when Yeats invokes Wolfe Tone, it is not for his labours, his persistence, his organisational powers, but for panache, bravura, all that constitutes that delirium of the style. His mind is fixed on one thing to the exclusion of all around it. Presumably that is why he ignores Fenianism in its organisational phase, when it nearly succeeded, and goes back several decades to praise its precursor in its romantic phase, gorily collapsing. Its present successors are not mentioned, of course; they are at work *now*, plotting and organising and continuing, arming and drilling and writing. But to mention *them* would be, perforce, either to redefine romantic Ireland or to confess that it is not in the grave after all.

I may sound unduly reserved about this poem; but I am merely trying to be observant. It is a very lively performance and in a sense an affirmative one, which deserves better than grudging notice. It comes across, oddly enough, a non-political poem, with very little calculation about it. The trouble is that, without a political reading, it doesn't mean anything very definite; and at the time, given the circumstances of its publication, in a newspaper, readers must have supplied that reading automatically; it must have seemed to them not only anti-Murphy but a combative statement contrasting one rebel group to another. If its energy calls up the past, it also increases the sense of distance from it.

Of all these poems, this is the one whose genesis it would be of interest to know. Jeffares plays down the lock-out as a factor, and points out that it was originally printed under the title 'Romance in Ireland/(On reading much of the correspondence against the Art Gallery)'.[33] But if Jeffares does not mention the lock-out, neither does the poem. It is only C.C. O'Brien's re-reading which has brought that into the foreground, and it does so by printing the whole of Yeats' letter of 1 November to the *Irish Worker*, attacking the use of 'religious passion' by 'the Dublin Nationalist newspapers' to break the unions and to attack parents trying to send their children to safety in England.[34]

This letter, then, and whatever provoked it, including the Archbishop's letter of 21 October, are part of the complicated campaign that several forces in Ireland, including Yeats and his associates, were by now waging against one another. It does not follow that they are causal factors in producing the poems I am dealing with, or that we need to refer to them in order to read those poems. It is possible to be *too* contextual, and to assign too much politics to a poet, however calculating.

Still, I do read it as a 'Poem to the Editor', by which I mean both that it is written as part of a network of texts and oral pressures and that it seems designed to produce an effect on a readership whose reactions will be political in character and will have a political significance. The world of Dublin, in and to which Yeats wrote, was a world of ephemeral publications (newspapers and pamphlets), meetings, speeches, and conversations held, repeated, and reported

555

5555555

555555555555

ad nauseam.[35] Interventions in controversies caused much immediate comment. The oral culture was served immediately by the print one, and in time the compliment was returned. The metropolis was also small enough for everyone to be known to everyone. Houses and pubs were extensions of the streets, places of report and assessment. A poem dated one day and published in the leading newspaper the next was in effect a poem to the editor, but to the power of *n*; and it could be at once deeply spontaneous and habitually calculating. Of Yeats' five poems, the first and second, separated by nearly nine months, are of this sort; and they are divided by a clearly calculating letter to the editor; the other three may have a similar effect, but a little more remotely: they are truly poems written in discouragement, and are to a degree appendages on the earlier poems.

It is not until 1916, three years later, that we shall see another group of poems to the editor coming from Yeats; and then, he is caught much more at a disadvantage by the historical events of which he writes, and he needs far more to have his poems discussed, memorised and quoted. They are not just poems to the editor but front-page poems, and all international papers will copy.

Notes and References

1. In A. Norman Jeffares and K.G.W. Cross (eds), *In Excited Reverie* (Macmillan, London, 1965), pp.207–78.
2. W.B. Yeats, *Poems . . .* selected with an Introduction and Notes by A.N. Jeffares (Macmillan, London, 1962); A.N. Jeffares, *A Commentary on the Collected Poems of W.B. Yeats* (London, Macmillan, 1968).
3. John Unterecker, *A Reader's Guide to William Butler Yeats* (Noonday Press, New York, 1959).
4. Conor Cruise O'Brien, 'Passion and Cunning: An Essay on the Politics of W.B. Yeats', in Jeffares and Cross (eds), *In Excited Reverie*, p.208.
5. Ibid., p.212.
6. Ibid., p.214.
7. Ibid., pp.218–19.
8. Ibid., p.222.
9. Ibid., p.225.
10. Ibid., pp.229–38. O'Brien's whole analysis of this episode is important.
11. Ibid., p.237.
12. Ibid., pp.252–6.
13. Ibid., p.258.
14. Ibid., p.259.
15. Ibid., p.264.
16. Elizabeth Cullingford, *Yeats, Ireland and Fascism* (Macmillan, London, 1981), p.47.
17. Ibid., p.55.
18. Ibid., p.81.

19. Allan Wade (ed.), *The Letters of W.B. Yeats* (Rupert Hart-Davis, London, 1954).

20. W.B. Yeats, *The Collected Poems of W.B. Yeats* (Macmillan, London, 1934), p.101.

21. 'All Things Can Tempt Me', ibid., p.109.

22. O'Brien, 'Passion and Cunning', pp.233–4.

23. Jeffares, *Notes*, p.107.

24. 1 January 1913, Wade (ed.), *Letters*, p.573.

25. Yeats, *Collected Poems*, p.120.

26. Ibid., p.122.

27. *Responsibilities*, January 1914, ibid., p.113.

28. Jeffares, *Commentary*, p.132.

29. Yeats, *Collected Poems*, p.122.

30. Ibid., p.123.

31. Ibid.

32. Ibid., p.121.

33. Jeffares, *Commentary*, p.129.

34. O'Brien, 'Passion and Cunning', pp.230–1.

35. See Oliver Gogarty, *As I Was Going Down Sackville Street* (Rich and Cowan, London, 1937); James Joyce, *Ulysses* (Shakespeare and Co, Paris, 1922); *et al.*

4 William O'Brien: Problems Reappraising his Political Career

Philip Bull

William O'Brien (1852–1928) was one of the principal leaders of the Irish parliamentary party during the period of Parnell's leadership and in the generation afterwards. An imaginative and vigorous writer and speaker, he was one of the most effective of Parnell's associates, and after the fall of the great leader he assumed, with John Dillon, the primary responsibility for the leadership of the party formed from the majority of those who had opposed Parnell. He made his most notable contribution to Irish politics in the late 1890s. Disillusioned with the factionalism and ineffectiveness of parliamentary nationalism, he gradually distanced himself from the parliamentary party, and began to establish a reputation for himself based on involvement in the problems of the farmers of the poverty-stricken areas of the west of Ireland, especially in West Mayo where he now lived. Through this work he began to lay the basis for a political revival which would make irrelevant the dissension-torn politics of the parliamentary party. The product of this was the United Irish League. Formed in 1898, this organisation quickly became the dominant political force in Ireland. Establishing its strength and vitality from the issue of land tenure, its wider political significance was evident from the beginning. Launched as part of the commemoration of the centenary of the 1798 rebellion, the wider nationalist purpose of the organisation was soon exemplified in the sustained conflict between its followers and the forces of government, a conflict which revived political hopes dormant since the fall of Parnell.

By 1900 the impact of the United Irish League had been sufficiently widespread throughout the country that it had largely usurped the role of other nationalist organisations, becoming itself the effective organisational arm of parliamentary nationalism. Its success forced the reunion of nationalist parliamentarians of rival factions, their concerns and disputes becoming rapidly untenable in the context of the spirit of unity and action which characterised the new League. This growing national role for the'organisation he had founded also ensured that O'Brien himself emerged as the dominant leader in the movement; these years marked, as F.S.L. Lyons wrote, 'the ascendancy of William O'Brien'.[1] Under his influence the restruc-tured and reunited nationalist movement mounted a national agi-tation during 1901 and 1902 which culminated in the Wyndham Land Act 1903, a measure which finally resolved the long and bitter conflict over land tenure in Ireland. With these successes behind him, O'Brien's political position seemed impregnable.

In fact, this was not so. By the end of 1903 O'Brien had resigned all his positions within the nationalist movement, and he was never again to exercise power or influence within its councils. This loss of position arose directly out of differing views as to the political significance of the Wyndham Land Act. O'Brien took the view — and it was endorsed by the National Directory of the movement — that the imminent removal of the economic ground of conflict between the nationalist majority and the minority landlord class inevitably involved a substantial shift in the strategy of the national-ist movement. A policy of 'conciliation' towards moderate sections of the landlord class was therefore adopted, based on the premise that the conference method which had been used to solve the land question was to be applied to the resolution of other problems in Irish life. For a number of leading nationalists such an approach to those whom they preferred to consider the 'hereditary enemy' was difficult to accept, and a powerfully led campaign was mounted to discredit the new policy. It was because of the damaging impact of this campaign on the unity and effectiveness of the movement that O'Brien resigned, thereby — as it was to turn out — isolating himself from the power centre of Irish nationalism for the rest of his career.

It is his resignation and its consequences which marks the most difficult problem in any assessment of O'Brien's political life. This action stands as a major turning-point both in his own career and in the way that the parliamentary nationalist movement subsequently developed. Looked upon retrospectively as an aberrant act by O'Brien — the staunch opponent of landlordism who had lost his wisdom in a surfeit of idealism — this moment has not been sufficiently recognised as the juncture at which the Irish parliamen-tary movement failed to adjust to circumstances fundamentally different from those which had shaped its past. Judgements about O'Brien's resignation have been taken out of the context of the options available to a parliamentary nationalist movement at that time. The significance and context of O'Brien's resignation must be examined before his career as a whole can be put into perspective and the basis from which the Irish parliamentary party evolved can be better understood.

How then, can we do this in a way which enables us to see that event in more than personal terms and in a context which elucidates the nature of the political realities from which it arose? What is proposed in this paper is to look at the underlying objectives of the revived nationalist movement from the time of the formation of the United Irish League in 1898 until 1903; assess the extent to which they were fulfilled or frustrated; set O'Brien's resignation in the context of that record; and finally attempt an explanation of the political significance of his action. The paper is an attempt to re-establish the importance of O'Brien's resignation as a political event, and to show how pivotal it is in the development of parliamentary nationalism.

The first objective we should examine in the revival of nationalism to which O'Brien so significantly contributed is the creation of a new and viable popular organisation. The fall of Parnell — and indeed the style of Parnell's leadership prior to that — had left nationalism devoid of the kind of popular organisation which was vital to its effectiveness. It was to fill this gap that O'Brien set about the creation of the United Irish League. This new body was an immediate and dramatic success. Beginning in West Mayo it had by the end of 1898 completely covered Co. Mayo and established many branches throughout the province of Connacht. By the end of 1899 its organisation extended throughout Ireland and its influence had become the dominant factor in nationalist politics. Its success was built around a campaign on behalf of poor farmers and against the grabbers of farms of the evicted and the graziers who were increasingly turning western agricultural areas into vast grass-lands. From its inception, however, the wider political purpose of the new organisation was perfectly clear. Its very name conjured up images of unity, of the Land League, and of the United Irishmen whose centenary the new organisation in part commemorated. And all those who took to the platforms of the new organisation constantly drew the contrast between its unity and effectiveness and the condition of the nationalist parliamentary representation. While drawing its inspiration and day-to-day activity from the agrarian cause, the United Irish League stood forth as a model for future nationalist political action.

In one respect in particular the UIL quickly exemplified what was to be an important element in the development of Irish nationalism. It embodied within its structure and in its actions a concept of alternative government, an expression of the legitimacy of Irish values and aspirations as opposed to those enforced by British law and government. This role for the League was greatly strengthened by British government reactions to its activities. Seeing the new organisation as a threat to the government's authority, the police were sent in to suppress it. This had the effect of instantly translating the League from an organisation involved in purely agrarian agitation into a nationalist force pitted in street conflicts with the forces of an alien government. This rapidly fulfilled O'Brien's purposes, both in clarifying the nationalist character of the organisation and in accelerating the popular response to it. The role was further consolidated in 1899 when the first democratic local government elections put control of many county and district councils in nationalist hands, often specifically the UIL, thus reinforcing the sense of legitimacy of the new organisation.

In one very important respect, however, the objectives of the founders of the UIL were frustrated. If the organisation were to play the role of an alternative government then it needed to be closely integrated with the nationalist parliamentary party. But it became apparent early in the life of the new organisation that leading parliamentarians were unwilling to involve themselves actively in its work. There were various reasons for this. The new organisation was clearly distrusted by the leaders of the Redmondite and Healyite factions as being too closely associated with O'Brien, and thus with the anti-Parnellite majority section. But even the leaders of O'Brien's own group of parliamentarians failed to lend significant support to the new organisation. Preoccupied with what they saw as their primary parliamentary roles, John Dillon and his colleagues paid lip-service to the work of the League while doing little to identify themselves with it. Thus the organisation was weakened in terms of its embodiment of a national purpose, and in particular its capacity to translate its local achievements into national politics was diminished.

The second major objective which underlay the revival of nationalist politics after 1893 was the reform of the parliamentary representation, and here the failure of the parliamentarians to involve
themselves in the work of the UIL seriously impaired the chance of
success. The record of the nationalist parliamentarians in the 1890s
was an abysmal one, and O'Brien — as demonstrated in a number
of his writings and speeches at this time[2] — was acutely aware that
unless there were significant reform at this level then the whole idea
of a parliamentary movement would be discredited. What he hoped
was that the identification of the best of the parliamentarians with
the work of the popular and ascendant UIL would serve to redeem
their reputations from an unfair association with the general body
of their number. In fact, their failure to so identify themselves had
the opposite effect. The neglect by virtually all parliamentarians of
this popular revival confirmed the growing public contempt for
them, a contempt from which increasingly none of them was
immune. This made exceedingly complicated and potentially dangerous the pursuit by the UIL of its goal of reform of the parliamentary
party. Subtly those involved in the organisation shifted from a belief
in renewal within the parliamentary ranks — reinforcing the better
MPs and getting rid of the worst — to a commitment to what came
to be called the policy of 'the clean sweep' — the absolute control
by the UIL of the selection of parliamentary candidates without
reference to any existing prerogatives of MPs. Such a policy, publicly
expressed as it was, could do nothing but aggravate the deteriorating
relationship between these two wings of the movement. Parliamentary leaders like John Dillon and Edward Blake, themselves sharing
most of the UIL criticisms of their colleagues, none the less became
defensive and began to deprecate the extent to which O'Brien and
others were publicly denigrating parliamentarians *en masse*.

It was in this context that the reunion of the Irish parliamentary
party occurred in January 1900. Such parliamentary unity was
obviously one of the consequences which it was hoped would flow
from the work of the UIL, but the form in which it occurred was
not in the interests of the organisation and served to frustrate the
aspiration for genuine reform. Frightened by the growing hostility
of the UIL, parliamentarians hurriedly patched up their institutional
differences, agreeing to a reunion which involved no substantial
reform or change in the form or functioning of the party and without
any decision as to the place which the UIL, as the only live nationalist
organisation, would play in relation to the party. Thus reunited,

the parliamentarians were able to assume a higher moral profile, deflecting the thrust of the UIL demand for reform. Public hostility to the parliamentarians having been so heavily focused on their lack of unity, it was now difficult to secure a hearing for the view that even though reunited they were still unregenerate. The general election in October 1900 showed how little had changed in the Irish parliamentary party as a result of reunion and how little impact the UIL had had on the shape of the new party. Of the 31 new nationalist Members of Parliament only six had been actively associated with the League's work prior to the parliamentary reunion. More serious an indicator of the League's failure was the extent to which those MPs who the League had been most determined to displace had found their way back into Parliament. In the last years of the old Parliament there had been only about 15 members of the party who could be relied upon to attend Parliament with regularity, and yet 49 of the nationalist members of that Parliament were back after the 1900 general election. As O'Brien was later to write of the parliamentary reunion of 1900 'The party was reunified, rather than reformed'.[3]

Central to O'Brien's original concept of a new political organisation was that it should secure the adherence of significant elements of the more extreme nationalists; this is the third of the major objectives of the nationalist revival in this period. The launching of the UIL had coincided with the biggest revival in non-constitutional separatist politics since the Fenian days of the 1860s. Much of this revival had been stimulated by the imminence of the centenary of the 1798 rebellion and O'Brien had seen the UIL as 'a *really* big '98 celebration'[4] which would help recover for constitutionalism some standing amongst more extreme nationalists. In this it was to some extent successful, but its achievement was greatly circumscribed by certain geographical and social limitations inherent in its structure. It was in the west, where the League was most successful and its conflict with the police most marked, that more extreme separatists were more readily drawn into its organisation. This was in part a product of local history. The legacy of the Land League was still strong there, and extreme nationalists were instinctively drawn to a campaign that so largely replicated the earlier movement. Also in the west the League was more successful than elsewhere in capturing the sentiment associated with the centenary of 1798. But these factors did not operate in the east of the country. In Dublin the revival of separatist sentiment was to be a powerful influence in the next phase of Irish history, but the League's position in Dublin was weak and it failed to tap this new and important expression of nationalism. Worse still, the League unintentionally alienated a group of younger nationalists who, disenchanted with the collapse of organised nationalism, were not necessarily antagonistic to parliamentary action *per se*. In a by-election in South Mayo early in 1900, a group of nationalists who were to be the nucleus of the later Sinn Fein put forward a candidate of their own against that of the League. This led to a conflict which, in terms of the League's own interests in the long term, would have been better avoided. The hostility so aroused, coinciding as it did with the reunion of the parliamentary party and the apparent reassertion of traditional political structures, drove these young and idealistic nationalists towards a more intransigent attitude to the parliamentary idea. Tom Kettle, a younger parliamentarian who was to pay a heavy political price for the alienation which was to occur, saw the South Mayo election as the point at which the incipient Sinn Fein had developed sharply away from the parliamentary tradition,[5] helping create the political divide which was to bedevil nationalist politics for the next ten years.

The fourth of the objectives which underlay the revival of nationalism after 1898 was the development of a broader political strategy around which pressure could be mounted against the British government, ostensibly on the land question, but with the potential for continuing nationalist purposes. The creation of the UIL had obviously been the first step in this, but after the reunion of the party in 1900 O'Brien attempted to focus the attention of the movement on the need to enlarge the scope of political action. The intensive land agitation carried on during 1901 and 1902 was the product of this intent. The basic form of the strategy of which this agitation was a part is clearly discernible in O'Brien's speeches and in the columns of the League newspaper, the *Irish People*. One of the most interesting features of this strategy is that it foreshadows in its main characteristics that later advocated by Sinn Fein. It relied heavily on the concept of passive resistance. Emphasis was placed on the parallel between boycotting in rural Ireland and the peaceful picketing which the law allowed to trade unionism in England. Any activity which gave a legal justification for police action against tenants, for example, was to be avoided; thus there were not to be rent refusals as in the Land League days. Where the execution of British government in Ireland left any room for moral attack it was to be pursued vigorously, and in this regard the court system and police action were to be primary targets of attack; jury-packing, for example, came under heavy fire in these years. The concept of alternative government, embryonically present in the Land League and more overtly evident in the early UIL, was now to become an explicit object of the strategy. A clear theory was evolving whereby the Irish parliamentary party, the UIL itself, nationalist controlled county and district councils and unofficial quasi-judicial League functions were to be seen as the embodiment of a communal and national ideal. There was also clearly emerging as part of this new strategy a more explicit sense of the need for an 'Irish Ireland'. There was advocacy of the wider use of the Irish language and of Irish pastimes and sports. Public encouragement was given for the purchase of Irish manufactures in preference to imported ones.

Although the agitation which gave expression to this new strategy left much of Ireland seriously disturbed during 1901 and 1902, its effect was much less significant than its devisers had hoped. Although the government heavily resisted the agitation, and there were many imprisonments, the main problems arose from the indifference or hostility of nationalists themselves. It was a peculiar misfortune that those younger nationalists who were evolving a theory similar in character failed to see the relevance to their purpose of what was actually a going proposition in the Irish countryside. The chance of making any active appeal to such nationalists was greatly reduced by the need to confront the mistakes and hostilities of those nationalists supposedly associated with the League. In O'Brien's absence abroad his associates introduced a damaging no rent strike on the De Freyne estate despite the clear incompatibility of this with the principles of the new strategy. A 'Settlement of Connaught Committee' intended to publicise the failure of British government in dealing with problems of congestion in the poor western districts had to be abandoned because of Dillon's refusal to participate. Finally, in August 1902 a triumvirate of Dillon, Redmond and T.P. O'Connor were responsible for a private, but powerfully presented, attack on O'Brien over the conduct of the national campaign; they claimed that the whole movement was being put at risk by too extreme an agitation in Ireland, which was turning English opinion against the nationalist cause.[6] This was the final blow to the attempt to create an aggressive agitation in which the commitment and involvement of all levels and all types of nationalists would serve as an intimidation against too fierce a government reaction. The leadership of the parliamentary wing of the movement had clearly indicated their refusal to support vigorous political agitation in Ireland.

The agitation had, however, been effective enough to bring about the realisation of the fifth of the main objectives underlying the nationalist revival of these years, the settlement of the land tenure question. The effect of land legislation from the 1870s onwards, and more particularly of Unionist government policy in the 1890s, had been to bring the landlord and tenant sides much closer together, both now being in basic agreement that the transfer of landownership from the landlord to the occupier was the best solution to the land problem. A major difference, however, remained as to the means of achieving this, the tenant interest being strongly committed to compulsory purchase and the landlords insisting that the process should be entirely voluntary. The central thrust of the 1901–2 agitation was to force the government and landlords to concede that a more radical initiative was required if any progress were to be made in land purchase. This it eventually achieved by bringing representatives of the majority of landlords to the negotiating table. The result was the Land Conference convened at the end of 1902, from which the basic terms of the Wyndham Land Act emerged.

The settlement of the land question had very important political implications for the Irish nationalist movement. Since the late 1870s that movement had organised itself on the basis of land agitation, putting the interests of the tenant farmers at the forefront of its programme. That had now obviously to change. This emphasis hitherto given to the land question in nationalist ideology and organisation had shaped the nationalist movement in a particular way, largely excluding from its purview Irish people who were landlords and thereby, to a great extent, Protestants as well. It was this materialist basis to the parliamentary movement which had turned some old Fenians like John O'Leary into opponents. It was consistent with some of the longer traditions of Irish nationalism that the opportunity should now be taken to remove as one of the defining features of nationalism the now redundant concern with the question of land tenure. This intent was the basis of the 'conciliation' policy which O'Brien devised and which was approved by the National Directory of the UIL on 8 September 1903. Put forward by O'Brien, it was a policy which enjoyed the full support of John Redmond, the party leader.[7] The move was the more timely by reason of the split which had occurred in the landlord ranks over the convening of the Land Conference, a split between those who remained intransigently Unionist and against the aspirations of the bulk of the Irish people and those who sought and welcomed the opportunity for communication and compromise.

One of the characteristics of O'Brien's political style affected the manner in which the new policy was put forward. Always very clear in his own mind about the direction which he thought appropriate for the nationalist movement, he acted upon his views too impulsively for others to follow easily. In turning apparently so suddenly and with such enthusiasm to a 'conciliation' policy O'Brien totally alienated two of his closest political associates, John Dillon and Michael Davitt. For O'Brien himself the abolition of landlordism represented the fulfilment of what had been the principal goal of his political life, leaving the path clear for the adoption of new, more specifically nationalist objectives. But for Dillon and Davitt the achievement of a peasant proprietorship was not an end for which they strove in itself. Davitt, a believer in land nationalisation, involved himself in land agitation to help destroy landlordism, not to create peasant proprietors, while for Dillon it was the means to a different end — the creation on the basis of agrarian discontent of a weapon to be wielded in the cause of Home Rule. Thus for neither of them did the abolition of landlordism and the creation of a peasant proprietorship open up new political goals, but removed the familiar and habitual ground on which their life's work was founded; as such it was deeply threatening to them. They reacted by launching a determined campaign, aided by Thomas Sexton and the *Freeman's Journal*, to defeat the new conciliation policy. It was the intensity of this campaign, and Redmond's failure as leader to respond to it, which brought about O'Brien's resignation on 4 November 1903.

Why did O'Brien resign? In the first place, he felt powerless in terms of his formal authority to react against the opposition to the new policy in any other way. He was neither leader of the party nor president of the UIL. Any public response by him, if not backed up by the party leader, would be depicted as a purely individual point of view. Redmond refused to take a strong stand on the issue. Unknown to O'Brien, Dillon had already put Redmond on the defensive in private correspondence by deftly exploiting his acute fear of public dissension.[8] The one and only card O'Brien had to play was his immense personal importance as the architect of nationalist revival and of the continuing strategy of the movement. Resignation was the only way he could play that card, but he did so hopeful that the manifest lack of any positive alternative to his own policy would force the movement back to a full endorsement of it. That was not, however, what happened.

The reaction to O'Brien's resignation involved, not the public debate about the issue which he had expected, but its successful suppression. Redmond, terrified of the implications of O'Brien's resignation for the unity of the movement, turned immediately to Dillon for support, and between them they ensured that there would be no debate in party organisations of the issues which had prompted O'Brien's resignation. Indeed, Dillon even advised that there should be no attempt to rescind formally the conciliation policy because to do so would provide an opening for its debate.[9] Thus an impression was created of continuity within the movement which obscured the real shift in power and strategy which had occurred, and O'Brien was left isolated and apparently himself the dissensionist. What in reality had happened was that the only remaining course open at that time for a constitutional nationalist movement had been frustrated, and the nationalist organisation had been redirected — not back to 'traditional lines' as Dillon and Davitt wanted to believe, but into a cul-de-sac from which there was to be no exit. It was here, it should be considered, that the ultimate failure of constitutional nationalism was determined.

The adoption of a 'conciliation' policy did raise some substantial problems for a movement which had become so accustomed to the language of antagonism with respect to the landlord class in Ireland, but quite apart from the need for an appropriate political response to the Land Act its adoption must be seen in the context of what had been the fate of alternative strategies in the preceding years. The most notable feature of the revival of nationalism in the late 1890s had been the UIL, but this organisation had been developed in the face of antagonism or indifference on the part of parliamentary leaders. The reunion of the parliamentary party in 1900 had been a product, not of the reforming zeal of the UIL, but of the intent of parliamentarians to thwart that reform. The UIL had been much less successful than had been hoped in attracting the support of more extreme nationalists, but the task had been made immensely more difficult by the constant need to take account of the criticism and indifference of the parliamentary wing of the movement; looking over its shoulder at the parliamentarians was not the posture best suited to attracting young nationalists like those involved in the beginnings of Sinn Fein. In all these frustrations the leadership of the parliamentary party had played a prominent part. In particular, John Dillon — critically placed to influence the course of events — had either neglected to take an active role in these vitally important political developments or had been hostile to them. Thus by 1902 it was evident to O'Brien that an aggressive nationalist agitation was no longer a viable possibility, and it is in the light of this that we must assess his role in relation to the Land Conference, the Land Act and the adoption of 'conciliation'. In these circumstances O'Brien was bound to react very strongly to an attempt by those who had systematically opposed or undermined an aggressive strategy to destroy the alternative which had been made possible by the settlement of the land question.

O'Brien's resignation had the effect in practice of eliminating his own influence on the course of events and undermining the viability of the policy he had sought to promote. Under concerted pressure from Dillon, Redmond cooperated in the practical dismemberment of the policy to which he had been as fully committed as O'Brien. No effective replacement for that policy was evolved. Dillon stressed repeatedly the need for a 'vigorous policy' if the party were to survive, and in the aftermath of O'Brien's resignation he was instrumental in giving a greater priority to issues such as the settlement of the west, the evicted tenants question, and the university question, but these were all matters either related to the events of the past or near to resolution. No strategy emerged which coupled political action in Ireland to long-term political goals. Dillon's advice that the party should draw its sustenance and inspiration from a continuation of land agitation was so lacking in realism, given the increasing impact of the new Land Act and the absence of political leaders willing to undertake the work and the risks associated with it, that he made little attempt in practice to follow it once he had taken from O'Brien the effective control of the movement.

It was towards a measure of Home Rule, wrested from a Liberal Party dependent at some later date upon Irish votes, that the hopes and energies of the party were now turned. Not only did this single-dimensional perspective greatly limit the tactical freedom of the Irish party in its dealings with British politicians, but so total a reorientation of the party's policy towards Westminster and the vicissitudes of British politics had serious implications for the party in Ireland. In the first place, such a course involved the abrogation, without any compensating concession from the Liberals, of one of the central principles on which the reunion of the party had been secured in 1900 — the freedom of the party from any alliances with British political parties. Many of those former Parnellites in the party who had originally demanded this principle had in practice since abandoned it. But many of the nationalists whom the UIL had hoped by its strategy to draw nearer to parliamentary nationalism were not likely to be attracted to a party which had stepped back in this way to the discredited anti-Parnellite tactics of the 1890s. Most seriously of all, a policy so dependent on the fluctuations of British politics and the necessities of parliamentary calculation turned the focus of the parliamentary party upon circumstances outside Ireland at a time when what was most evident within Ireland was the growing emphasis on self-reliance and the distinctiveness of the Irish identity as sources of cultural and social, as well as political, inspiration.

A party which had of deliberate purpose reversed a policy of conciliation towards a minority class had not by so doing restored itself to the position in which it had stood prior to the adoption of that policy. Had the conflict embodied in the land agitation been continued unimpeded by recourse to conference the door to reconciliation would have remained open; as it was, the landlord class, Unionist opinion in general, and indeed Protestants as such, could hardly obliterate from their memories the deliberate action of the nationalist party against, not tangible grievances, but the very principle of conciliation and cooperation. Unionist extremists could not have been better provided with arguments against Home Rule than by the treatment meted out to those nationalists who, in face of the removal of the last great economic barrier between the two major communities in Ireland, had attempted to evoke a climate of tolerance and reconciliation. O'Brien's resignation had opened the way to a development which greatly compounded the effects of this abandonment of conciliation on the perceptions by Protestants of the nature of the demand for Home Rule. The UIL organisation, on which much of the vitality of nationalism had depended since 1898, was effectively split by the events of late 1903. Many of those who hoped to see it assume a new political role in the aftermath of the settlement of the land question lost their enthusiasm and commitment to that body once that larger purpose had been abandoned. Others in the organisation retained their commitment to it, but in many cases this was founded upon a much lesser concept of the role of that organisation in the pursuit of nationalist objectives. But in the north, and particularly in Belfast, no such crisis occurred,

and the UIL organisation weathered the storm of O'Brien's resignation with equanimity, its leadership having been bitterly opposed
to the course which O'Brien had followed since the Land Conference.
It was this vigorous and effective organisation, based not on the
agrarian issues which characterised the League elsewhere in the
country but on the sectarian issue endemic to Belfast politics,
which came to fill the vacuum created in national politics by the
neutralisation of the nationalist purpose which underlay the conciliation policy. In its train went the Ancient Order of Hibernians,
which came to give its distinctive character to the largely political
machinery functions of the UIL. Both a cause and a symptom of the
domination of the parliamentary party by these northern sectarian
influences, the alienation of large areas of Munster from the parliamentary party further diminished its claim to speak for Irish nationality. In the face of the reality of this basis of the parliamentary party,
the denials of its leaders that it was sectarian were of little avail in
the ears of those Protestants who saw at closer hand the 'orangeism'
of their opponents. As the *Irish Worker* was later to declare, 'To
Brother Devlin and not to Brother Carson is mainly due the progress
of the Convenanter movement in Ulster.'[10]

O'Brien's resignation marked the end of his effective political
authority. As such it may be seen as a tactical error on his part,
bringing unnecessarily upon him the long period of political frus-
tration which was to follow. More usefully we may take that
resignation as an act to which there was no real alternative if O'Brien
were to try to ensure that the methods adopted in the nationalist
movement were appropriate to its long term political goals. His
resignation was a desperate attempt to awaken from the pattern of
the past a political leadership which held responsibility for respon-
ding to new circumstances. As such it was a failure. But it is an
event which must be taken more seriously, not only in terms of the
development of O'Brien's political ideas and policies, but as the
juncture at which the parliamentary party was set in a mould which
shaped the rest of its history.

Notes and References

1. F.S.L. Lyons, *The Irish Parliamentary Party, 1890–1910* (Faber and Faber, London, 1951), p.90.
2. See especially his speech in Belfast on 6 October 1897, *Freeman's Journal*.

3. William O'Brien, *An Olive Branch in Ireland and its History* (Macmillan, London, 1910), p.123.

4. O'Brien to J.M. Tuohy, 6 January 1898, National Library of Ireland, Tuohy Papers, MS 3883 (10).

5. T.M. Kettle, 'Would the "Hungarian Policy" Work?', *New Ireland Review*, vol.22 (February 1905), p.322.

6. T.P. O'Connor to O'Brien, 12 August 1902, University College, Cork, O'Brien MS AM 139–43.

7. Redmond to Dillon (copy), 25 September 1903, National Library of Ireland, Redmond Papers, MS 15182 (4).

8. Dillon to Redmond, 2 and 8 October 1903, National Library of Ireland, Redmond Papers, MS 15182 (5); Redmond to Dillon, 7 October 1903, Trinity College, Dublin, Dillon Papers, MS 6747 (49).

9. Dillon's Journal, 28 November 1903, Trinity College, Dublin, Dillon Papers, MS 6542; Dillon to Redmond, 25 December 1903, National Library of Ireland, Redmond Papers, MS 15182 (5).

10. Quoted in R.M. Henry, *The Evolution of Sinn Fein* (Talbot Press, Dublin, 1920), p.98.

5   Murder as Metaphor: Griffin's Portrayal of Ireland in the Year of Catholic Emancipation[1]

Tom Dunne

In 1829, Gerald Griffin, 26 years old, from a provincial middle-class Catholic background and author of two well-received collections of Irish 'tales', published two new works. The first, *The Collegians*, arguably the most important and certainly the most popular nineteenth-century Irish novel, was based on a sensational murder case, and became, in turn, the basis of an even more popular melodrama by Boucicault. The second comprised two short novels in tandem; a crude romance, with interesting political undertones, *The Rivals*; and a very powerful study of the conflict between a perverted official violence and the communal-based violence of Whiteboyism, called *Tracy's Ambition*.[2]

In that same year a revolution in Irish political life, under the leadership of Griffin's class, resulted in the notable victory of Catholic Emancipation.[3] Griffin's three novels of Emancipation year, while written, in part, to promote the Catholic cause, did not address themselves directly to the issues of the campaign (as did some of the novels of the other major Catholic writers of the period, John and Michael Banim),[4] nor did they radiate the self-confidence, or the Catholic nationalism, of much of the campaign's rhetoric. They portrayed, rather, a society in chaos, lawless and violent, morally bankrupt and culturally confused. This is the dark underside of the Catholic mind, the vision of social realities which fuelled the movement for constitutional reform. Endemic violence had been a constant of Irish life for 70 years, until the Catholic Association had managed to channel popular grievances into the new form of peaceful mass politics. The deflection of class antagonism was a prime aim of the movement, and the threat of renewed popular violence, should Emancipation be denied, was as much a real fear of the Catholic leadership as a potent argument in the appeal to British opinion. These novels, therefore, afford important insights into Catholic social and political attitudes, which are inadequately reflected in the speeches and writings of the political leadership. It is not necessary, even if it was possible, to establish how representative Griffin was of middle-class Catholic opinion, although the immense popularity of his books may offer some indication. A novelist's representative character is different from that of the politician, though also shaped in part by sensitivity to audience-response. The merits of novels as sources of evidence for the historian are various, reflecting the rich complexity of the genre. The novelist is, inescapably, a historian of his own time and society, most particularly in his reflection of its cultural ethos. In the early nineteenth century, the dominance of the realist mode also made him pay particular attention to social and political contexts.

Griffin's background and experience help to explain why his work reflected especially the fears and insecurities of his class.[5] A series of traumatic events exacerbated a natural hypersensitivity, most notably his inadequate education; the emigration to North America of most of his very close family, including his parents, when he was 17; his loneliness and poverty as an *emigré* writer in London, where he went to seek his fortune as a playwright before he was 20. Socially, his father's repeated failures in business, and his own dependence on his elder brothers, contrasted painfully with his expectations. Emotionally, he found it difficult to make and sustain friendships outside his family circle. Part of the strength of his fiction came from the way he used it to explore his own psychology, many of his heroes being tortured 'sensitives' like himself, notably Hardress Cregan in *The Collegians*. Many of them also reflect the social flux out of which the Catholic middle class had emerged, for example, Kyrle Daly, the other 'collegian' or college friend of Cregan's, the Trinity-educated son of a Catholic middleman, who aspired to marry the heiress of the leading local gentry family. The Limerick countryside, in which Griffin spent most of his childhood and much of his adult life, also shaped his work; the evocation of its scenery being central to his romanticism, and its intense social conflict a major factor in his obsession with agrarian violence. Next to Tipperary, the most disturbed county in Ireland during this period, it was one of the main areas of operation of the new system of special constabulary and stipendiary magistrates introduced to deal with agrarian secret societies in 1814–15, and despite this (or, as Griffin argued, because of it) it was a major centre of Rockite disturbances in the widespread Munster 'rebellion' of 1821–23.

The assassination in Limerick in 1821, of the unpopular special magistrate, Going, led to a reassessment of the system, and almost certainly inspired Griffin to write *Tracy's Ambition*. Limerick violence was also notably sectarian, featuring attacks'on Palatines as well as tithe-proctors, and it has been identified as a major centre of millenarian belief in the early 1820s. In 1828, when Griffin was writing *The Collegians*, it was one of the areas where maverick peasant mass meetings caused concern to the leadership of the Catholic Association, as threatening their social control.[6]

The themes and approach of Griffin's fiction were also determined by its political intent. In common with contemporaries like Maria Edgeworth, Lady Morgan, the Banims, he wrote not only to influence public opinion, but to urge specific reforms on government. For this remarkable group of novelists, fiction was 'politics by other means'.[7]

The contrast with contemporary English writers was striking, and reflected Ireland's very different historical experience. English society may not have been so peaceful as the novels of Austen or Thackeray suggested, but, in comparison with Ireland, it was characterised by a remarkable cultural and social cohesion, political stability and an absence of major racial or religious divisions. It seemed also at ease with its past, its history largely taken for granted in fiction as a shared experience, and reflecting the confidence and prosperity of an imperial power. Ireland, by contrast, was an intensely colonial society, one dominated by both the memories and the consequences of a recent, radical and traumatic experience of colonisation. This meant that the colonist Ascendancy's monopoly of power through religious discrimination was the main issue of politics; that the colonial land settlement was a major complicating factor in class conflict; and that competing historical interpretations were an obsessive feature of public controversy. These were also the dominant themes of Irish fiction, as in Maria Edgeworth's complex critique of landlordism as the critical factor in colonial rule,[8] the manipulation of history in contrasting ways by Lady Morgan and John Banim,[9] and Gerald Griffin's concern with the roots of Irish lawlessness and violence. There are interesting parallels with modern African fiction, the novels of Edgeworth having much in common with those of white colonials like Camus, while those of 'native' writers like Griffin can be compared to the work of black Africans such as Chinua Achebe, the title of whose first book, *Things Fall Apart*, comes from a Yeats poem, and could serve as a text for Griffin's work.[10] Irish fiction in this period was colonial in terms of the writers' perception of their audience, as well as in its themes. All of them addressed their books primarily to English readers, partly for obvious economic reasons, but also to make educated English opinion aware of Irish realities, and to counteract the dominant and damaging negative image of Ireland in England. This was in a long-established tradition of Irish writing from all communities,[11] and one given added impetus by the Act of Union in 1800, which more clearly located the centre of Irish political power at Westminster, while making Irish affairs of more direct concern to English politics and English public opinion. Debates in Parliament, government commissions and reports, travellers' accounts, all made the horrors of Irish poverty and violence better known in England, reinforcing the traditional negative stereotypes. The first generation of Irish Catholic novelists were counter-propagandists, presenting the case of the victims of the colonial system to its ultimate rulers. The fact that they wrote in the language, and used the literary forms of the imperial culture, created notable tensions in their work. So also did their ambivalent attitude to the imperial system, the fact of which they accepted and exploited, while resenting its unjust operation by the Irish colonist class. They were not nationalists, but advocates of the application of social and political reforms, on liberal-humanitarian grounds, to a chaotic and crisis-ridden colonial society.

Griffin had outlined two possible approaches for the colonial novelist in his introduction to *Tales of the Munster Festivals* (1827). This took the form of a dialogue between the author and 'a sour old man', a Gaelic antiquarian. The former argued that 'the conscientious novelist' could improve understanding between 'neighbouring nations', and by depicting reality, 'furnish the statesman and the legislator with an index to the dispositions and habits of the people he was to govern'. The antiquarian dismissively compared this approach to that of

the music master in Molière . . . who attributes all the wars, famines and pestilences . . . to a want of the general diffusion of musical knowledge. You seem to have the same faith in the influence of novels. . . . You would, I suppose, have a typhus fever or a scarcity of potatoes remedied by a smart tale, while you would knock a general insurrection on the head with a romance in three volumes.

In his view, 'a ruined people stood in need of a more potent restorative' which the novelist would find in 'the Ireland that once was'.[12] During the next three years, however, Griffin ignored both the appeal to the past, and the implication that he should be more concerned to promote Irish morale than to inform English consciences. But he then abandoned his characteristic didactic realism for a romantic historical novel, *The Invasion*, set in a pre-colonial golden age and thus elaborating on an important motif of Gaelic poetry from the mid-seventeenth century.[13] Before doing so, he wrote a reflective conclusion on his work to date, at the end of *Tracy's Ambition*, and this included the clearest statement of both his political intent and his colonial perspectives. Commenting that 'the Irish peasant has, by a combination of circumstances, become better known within the last few years to his English rulers, than he has been since the Conquest', he declared that the objective of his writings had been to further this process by depicting 'the character and condition of the Irish peasant as he is'. Urging political reform 'upon the attention of his governors', Griffin's appeal was unambiguous.

> Will England then, remain insensible to the personal afflictions, to the continued agonies of this long-suffering and long-neglected class of men? . . . Will England continue to wear this burthensome conquest around her neck, like the painful ornaments borne by some Indian princess, serving no other purpose, but to exhaust her strength and to embarrass her in her relations with foreign countries?

The conservative as well as colonial bias of Griffin's politics was clear in this fascinating manifesto, particularly in the way in which his compassion for the peasantry was combined with a strong fear and obvious distaste, and his view of the landlord class, once reformed, as their 'natural protectors'.[14] His concern to avert social revolution as well as to end injustice by timely reform, resembled that of the leadership of the Catholic Association, though he was critical on occasion of their rhetorical excesses.[15] It is interesting, in this regard, to note the silences as well as the themes in these novels, in particular the absence of Catholic sectarianism in his portrayal of peasant violence, and the confining of his critique of the Ascendancy to its down-at-heel squireen element. These should be kept in mind during the analysis which follows, of Griffin's dominant theme, that social injustice, and the systematic abuse of the law by elements in the official and Ascendancy classes, were the root cause of the alienation of the peasantry.

Given that two, at least, of the novels in question will be unfamiliar to most readers, it may be useful to give brief outlines. Set nominally in the 1770s, *The Collegians* was based on a celebrated murder that happened in Limerick, when Griffin was 16, the same age as the victim. The case caused a sensation mainly because it involved a member of a local gentry family, who had seduced a girl from a poor background, and then murdered her, with the help of his boatman. Both men were executed despite the efforts of Daniel O'Connell, who defended, to pin the blame solely on the servant. In his central story of Hardress Cregan's passion for Eily O'Connor, their secret marriage, the young man's inability to face the social consequences, and his commission to Danny Mann to 'get rid' of Eily, Griffin stuck close to the original.[16] Like O'Connell, though in a different manner, he made the gentry figure a sympathetic character, while the servant was darkly evil, and he even succeeded, where the great lawyer had failed, by having Cregan exiled rather than executed. The great strength of this novel is that Griffin focused on the class element which was fundamental to the tragedy, so that, in Thomas Flanagan's words, 'the crime is made to serve as a mirror of the culture in which it occurred'.[17] A wide range of social class and class relationship is depicted, the main emphasis throughout being on the attitudes of all classes to the law. Also of interest is the fact that all the main characters, except for one of the appalling squireens, are Catholic, and that the only family included from the higher reaches of the Ascendancy is portrayed in positive terms. The novel has a second important dimension, as indicated by the title. This is the contrast in philosophy and psychology between the college friends, Cregan and Daly, the former a tortured romantic, 'an impassive slave to his imagination', the latter a worthy, if dull rationalist. This is clearly another projection of the conflict within the author's own mind, and it is an indication of his complexity, that having made Cregan the more interesting and sympathetic character of the two, he then was upset at the tendency of his readers to prefer him.[18]

Cregan and Daly are also rivals in love, and this theme is repeated in the crudely melodramatic story, *The Rivals*. These are the quiveringly sensitive and insufferably priggish 'patriot', Francis Riordan and the unscrupulous and tyrannical magistrate, Richard Lacy. Both

appear to be Catholic, but the heroine is a Methodist, Esther
Wilderming. The main interest in the story lies in the victimisation
of the peasantry by a corrupt magistrate and their defence by the
patriotic hero; and in peasant antagonism to the law, and to the
'Peelers', or new police force. These themes are reworked superbly in
the very fine *Tracy's Ambition*, the story of a prosperous Protestant
middleman, popular with his tenantry, in part because of his Catholic wife. He hopes to rise socially by means of a government
appointment, and to this end becomes an ally of Dalton, the special
magistrate, sent to the area with a company of police to put
down the Rockite agrarian secret society. The alliance ruins Tracy
financially and estranges him from the peasantry. Dalton is unscrupulous and abrasive, and his activities, together with those of the police,
push even hitherto law-abiding tenants into murderous violence. As
in *The Collegians*, the victims are the innocent, Tracy's wife and
Dalton's son. This short novel is a brilliant indictment of the
corruption of law by the colonial system, and a sympathetic explanation of the roots of the peasant violence which was so shocking
to English opinion.

The depiction of class in these three novels naturally reflects
Griffin's own background. Thus, the squireen class who are the
villains of *The Collegians* are introduced to the reader by the upright
Catholic middleman, Mr Daly, and his son Kyrle, who view them
with either derision or contempt — the Cregans as vulgar *arrivistes*,
Creagh as 'a notorious duellist' and social parasite. Connolly a
drunkard and incurably dishonest. Clearly, Griffin shared the hope
that Kyrle Daly expressed to Creagh, that 'the time will come when
you and your mean and murderous class shall be disposed and
trampled on as you deserve'.[19] The type reappears in the 'true wild
Irishman', Purtill, and to a lesser degree in Dalton's son, in *Tracy's
Ambition*, both of them also practitioners of the 'bloody science' of
duelling, stressed by Griffin as the defining characteristic of the
class. It is much discussed as well as practised in *The Collegians*,
and was important in the corruption of Hardress Cregan.[20] The
increasingly political nature of Griffin's writing over the three novels
can be seen in the fact that while the squireens operated as individuals, or as a class, in *The Collegians*, in the two later novels, they
featured mainly as corrupt administrators of the law. Similarly, their
abrasive and contemptuous attitude to the peasantry, articulated
vehemently by Dalton in *Tracy's Ambition*, had been conveyed on
the level of symbolic action in *The Collegians*, as in the hunting of

Danny Mann by the drunken squireens, who compete to 'pink the rascal' with their swords.[21] Dalton's long diatribe against 'the people', as 'a base, fawning, servile, treacherous, smooth-tongued and blackhearted race of men; bloody in their inclinations debauched and sensual in their pleasures, beasts in their cunning and beasts in their appetites', was accompanied by some real understanding of the roots of peasant violence, as due to 'bad education, poverty and a fierce and ignorant enthusiasm'.[22] As with the character of Hardress Cregan, it may not be too fanciful to see in Dalton's attitude, a projection of the dark side of Griffin's own mentality. We will find the same mixture, with the proportions and emphases reversed, in Griffin's portrayal of his peasant characters.

No such shadows, however, darkened the minds of Griffin's middle-class heroes, best represented by the Dalys, 'a very respectable family in middle life'; and his affectionate description of their lifestyle is clearly an idealised account of his own childhood.[23] While he failed to give them a central importance in the events of *The Collegians*, he emphasised their pivotal and mediatorial role in society. The middleman system, he argued, was 'both natural and beneficial', because, in the absence of a resident gentry in many areas, wealthy farmers assumed 'the feudal authority which distinguished their aristocratic archetypes'.[24] Their role in this 'troublesome country', according to Abel Tracy, was to mediate between 'our castle-holders above us and our cabin-holders below'.[25] When Tracy fails in this role, he becomes the object of peasant violence, while Francis Riordan in *The Rivals* is a hero precisely because he persists as a champion of the poor, at great risk to himself.[26] The Dalys are depicted as paternalistic, and very class-conscious. The wonderful description of Mrs Daly's wake, for example, emphasises the distribution of people throughout the house according to class, and a very heavy atmosphere of decorous and deferential behaviour. Despite their popularity, the Dalys feel threatened, and in their living-room, among the cherished symbols of civilised life, was an awesomely stocked gunrack, which, the author commented, 'manifested Mr Daly's determination to maintain, if necessary by force of arms, his claim to the fair possessions which his honest industry had acquired'.[27] The threat, clearly, came from below, the family being intimate with the local gentry, to the extent that Kyrle could aspire to marry Anna Chute, which indeed he does in the end, a telling comment on the social aspirations of Griffin's class.

It is also an interesting fact that Griffin's portrayal of 'the peasantry', as he described both urban and rural poor, was more vivid and varied than that of his own class. His peasant characters ranged from the innocent and the honest, through the comic, the picturesque and the homespun philosophical, to the devious and the murderous. While sympathetic overall, his depiction of this class had interesting negative aspects, sharing the ambivalence of the Catholic Association leadership, so well captured in Richard Lalor Sheil's description of their followers as 'this vast body of fierce, of fearless and desperate peasantry'.[28] Awareness of the Irish peasant stereotype expected by his English readers gave a literary, as well as a class and political, bias to Griffin's typology. His critique in the afterword to *Tracy's Ambition*, of the manner in which the Banims had satisfied the 'alarmed interest' and 'strong curiosity' of the English public regarding the Irish poor, is revealing of his own mixed feelings.

> They were the first who painted the Irish peasant sternly from the life; they placed him before the world in all his ragged energy and cloudy loftiness of spirit; they painted him as he is, goaded by the sense of national and personal wrong, and venting his long pent up agony in the savage cruelty of his actions, in the powerful idiomatic eloquence of his language, in the wild truth and unregulated generosity of his sentiments, in the scalding vehemence of his approaches and the shrewd biting satire of his jests. They painted him also, such as he is sometimes found . . . mean, cringing, servile, crafty and sycophantic.

The similarity in perspectives to Dalton's diatribe is striking, however different the tone, and while Griffin went on to claim that his fiction, by contrast with that of the Banims, had attempted 'to furnish a softening corollary . . . to bring forward the sorrows and the affections more frequently than the violent and fearful passions of the people',[29] it was the latter which obsessed him.

He also managed to exploit the humorous aspects of the stereotype with particular success, though this also had a serious purpose. Following in the tradition begun by Edgeworth, Griffin depicted Irish peasant speech, whether humorous, flattering or servile, as the survival mechanism of a vulnerable class, and the product of an understandable cultural confusion following linguistic change.[30] Take, for example, his different depictions of the servile peasant. Lowry Looby, that wonderfully named servant of the Dalys in *The*

Collegians though physically grotesque, was characterised by both an 'excellent honesty', and a shrewdly comic loquacity, including, 'the national talent for adroit flattery', which he employed 'under the disguise of a simpleness which gave it a wonderful efficiency'. This complex persona, Griffin tells us, was 'the effect in great measure of habitual penury and dependence'.[31] By contrast, the handsome Kerry giant, Myles Murphy, exploited a totally confident as well as richly humorous flattery in order to have his ponies released from the pound at Castle Chute, causing Anna Chute to ask, 'Could any courtier make interest more skilfully?'[32] The devious and utterly amoral Phil Naughten, another Kerry 'mountaineer', fighting for his life in court before the same audience, months later, answered the magistrate in Irish, was 'humble, timid and deprecating', and with equal success, exploited 'the assumed simplicity, and the inimitable subtleties of evasion and will, which an Irish peasant can display, when he is made to undergo a scene of judicial scrutiny'.[33] Griffin also manipulated peasant speech successfully, in balancing peasant violence with explanations by sympathetically drawn peasant commentators. Thus, Moran, Abel Tracy's deferential tenant, described the Rockites who 'murdered the mistress', as 'a set o' poor boys . . . distressed and sazed an' driven out o' house an' home, without either country or carakter or religion, an' they grow desperate'[34] — an explanation which Griffin's depiction of society in the novel had already conditioned his English readers to accept. The most important of these peasant guides to the dark side of Irish life, Morty Shanahan, so impressed Tracy with his explanations of poverty and violence that the middle-man changed his 'long-established but lightly founded opinions'. Shanahan's views had particular force because he had appeared throughout as an honest man, who refused to join the Rockites despite intense provocation. This also made his murder of his friend, the magistrate's son, particularly shocking, and a challenge to the stereotype of the Irish assassin.[35] For Shanahan murder became the only redress for intolerable injustice in a situation where the law was abused systematically as an instrument of both class warfare and colonial rule.

Griffin's savage appraisal of the Irish legal system was the basis of his social critique. In *The Collegians*, both the gentry and the administrators of the law, treat it with contempt. Their passion for duelling was the only idea of justice subscribed to by the 'half-sirs', a violent alternative code to the official one, comparable to that of the agrarian secret societies. One of them, Hepton Connolly, treats the law as a game, confident of having a majority of his relatives on any jury, and as a group they draw their swords when that class immunity is breached at the end of the novel, and soldiers invade Castle Chute to arrest Hardress Cregan.[36] The English commanding officer, Gibson, forced to act on that occasion by the weight of the evidence, had up to then regarded the whole business with amusement, while the magistrate Warner, was mainly interested in his fee.[37] In *The Rivals* and *Tracy's Ambition*, this situation is made infinitely worse by the operation of the Insurrection Act, under which even the inadequate ordinary processes of law were suspended, and a system of special magistrates, aided by the new police force, operated what Griffin described as a form of official terror.[38] Abel Tracy called it 'a self-constituted inquisition' against a 'despoiled, degraded, wretched, unhappy people'. Repenting that he had become 'one of the scourgers and oppressors of my country men', his reflection on his experience was an indictment of the whole system.

> I have seen fathers torn from their families, innocent hearths made desolate, the judgement of the law inflicted on the offending, and punishment, appointed only for extremity, used as preventatives. . . . The corruption of Grand Juries . . . the oppression of all, from the legislature which frames the law to the vilest constable who puts its provisions into effect against the people, all have shocked my observation.[39]

Thus, the villains in both the later novels were special magistrates. Richard Lacy, in *The Rivals*, 'became an object of terror to the peasantry and of high favour at the Castle. He filled the gaols and transport ships with victims'.[40] Lacy's abuse of the law, including an attempt to frame a law-abiding peasant family, pales beside the systematic illegality of Dalton, 'this croppy-gardener, this weeder-out of disaffection', as Abel Tracy calls him.[41] Griffin's depiction of the new police force, or 'Peelers' was in line with the systematic campaign conducted against them by O'Connell and the Catholic Association.[42] Formed 'for the purpose of overawing the discontented peasantry',[43] they quickly became 'a hated race', according to *The Rivals*, where a pub audience greeted the satire, 'The peeler and the goat' with savage enthusiasm.[44] In *Tracy's Ambition* there are several descriptions of them in action, shooting one of a Rockite gang; protecting Tracy from threatened violence; jeering at the ramshackle Yeomanry Corps, to which Tracy belongs, and even locking them up for not having a pass after curfew. The most graphic and damning description of their activities was of their part in the arrest of Morty Shanahan on the basis of 'evidence' planted by Dalton — 'a party of the all-formidable police . . . laughing and enjoying amid this scene of distress, the delicious consciousness of power'. Little wonder, as Tracy believed, that 'scenes of strife . . . usually followed the appearance of these awful protectors of the peace'.[45]

This wholly damning view of the magistracy and police, as well as reflecting common Catholic attitudes, served to underline the main point about Irish violence which Griffin wished to impress upon his English readers — that it was due to peasant alienation from an oppressive legal system. The theme of alienation was one much stressed by Irish and English politicians who favoured Emancipation,[46] and was addressed directly by Griffin, in a relatively rare use of his authorial voice, to introduce the key court scene in *The Collegians*.

> The peasantry of Ireland have, for centuries, been at war with the laws by which they are governed. . . . There is scarcely a cottage in the south of Ireland where the very circumstances of a legal denunciation would not afford, even to a murderer, a certain passport of concealment and protection.[47]

In fact, Danny Mann, the murderer, only paid the penalty because he gave himself up to the authorities after a row with his young master. In doing so, however, he did not expect mercy — 'If I did, it isn't in courts I'd look for it.' His contempt for what he called 'your laws' was total, and listing the use of the gallows and transportation against innocent and guilty alike, he commented in a significant phrase, 'they teach us something of the laws, we thank 'em'.[48] Danny himself may evoke little sympathy, but his point is borne out by the case of Morty Shanahan, driven to murder by the magistrate's abuse of his position, having tried hard 'to do what's right and to be said by them that knows better than me'.[49] Agrarian secret societies, like the Rockites, were, therefore, alternative systems of 'justice', which the peasantry were driven to develop by the failures of the official system. As Shanahan's mother told Abel Tracy, 'there is no law for the poor in Ireland, but what they make themselves'.[50] While Danny Mann despised the state law, he was imbued with 'the peculiar notions of honour and faith held among the secret societies of the peasantry'. Thus, while he knew that his execution for murder would normally be the subject for popular ballads rather than disgrace, in his case his name would be reviled as an informer, something 'despised and detested by the Irish peasantry beyond all social ills'.[51]

In his earlier abortive examination by the magistrate, he and his family had illustrated some of the common stratagems evolved by the peasantry to survive involvement with the legal system — the use of flattery, feigned stupidity, or the evasion of the oath by kissing the thumb instead of the Bible.[52] By contrast, some of the more admirable peasant characters in these novels were upholders of the law, like Lowry Looby, who believed that not even the King could 'lay a wet finger on me, without the Jury, be course of law'. More pragmatically, Davy Lanigan in *The Rivals* concluded a classic O'Connellite denunciation of the penal laws with a fine paraphrase of O'Connell's pacifist argument, urging his hearers 'to observe the laws in the strictest manner' and 'to live pacable with those savages that daily want to raise us to rebellion'. His warning 'to beware of any secret societies', was on the basis that they only led to 'violating the laws an' going headlong to the gallows'.[53]

An amusing but significant feature of Philip Naughten's attempt to survive his court appearance in *The Collegians* was what John Cronin has called a 'cunning bilingualism'.[54] The complex cultural and socio-economic pressures by which the language of the colonial power replaced Irish, and the consequences of the massive cultural revolution involved, have been little studied.[55] It features in many early nineteenth-century novels. Griffin in particular using it to emphasise the polarised and colonial nature of Irish society. In this period, the poorer classes, while rapidly acquiring English as the language of survival, were still mainly Irish-speaking, so the fact that the legal system operated entirely in English was important in peasant alienation. Naughten had answered the magistrate's opening question in Irish, and the following dialogue ensued.

> 'Answer me in English, friend. We speak no Irish here. Is your name Philip Naughten?'
> 'Tha', wisha vourneen — '
> 'Come, come, English. Swear him to know whether he does not understand English. Can you speak English fellow?'

'Not a word, plase your honour.'

A roar of laughter succeeded this escapade, to which the prisoner listened with a wondering and stupid look. Addressing himself in Irish to Mr Cregan, he appeared to make an explanatory speech, which was accompanied by a slight expression of indignation.

'What does the fellow say?', asked Mr Warner.

'Why', said Cregan with a smile, 'he says he will admit that he couldn't be *hung in English before his face*, but he does not know enough of the language to *enable him to tell his story* in English.'[56] [Griffin's italics]

In other words, while he had enough English to understand the gravity of his situation, he had not enough to explain himself properly. Note that *Cregan* acts as interpreter and it is Houlahan the clerk who 'thought it *genteel* not to know Irish'. This is Griffin at his best, using the comic potential of peasant speech to make a serious point. The distinction made by Naughten was crucial. Peasant bilingualism, besides being 'cunning' was also imperfect and potentially lethal. Throughout these novels, there are many comments on peasant difficulties with English, as well as revealing references to their continued use of Irish, particularly in situations of emotional stress, danger or illegal activity.[57] In a sense, this is a form of linguistic Whiteboyism, a feature of the peasants' secret and frightening world, outside not only the law, but the dominant culture.

'My brain is sick with horrors',[58] Griffin wrote to John Banim, after completing *The Collegians*, and it is hardly surprising that after 1829 he sought refuge from 'an intolerant present in a richly romanticised past'.[59] Long-interested in writing Irish history, his view of it was characteristically dark, 'a miserable and shocking succession of follies, excuses and tyrannies', and he left it to others to depict what he felt was its main feature, 'the convulsions of a powerful people, labouring under a nightmare for ten centuries'.[60] He turned instead to the pre-colonial golden age of saints and scholars, and did considerable research for an historical novel, published in 1832 as *The Invasion*.[61] A book of interest now mainly for the fictional use made of recent historical and antiquarian research, it was an exercise in nostalgia typical of much colonial literature. Comparison with the hasty retreat from mass agitation into the cosier world of Westminster by the leadership of the

Catholic Association may be a little forced, but there is no doubting the relief of the latter at no longer having to justify their nervous boast, most famously expressed by Sheil, that they were 'masters of the passions of the people'.[62] Griffin's powerful evocation of the violent and divided society whose energies they had harnessed, underlined both the extent and the precariousness of their achievement. Sharing their aim of alerting English opinion to the nature and consequences of Irish alienation, his overriding artistic concerns, and the rich potential of his literary genre, produced more complex contexts, and more subtle texts than can be found in the rhetoric or correspondence of politicians. These novels underline how assimilated as well as assimilationist the Catholic middle class was, Griffin's silences being as eloquent in this respect as his prose. Largely absent is the impelling and burning sense of Catholic servitude, so striking an element of O'Connell's campaign. Completely absent is the sectarian basis of agrarian violence. O'Connell's scarifying anger at the Irish Ascendancy is narrowed here to the debauched petty tyranny of a sub-class, and that, largely Catholic. Griffin concentrated instead on the peasant threat, as Maria Edgeworth had done, and with unexpectedly similar perspectives. While providing compelling arguments for reform for Ireland's colonial rulers, he also revealed the fearful fascination of his own class with the teeming millions, who dominated the mental, as well as the physical worlds of pre-Famine Ireland.

Notes and References

1. I am indebted to the undergraduates who took my course on the pre-Famine novel during the past four years, and especially to Ruth Burke. Valuable criticism and encouragement came from Kevin Barry, Clare O'Halloran and Fergus O'Ferrell, while Veronica Fraser was a patient and efficient typist. I am grateful to the Cultural Relations Committee of the Irish Department of Foreign Affairs, and to University College Cork, for funding in aid of travel and research.

2. Gerald Griffin, *The Collegians*, 1st edn (3 vols, Saunders and Otley, London, 1829); *The Rivals. Tracy's Ambition*, 1st edn (3 vols, London 1829).

3. Cf. J.A. Reynolds, *The Catholic Emancipation Crisis in Ireland* (London, 1970; reprint of 1954 Yale UP edn).

4. John and Michael Banim, *Tales by the O'Hara Family*, 1st ser. (3 vols, London, 1825); *Tales by the O'Hara Family*, 2nd ser. (3 vols, London 1826); *The Boyne Water*, 1st edn (3 vols, London, 1826)

5. Cf. *The Life of Gerald Griffin*, by his brother, 2nd edn (London, 1857); John Cronin, *Gerald Griffin 1803–1840. A Critical Biography* (Cambridge UP, Cambridge, 1978).

6. For the background to Limerick in the 1820s, see Galen Broeker, *Rural Disorder and Police Reform in Ireland, 1812–36* (Routledge and Kegan Paul, London, 1970); Michael Beames, *Peasants and Power. The Whiteboy Movements and their Control in Pre-Famine Ireland* (Harvester, Sussex and New York, 1983); Samuel Clark and James S. Donnelly Jr (eds), *Irish Peasants. Violence and Political Unrest 1780–1914* (Manchester UP, Manchester, 1983).

7. The phrase is Oliver MacDonagh's, used in relation to the historians of this period. Oliver MacDonagh, *States of Mind. A Study of Anglo-Irish Conflict 1780–1980* (George Allen and Unwin, London, 1983), p.6.

8. Cf. Tom Dunne, *Maria Edgeworth and the Colonial Mind* (O'Donnell Lecture, National University of Ireland, 1984).

9. Cf. Tom Dunne, 'Fiction as "the best history of nations": Lady Morgan's Irish novels', in T. Dunne (ed.), *The Writer as Witness: Literature as Historical Evidence* (Historical Studies XVI), forthcoming.

10. For Camus as a colonial writer, cf. C.C. O'Brien, *Camus* (Collins, London, 1970); Chinua Achebe, *Things Fall Apart* (Heinemann, London, 1958).

11. E.g. R. Stanihurst, *The Description of Ireland*, in L. Miller and E. Power (eds), *Holinshed's Irish Chronicles* (Dolmen Press, Dublin, 1979); S. Ceitinn, *Foras Feasa ar Eirinn*, P.S. Dineen and D. Comyn (eds) (4 vols, Irish Texts Society, 1902–14); W. Molyneux, *The Case of Ireland's being bound by Acts of Parliament in England, Stated* (J. Ray, Dublin, 1698).

12. G. Griffin, *Tales of the Munster Festivals, containing Card Drawing; The Half-Sir; and Siul Dhuv, the Coiner*, 1st edn (3 vols, London, 1827), pp.vii–xxiii.

13. G. Griffin, *The Invasion*, 1st edn (4 vols, London, 1832); Tom Dunne, 'The Gaelic Response to Conquest and Colonisation: the Evidence of the Poetry', *Studia Hibernica*, no.20 (1980), pp.7–29.

14. Griffin, *The Rivals. Tracy's Ambition*, vol.3, pp.293–302.

15. *Life*, by brother, pp.147–9, 189–93, 238–9, 298–9, 314; Cronin, *Gerald Griffin*, p.72.

16. Cronin, *Gerald Griffin*, pp.51–2.

17. Thomas Flanagan, *The Irish Novelists, 1800–1850* (Columbia UP, New York, 1959), p.220.

18. Griffin, *The Collegians*, vol.1, p.128; *Life*, by brother, p.225.

19. Griffin, *The Collegians*, vol.1, pp.57–8, 117–23; vol.3, pp.18–19.

20. Ibid., vol.3, pp.18–19; vol.2, pp.47 ff., 243; vol.3, pp.95–6.

21. Ibid., vol.2, pp.229–37.

22. Griffin, *The Rivals. Tracy's Ambition*, vol.2, pp.183–4, 188-97, 273–5.

23. Griffin, *The Collegians*, vol.1, pp.37–85.

24. Ibid., vol.1, pp.84–6.

25. Griffin, *The Rivals. Tracy's Ambition*, vol.2, p.112.

26. Ibid., vol.1, p.169; vol.2, pp.64 ff.

27. Griffin, *The Collegians*, vol.3, pp.34 ff.; vol.1, p.38; *The Rivals. Tracy's Ambition*, vol.1, p.142.

28. Reynolds, *Catholic Emancipation*, p.140.

29. Griffin, *The Rivals. Tracy's Ambition*, vol.3, pp.297–8.

30. Dunne, *Maria Edgeworth*, pp.17–20.

31. Griffin, *The Collegians*, vol.1, pp.62–5.

32. Ibid., Ch.9.

33. Ibid., vol.3, pp.188–92, 179–80.

34. Griffin, *The Rivals. Tracy's Ambition*, vol.3, pp.5–6.

35. Ibid., vol.3, pp.161–77; Richard Ned Lebow, *White Britain and Black Ireland: the Influence of Stereotypes on Colonial Policy* (Institute for the Study of Human Issues, Philadelphia, 1976); L.P. Curtis, Jr, *Anglo-Saxons and Celts: A Study of Anti-Irish Prejudice in Victorian England* (New York UP, Connecticut, 1968).

36. Griffin, *The Collegians*, vol.1, pp.121–3; vol.3, pp.293–300.

37. Ibid., vol.3, pp.188, 240, 293.

38. Griffin, *The Rivals. Tracy's Ambition*, vol.1, pp.36–7.

39. Ibid., vol.2, pp.272–5, 310–11.

40. Ibid., vol.1, p.165.

41. Ibid., vol.2, pp.127, 268; vol.3, pp.44 ff.

42. Broeker, *Rural Disorder and Police Reform*, pp.164 ff.

43. Griffin, *The Rivals. Tracy's Ambition*, vol.1, p.164.

44. Ibid., vol.2, p.45; also, vol.1, p.169.

45. Ibid., vol.2, pp.142 ff., 155 ff., 215 ff., 267–8.

46. E.g. Reynolds, *Catholic Emancipation*, p.140 (Sheil); Broeker, *Rural Disorder and Police Reform*, p.174 (Anglesea).

47. Griffin, *The Collegians*, vol.3, pp.179–80.

48. Ibid., vol.3, pp.245–7; cf. also *The Rivals. Tracy's Ambition*, vol.2, p.296.

49. Griffin, *The Rivals. Tracy's Ambition*, vol.3, p.156; cf. also, vol.2, pp.153–4, 265.

50. Ibid., vol.2, pp.206–7; cf. also, *The Collegians*, vol.1, pp.149–50.

51. Griffin, *The Collegians*, vol.3, pp.252–3.

52. Ibid., vol.3, pp.180 ff.

53. Ibid., vol.1, p.300; *The Rivals. Tracy's Ambition*, vol.2, p.41.

54. John Cronin, *The Anglo-Irish Novel. Volume one, the Nineteenth Century* (Barnes and Noble Books, Belfast, 1980), p.71.

55. An important demographic study is Garret FitzGerald, 'Estimates for Baronies of Minimum Levels of Irish Speaking among Successive Decennial Cohorts: 1771–1781 to 1861–1871', *Proc. Royal Irish Academy*, vol.84, C, no.3, 1984.

56. Griffin, *The Collegians*, vol.3, pp.189–90.

57. For difficulties with English, cf. *The Collegians*, vol.1, p.111; *The Rivals. Tracy's Ambition*, vol.1, pp.1–3; vol.3, p.59, etc. For use of Irish, cf. *The Collegians*, vol.1, p.155; vol.2, pp.13, 150–1; *The Rivals. Tracy's Ambition*, vol.2, p.201, etc.

58. *Life*, by brother, pp.192–3.

59. Cronin, *Life of Griffin*, p.88.

60. *Life*, by brother, pp.285–90; cf. also *The Rivals. Tracy's Ambition*, vol.3, p.110.

61. *Life*, by brother, pp.231 ff.; Cronin, *Life of Griffin*, pp.86 ff.

62. Reynolds, *Catholic Emancipation*, pp.159–60.

6   The Overflow of the Deluge: Anglo-Irish Relationships, 1914–1922

David Fitzpatrick

'Bloody frivolity', so W.B. Yeats dismissed the war in August 1915, a few days after the destruction of the 10th (Irish) Division at Suvla Bay.[1] Irish politicians, poets, novelists, and above all historians, have generally shared his indifference to Ireland's war experience. Their most effective gesture of dismissal has been silence rather than the Yeatsian sneer. Ireland produced one war poet who is remembered (Francis Ledwidge),[2] one novelist whose war sketches were long forgotten (Patrick MacGill)[3] and one war historian whose book is out of print (Henry Harris).[4] School histories of the period usually allude to the war only as an external factor which deluded John Redmond, split the Irish Volunteers, threatened conscription, and hence reactivated the republican spirit. The shadow of war could not, of course, be eliminated completely from modern Irish memory: there were the shadows of Lieutenant Robert Barton, later a minister of Dáil Éireann, guarding the internees after Easter 1916; of Commandant Tom Barry, who received his military training in Mesopotamia; of Ernie O'Malley, who used to laugh at the Irish Volunteers and longed to follow his brother into the 'Pals' battalion of the Dublin Fusiliers but didn't.[5] There were the shadows of the quarter-million Irish soldiers (some said half a million), swamping the 3000 heroes of the Flying Columns; and of the 30,000 fatalities (though Kerry folk believed that 'only one in every hundred Irish soldiers survived the war'), outnumbering civilian casualties in the War of Independence by about 20:1.[6] Yet Irish historians, even today, have scarcely come to grips with the war as an agent of social, economic, administrative, political and mental revolution: an agent dwarfing all others in the period 1914–18 and leaving its imprint on the subsequent independence struggle. The war is still 'bloody frivolity', the fight for freedom 'bloody sacrifice'.

This chapter explores one dusty corner of a neglected topic: the impact of war on Anglo-Irish relationships. In its broadest sense, the relationship between Ireland and Britain coloured every aspect of Irish life, whether political, economic or imaginative. Just as the war affected every facet of life, it also transformed Anglo-Irish relations, generally for the worse. But my concern is restricted to its impact on *personal* relationships between people in the two islands, who for various reasons were brought into immediate contact with each other. By increasing personal mobility, war added to the risk that hereditary enemies would meet, so testing out the abstract assumptions, attitudes and stereotypes which each nation had developed concerning the other. These abstract conceptions drew strength from their timelessness, being strikingly impervious to the rapidly changing political context of the early twentieth century. Augustine Birrell, the last great reforming Chief Secretary, told the Hardinge Commission in 1916 'of the old hatred and distrust of the British connection, always noticeable in all classes and in all places, varying in degree and finding different ways of expression, but always there'.[7] British contempt for Irish character and political backwardness, also the product of a polemical reading of history rather than of observation, was equally persistent despite the absence of insurrection for half a century after the Fenian rising.

It would be naïve to suppose that knowledge acquired from personal interaction could undermine ignorance hardened into racial and national abstractions. The solution to the Anglo-Irish problem was not compulsory foreign holidays, or even universal conscription into mixed regiments. Yet the responses of Irish immigrants to their experiences in wartime Britain, and those of British soldiers and administrators to posting in Ireland, reveal unexpected nuances of the Anglo-Irish relationship. The mode of interaction was determined not merely by presuppositions and events, but also by the context of meeting, just as the outcome of a football match is affected by its location at home, away or on neutral ground. In Ireland, a majority confronted its British masters; in Britain, an Irish minority competed for employment within the working class; in the army, Irish and British masters and workers were disoriented alike. Let me first examine the consequences of dressing both nationalities in the same uniform.

At the outbreak of war, about one-tenth of the Regular Army of 200,000 was Irish-born, the proportion being slightly higher for reservists. Ireland's contribution to army recruiting had altered little over the previous half-century, being significantly less than its share of the United Kingdom's population. The celebrated over-representation of Irish natives in the army is attributable to heavy recruitment among working-class immigrants in Britain, which masked sluggish enlistment in Ireland itself. In the early 1860s over two-fifths of Irish candidates were inspected in British depots, the proportion having fallen to one-eighth by the eve of war.[8] Thus one element of the Irish stereotype, bellicosity, failed to drive the non-emigrant Irish into whatever army might beckon them. After 1914 Irish military participation multiplied, and the 50,000 regulars and reservists were supplemented by at least 130,000 volunteers enlisted at Irish depots. Yet recruiting within Ireland remained relatively slow throughout the war, the disparity being sharply widened after the application of conscription to Britain alone in 1916. Irish recalcitrance was widely ascribed to another element of the national stereotype, incurable disloyalty. In fact, most of the disparity between Irish and British volunteering rates may be explained by the scarcity of urban adult males who constituted the most likely material for the army. Catholics in most Irish countries were as likely to join up as their Protestant neighbours, and recruiting in Ulster was scarcely brisker than in Dublin.[9] The army had never been a favoured occupation for farmers' sons with 'prospects', and rural Ireland's wartime prosperity accentuated their reluctance to abandon butter for guns. Fear of 'press-ganging' swept villages in Kerry: the advent of a motor-car with lights sent the lads into hiding until news came that it belonged to a doctor.[10] In Ireland, perhaps even more than in Britain, economics rather than sentiment determined recruiting levels: if loyalty failed to entice Kerry farmers' sons into the army, disloyalty failed to keep urban *lumpen* proletarians out of it.

In urging Home Rulers to participate in the war, John Redmond had hoped to eradicate lingering national and religious hostilities through the agency of personal contact. If Ulstermen, Home Rulers, Englishmen and Scotsmen fought together, their growing comradeship and mutual admiration would allay their mutual suspicions and those of politicians at home. Redmond's model of reconciliation was that of 'multi-culturism' rather than the 'melting pot': he urged that Irish soldiers be formed into distinctive units under Irish officers rather than being dispersed throughout the armed forces. This programme was never put properly to the test. The War Office, suspicious of clumps of Irishmen in barracks and impatient of attempts to interfere with its management of army hierarchies, scotched Redmond's proposal for sanction of the Irish Volunteers as a home defence force. It approved the creation of three distinctively Irish divisions and one brigade (the 'Tyneside Irish'), but ensured that only the 36th (Ulster) Division drew its officers from its own recruiting area. As casualties depleted these 'Irish' units, they were rapidly diluted with British reinforcements. Only at the very end of the war was a thoroughly green Irish brigade approved, to be led exclusively by serving Irish officers. Its organiser was Arthur Lynch, who had once led another brigade on behalf of the Boers and appealed to Irishmen to join up as friends of France rather than Britain. The Brigade was to have six pipers dressed in Irish kilts, a head-dress 'of colonial type, with a green band and with a green and white hackle', and a hat-badge representing the Irish wolfhound.[11] But the armistice aborted multi-culturism in the British army, and Irish soldiers were unable to avoid immediate contact with British men and officers in their own brigades.

There is little evidence that Irish and British soldiers combined against each other on national lines. No Irish detachments mutinied with the exception of Connaught Rangers in the Punjab in June 1920. Sir Roger Casement was greeted with incredulity and abuse by Irish prisoners of war at Limburg when he attempted to raise a revolutionary Irish brigade in 1915. To those actually involved in war, ethnic hostilities engendered in peacetime seemed feeble and irrelevant when compared with shared hatred of the Hun or even shared Gallophilia. A characteristic chapter opening in MacGill's *The Great Push*, which is by no means a eulogy of war, runs as follows: 'As I was sitting in the Café Pierre le Blanc helping Bill Teake, my Cockney mate, to finish a bottle of vin rouge . . .'. In the more common genre of recruiting propaganda veiled in fiction, Sergeant Michael Cassidy, R.E., is even allowed to express healthy contempt for British shirkers, effete in their mauve socks and purple cuffs: '"Ah! but 'tis cruel, sir", he said, turning to me. "'Tis cruel to think of them pimply little beasts creeping about the country, and then remember what the lads are doing over the water. To think that Mr. O'Rourke gave his life for such as them".'[12] The loyalties and contempts of serving soldiers were common to Irish and British alike, reflecting their shared subjection to a military code which was alien to home life in both islands.

Shared alienation became all the more obvious upon demobilisation. Irish soldiers at home on furlough had seldom been subject to local hostility despite growing opposition to recruitment: in the

Clare of June 1918, 'boys of military age, even prominent members of Sinn Féin clubs, do not boycott natives of their parish home on leave but foregather with them and listen with interest to their stories of modern warfare'.[13] But the demobs of 1919, in Ireland as in Britain, quickly became resentful of the indifference of employers and fellow workers to their sacrifice. Former soldiers in Ireland joined several competing protective associations, thus underlining their alienation from existing institutions. The Irish Transport and General Workers' Union, which in 1916 had as many members in the trenches as in Ireland, resolved three years later 'that men who are no longer in the army, but in civil employment, are a menace to the Labour movement as a whole, if they remain unorganised outside the trade unions, or become organised in associations which are promoted and patronised by their industrial enemies'.[14] One former Connaught Ranger wrote to *The Republic* that 'the English Government seems to have thrown those of us now demobilised aside as of no further use, and the Republicans do not seem to be interested in whatever part we play in the country's future'.[15]

Alienation was expressed in many ways: by grumbling, by organising apart, by drinking, even by maliciously injuring houses. In Clare there was the case of Thomas Crotty, who got drunk, broke his father's windows, 'put the blessed candle all around the floor', and later explained that 'the cause of this row is that my father and the rest of them are Sinn Féiners, and since I came home they are always going on to me for joining the Army'.[16] For other returned fighters, the least unattractive option seemed to be recruitment to some other fighting force. Irish recruitment to both the New Army of 1919 and the newly militarised RIC was well above pre-war levels, and numerous ex-soldiers joined the Flying Columns of the IRA. Their restlessness and discontent was mirrored by that of British ex-soldiers, many of whom found an acceptable alternative to unemployment in the Black and Tans.

My second theatre of wartime interaction is Britain, where the Irish immigrant population had been in slow decline for several decades. In 1911 there were about half a million Irish natives living in Britain, accounting for only 4 per cent of the Scottish population and one per cent of the English. Despite the gradual reduction of immigrant pauperism and deprivation during the later nineteenth century, Irish workers were still concentrated in unskilled and manual employment in the major cities of northern England and southern Scotland. Irish settlers continued to evince their social alienation through excessively high crime rates, though their choice of crimes differed little from that of their British working-class neighbours. Though largely excluded from middle-class occupations except teaching and nursing (for women), the immigrants had become increasingly assimilated into working-class institutions and patterns of protest. They were now known as strike-makers rather than strike-breakers, the old Irish residential enclaves had mostly disappeared, and the United Irish League of Great Britain had become in effect a faction with the Liberal Party. As one ex-Fenian had observed with regret: 'They have children born to them on English soil, all their worldly interests are centred in England, and their prospects in life are practically bounded by the English shore'.[17]

The effect of war was almost certainly to reverse the decline in movement from Ireland to Britain. By March 1918, daily traffic across the Irish Sea was nearly 3000, of whom about one-third were civilians. The greater shortage of labour in Britain encouraged Irish workers to migrate to Britain to work in munition factories and also, as in the past, on farms at harvest-time. Irish labour was obtained by the Ministry of Munitions not only through employment exchanges, but also through direct recruiting by officials, agents and contractors. These irregular methods were eventually banned, but demand for Irish labour remained strong enough to provoke a Ministry of Labour complaint that Irish restriction of travel permits was inhibiting the supply of labour. The Irish inundation caused resentment among British workers, whose protests echoed those of the nineteenth century when Irish immigrants were detested as disorderly intruders. It was reported from Scotland that 'the introduction of Irish labour . . . which has been possible because of the military conditions in Ireland, has always been resented, and it has been stated that any measure terminating such immigration should be welcomed by organised labour'.[18] The effect of renewed wartime immigration was to reinvigorate working-class antipathy towards the Irish, but also to obtain grudging approval from government and employers aware that Irish labour was often indispensable.

Nationalist organisers in Britain responded to this partial reinforcement of British hostility by emphasising the patriotism of Irish settlers and their disjunction from the growing rebelliousness of their connections at home. As in pre-war years, the Irish in

Britain were particularly prone to join the army, and in Newcastle upon Tyne no less than 5500 men joined four battalions of the 'Tyneside Irish' within two months of War Office sanction for the brigade. By February 1915 T.P. O'Connor was urging Redmond to assert publicly that 'we had already raised 115,000 Irishmen in Great Britain'. Catholics in Britain (most of whom were of Irish extraction) scarcely ever expressed conscientious objection to military conscription, showing no signs of solidarity with the Irish campaign of 1918.[19] Nor was the end of the war marked by the general displacement of 'Constitutionalism' by 'Republicanism' among immigrants. In Liverpool the UIL actually increased its representation on the city council between 1918 and 1923, while the new ISDL of Great Britain was only sporadically successful in organising Irish settlers and dared not adopt an overtly republican programme. Thus the Irish in wartime Britain, far from constituting a disruptive faction in society or in politics, took care to demonstrate their 'patriotism' in words and often in deeds. Earlier experience of the costs of social ostracism caused most immigrants to tread warily in a volatile environment. In the words of T.P. O'Connor in 1917, partial integration into the 'British environment' had made the expatriate Irishman 'broader in his outlook' than his fellows at home. He now occupied 'a curious middle place' in British life.[20]

Immigrant assimilation, if not broadness of outlook, was betokened by the solidarity of British and Irish workers in their fear and dislike of the new immigrants of the late nineteenth and early twentieth centuries. The Jewish influx of 1870–1907 had united the working class in its anti-Semitism. As a midwife of London's East End had recollected in 1902: 'it used to be a street occupied by poor English and Irish people. In the afternoons you would see the steps inside cleaned, and the women with their clean white aprons sat in summer times inside the doors, perhaps at needlework, with their little children about them. Now it is a seething mass of refuse and filth . . .. They are such an unpleasant, indecent people.' Cartoonists had sharpened their focus from forehead and chin to nose, and the 'poor Irish people' had enjoyed a shove up the ladder of civilisation.[21] The war brought further immigration of Chinese, West Indian and other exotic peoples into British ports, where British seamen and Irish dockers found common cause in assaulting the newcomers. Thus in Cardiff, one-third of those arrested in 1919 for attacking black seamen (mainly resident in quarters once identified as Irishtowns) had 'Irish' names.[22] The Irish in Britain, as in

America, discovered that shared hatred could be twisted into mutual trust, and the war was fertile for hatred.

Ireland itself played host to an equally vulnerable and embattled immigrant minority, that of the 'British garrison'. The number of British residents in Ireland had trebled between 1841 and 1911 to 125,000. The British in Ireland were in some respects reminiscent of the Irish in Britain: predominantly male and adult, with a strong Scottish element, and heavily clustered in the major cities. But their functions and occupations were quite dissimilar. In 1861, the last census for which their occupations were recorded, nearly three-fifths of occupied British men in Ireland were soldiers, naval ratings or sailors. British immigrants were also hugely over-represented as hatters, inland revenue officers, engineers, coastguards, merchants, stewards, commercial travellers and gentlemen (in that order), with more than their share of professional men, clerks and drapers.[23] The British component of Ireland's administrative, military and middle classes was even more important than the Irish component of Britain's working class. During the war the British military garrison fluctuated wildly in size as units were trained, transferred or replaced. In November 1914 the available striking force consisted of 400 cavalry, 2000 infantry and four guns; whereas by late 1918 there were 100,000 soldiers in Ireland, most of them British.[24] The number of British administrators presumably grew as new departments and councils were convened, but the major extension was delayed until spring 1920 when a team of Treasury 'high-fliers' under Warren Fisher and John Anderson was sent to Ireland to control the 'old Castle gang'.

Before the war, the British 'garrison' had been treated with indulgence if not affection. Soldiers had won friends among shop-keepers, publicans and girls bored with waiting for emigration or an Irish 'match', while administrators had walked unmolested through city streets and squares. Growing disaffection after the Rising did not place British visitors in immediate physical danger. British contempt often irritated the natives, as in March 1918 when a military lorry ran into the pony trap driven by Conor Clune (later an innocent victim of the 'Bloody Sunday' reprisals). 'What vexed me entirely was the manner in which the soldiers treated us. The officer laughed at us and the soldiers gave us no assistance to extricate the horse. All they did was to say more than once "Cut the f—king harness. Hurry up with the f—king mess we can't wait here all the f—king night".'[25] Yet Irish distaste for British arrogance faded during the following month when rumours swept Ireland that Ghurkas were being drafted into Ireland, an insult necessitating national unity against an 'invasion, backed by the menace of uncivilised forces'. The alarm eventually reached the UIL in Australia, which induced the Governor-General to request an explanation: this revealed that 'the rumour started from the fact that a sentry belonging to an English Regiment, who was on duty at Broadstone Station is of somewhat dusky hue'.[26] When guerrilla fighting was intensified in 1920, the Volunteers refrained from attacking British officials, judges or even off-duty soldiers and policemen, and directed their most ferocious campaign against the predominantly Irish constabulary. Soldiers and officers were treated with relative respect, as in the case of Brigadier General Lucas who was captured near Fermoy in June 1920. According to a Castle official, Lucas 'was well treated and got some fishing and night poaching'.[27] The general played bridge with his guards every morning till 2 a.m. and drank a bottle of whisky daily which they 'hated like hell to pay for'. This rare rich Anglo-Irish relationship was cut short when Michael Brennan decided to reduce his column expenses by inducing Lucas to escape from custody.[28]

The indulgence shown by Irish nationalists towards the 'garrison' was not fully reciprocated. British visitors, then as now, were often more interested in Irish bloodstock or snipe than people. A fortnight before the outbreak of war, an officer at the Curragh lamented that 'there will probably be no hunting next season, on account of Home Rule, which will be a great loss to the country. It will also stop all steeple-chasing, etc. The small owners say they will allow no soldiers to ride over their land, and as two thirds of the fields are soldiers it will stop all hunting'.[29] From Easter 1916 onwards, military indifference to Irish people hardened into hatred for the protectors of those who were stabbing the Empire in the back. A year before his own appointment as Irish army commander, Nevil Macready commiserated with Macpherson upon his assumption of the Chief Secretaryship thus: 'I cannot say I envy you, for I loathe the country you are going to and its people with a depth greater than the sea, and more violent than that which I feel against the Boche'. As GOC, Macready called upon his troops to maintain discipline 'even in face of provocation such as would not be indulged in by the wildest savages of Central Africa'.[30] Most soldiers eschewed all contact with the Irish. An officer of the Essex regiment at Bandon recalled that 'we had no social contact with any civilians of whatever political beliefs', while his colleague B.L. Montgomery 'regarded all civilians as "shinners", and [I] never had any dealings with them'.[31] This attitude gained official expression in the training manual 'Notes on Guerrilla Warfare in Ireland', which advised 'that no inhabitant or civilian employee is really to be trusted . . ... Individuals cutting peat in the bog may not be as harmless as they appear to be.' Suspicion extended even to cows, which might carry removable horns, to animals whose ears might contain ammunition, and to 'mangolds, turnips, etc.'.[32] Military paranoia was in fact an essential psychological adjustment for soldiers faced with seemingly universal disaffection: only by dehumanising the enemy could they engage in this 'image of war' without suffering intolerable guilt and shame.

For administrators, charged with conciliation rather than repression, the difficulty of achieving personal contact with Irish people was perhaps still greater. Administrators like Birrell had worked hard to 'govern Ireland according to Irish ideas', digesting shelves of Irish history and literature in preparation, taking educative motor tours under the guidance of Henry Robinson, searching for the Irish soul at the Abbey. By Macpherson's time, official desire to learn about Ireland had dissipated, and he was reputed to have spent only three days in the country between the 1919 Horse Show and his resignation as Chief Secretary just after the 1920 Spring Show. The sense of isolation among Castle officials, already evident during the war as police information dried up, became acute upon the arrival of the Treasury squad in 1920. Officials were increasingly confined to the Castle and the Phoenix Park lodges, being obliged to relax upon uneven makeshift tennis courts in Lower Castle Yard, or by dipping into the typing pool outside Lower Castle Gate. Mark Sturgis, always resentful of his enforced 'internment', began 'to believe that these mean, dishonest, insufferably conceited Irishmen *are* an inferior race and are only sufferable when they are whipped — like the Jews'.[33] Revolver practice rather than receiving Irish guests became his chief preoccupation, though in the cheery vision of Greenwood, the Chief Secretary, this only contributed to 'the stimulating atmosphere of this country' and showed that Lady Greenwood 'turns out to be a better revolver shot than I am, which is really fine'.[34] The truce brought about renewed personal contact without endearing Irish Republicans to Sturgis and his colleagues. Upon meeting two liaison officers at the Gresham Hotel, Sturgis felt 'sick' because of McAlister's 'most offensive habit of sniffing' and found

O'Duffy 'stupid and rather truculent'. He offered O'Duffy a cigarette and matches, after which both officers 'quite unconsciously picked my matches to pieces by the dozen all the time they were speaking'. At times Sturgis relished the atmosphere of 'intrigue, plot and counter-plot with a small spice of danger all mixed up with the life of something like a big country house [party: deleted] in the old days', and wondered if he could ever settle down again in a London office.[35] But the memorable contacts of British soldiers and administrators in revolutionary Ireland were usually with each other rather than with the people of Ireland. The experience of the British 'garrison' during and after the war strengthened and embittered their hostility to the subject people. If the Irish experience in Britain and the British army did a little to break down Irish Anglophobia, the British experience in Ireland left both parties with an enhanced desire for separation.

Notes and References

1. Yeats to Henry James, 20 August 1915, in Allan Wade (ed.), *The Letters of W.B. Yeats* (Rupert Hart-Davis, London, 1954), p.600.

2. Francis Ledwidge, *Last Songs* (Herbert Jenkins, Dublin, 1918).

3. Patrick MacGill, *The Great Push: an Episode of the Great War* (Herbert Jenkins, London, 1916).

4. H.E.D. Harris, *The Irish Regiments in the First World War* (Mercier Press, Cork, 1968).

5. Tom Barry, *Guerrilla Days in Ireland* (Anvil Books, Tralee, [1962]); Ernie O'Malley, *On Another Man's Wound* (Rich and Cowan, London, 1936), pp.26–8.

6. Irish Folklore Archive, University College, Dublin, MS 1237, pp.259–59A (Ó Dálaigh, Dunquinn).

7. Royal Commission on the Rebellion in Ireland, *Minutes of Evidence*, HC Papers 1916 Cd. 8311, xi, min. 520.

8. British Army, Medical Department, *Annual Reports* for 1860–63, 1911–13, HC Papers, *passim* (data available only for these years); cf. H.J. Hanham, 'Religion and Nationality in the Mid-Victorian Army', in M.R.D. Foot (ed.), *War and Society* (Elek, London, 1973), pp.159–82; Peter Karsten, 'Irish Soldiers in the British Army, 1792–1922', in *Journal of Social History*, vol.17, no. 1 (1983), pp.31–64.

9. See Appendix below.

10. Irish Folklore Archive, University College, Dublin, MS 1319, pp.217–21 (Ó Muircheartaigh, Corkaguiny).

11. Macpherson to House of Commons, *Debates*, 5th series, vol.110, col. 899.

12. MacGill, *The Great Push*, p.22; 'Sapper', *Sergeant Michael Cassidy, R.E.* (Hodder and Stoughton, London, 1915), p.63.

13. Edward Lysaght, Diary, 3 June 1918, National Library of Ireland, MacLysaght Papers, MS 4750, p.317.

14. ITGWU, *Annual Report* (Dublin, 1919), p.145.

15. *The Republic*, vol.1, no. 10 (23 August 1919), p.118.

16. *Clare Champion*, 11 January 1919.

17. J. O'Connor Power, 'The Irish in England', in *Fortnightly Review*, vol.27, no. 159 (1880), p.418.

18. Reports and memoranda, PRO, London, CO 904/169/4; MUN 5/57: HR 320/31; HO 45/10957: 54b; MUN 2/15.

19. Felix Lavery (compiler), *Irish Heroes in the War* (Everett and Co., London, 1917); O'Connor to Redmond, 27 February 1915. National Library of Ireland, Redmond Papers, MS 15215; Alan Wilkinson, *The Church of England and the First World War* (SPCK, London, 1978), p.315; John Rae, *Conscience and Politics; The British Government and the Conscientious Objector to Military Service, 1916–1919* (Oxford UP, London, 1970), pp.80, 250–1.

20. Lavery, *Irish Heroes*, pp.31–2.

21. John A. Garrard, *The English and Immigration 1880–1910* (Oxford UP, London, 1971), p.51.

22. Neil Evans, 'The South Wales Race Riots of 1919', *Llafur*, vol.3, no. 1 (1980), p.23.

23. Census of Ireland, *General Report*, HC Papers 1863 C. 3204–IV, lxi, pp.530–59. For each major immigrant occupation, an 'Index of Over-Representation' was calculated by dividing the proportion of British-born workers in that occupation by the proportion of all workers in Ireland. The index was calculated separately for occupied persons of each sex, omitting members of the army and navy. Among women, over-representation was greatest among governesses, teachers, ladies, milliners and annuitants.

24. Friend to Kitchener, 16 November 1914. PRO, London, 30/57/60: WK 12.

25. Clune to Lysaght, 31 March 1918. National Library of Ireland, MacLysaght Papers, MS 2649.

26. Memoranda of April–July 1918. State Paper Office, Dublin, RP 20554/1918.

27. Mark Sturgis, Diary, 15 August 1920. PRO, London, 30/59/1, p.23.

28. Michael Brennan, *The War in Clare, 1911–1921: Personal Memoirs of the Irish War of Independence* (Four Courts Press, Dublin, 1980), pp.54–6.

29. Lt. R. Macleod, letter of 20 July 1914, 'An Artillery Officer in the First World War', pp.39–40, King's College, London (Centre for Military Archives).

30. Macready to Macpherson, 11 January 1919, Bodleian Library, Strathcarron Papers, MS Eng. Hist. c490/70; GOC in C, General Routine Order, 25 February 1921, in PRO, London, CO 904/168/2.

31. F.A.S. Clarke, 'The Memoirs of a Professional Soldier', Ch. 6, p.8, King's College, London (Centre for Military Archives); Montgomery to Percival, 14 October 1923. Imperial War Museum, Percival MS 4/1.

32. 'Confidential. History of the 5th Division in Ireland', Imperial War Museum, Jeudwine Papers, 72/82/2.

33. Henry Wilson, Diary, 1 April 1920. Imperial War Museum, HHW 29; Sturgis diary, 3 September 1920, PRO 30/59/1, p.49 (text later amended by addition of 'almost' before 'begin to believe').

34. Greenwood to Davies, 20 September 1920. House of Lords Library, Lloyd George Papers, F/19/2/20.

35. Sturgis Diary, 11 October 1921, PRO 30/59/5, pp.55–6; 9 November 1920, PRO 30/59/2, p.119.

Appendix (A): Ireland's Contribution to the British Army in the First World War

Category	Date	Ireland	Britain	%I:UK
Regular army	1 Oct.1913	20,780	207,641	10.01
Army reservists mobilised	Aug.1914	17,804	121,918	12.74
Special reservists mobilised	Aug.1914	12,462	46,603	21.11
Enlistments (excluding officers)	1914	44,134	1,142,223	3.72
	1915	46,371	1,233,991	3.62
	1916–18	43,697	2,460,486	1.74
Male population aged 20–39 (000s)	1911	649	6,307	9.33
Males occupied outside farming (000s)	1911	697	11,494	5.72
Total population (000s)	1911	4,390	40,831	9.71

Appendix (B): Provincial Comparisons

Percentage RC	Dublin	Leinster	Munster	Ulster	Connacht	Ireland
Reservists 1914	n.a.	95.3	96.2	43.5	93.4	67.2*
Enlistments 1914	n.a.	88.5	94.7	20.6	92.8	40.4*
Enlistments 1915	80.3	87.9	93.2	32.0	90.5	61.4 [57.2*]
Enlistments 1916	n.a.	90.2	94.4	31.9	90.5	58.4*
Total of above	n.a.	89.8	94.3	29.4	91.6	53.7*
Population 1911	83.1	85.9	94.0	43.7	96.2	73.9 [73.2*]
Males occupied outside farming 1911	79.0	80.1	88.7	34.2	92.5	66.0 [63.5*]

Ratio of reservists and enlistments (1914–15 only): males occupied outside farming

Percentage	17.5	9.1	11.2	22.3	10.3	15.7
						cf.Britain: 21.7

Notes:

Statistics for mobilisation in part (A) refer to those enlisted (and passed as fit) in Ireland and Britain respectively, not to the nationality of soldiers. Figures include army and territorial force only, and exclude officers.

Statistics in part (B) are derived from police returns of army recruiting in Ireland by country and province of origin, and include Irish residents who were attested in Britain. These returns generally show slightly higher numbers of recruits.

Percentages marked* refer to Ireland excluding the Dublin Metropolitan Police district, for which returns of recruiting by religion were not always available.

Sources:
British Army, *General Annual Reports* for 1913–19, HC Papers 1921 (Cmd. 1193), xx: recruiting returns in State Paper Office, Dublin, RP 21680/1916; Census of Ireland for 1911, HC Papers 1912–13 (Cd. 6049–52, 6663), cxiv-cxviii.

7   Daniel Mannix and the Cult of Personality

James Griffin

> Verdun is now in the very air. Will it interest any of us that the
> first ten bishops of Verdun were irishmen? What wonder the
> fighting there is so excellent?
>
> (Melbourne *Advocate*, 15 July 1916)

> When I think of Archbishop Mannix as I do very often these
> days, I feel like praying to him more than praying for him. I feel
> like applying to the beloved, noble, dead Archbishop the opening
> words of the Easter Mass, 'I arose and am still with you, Alleluia'.
>
> (Bishop Patrick Lyons of Sale, Victoria, formerly Melbourne
> diocesan Vicar-General, preaching at the Month's Mind Solemn
> Pontifical Requiem Mass for Archbishop Mannix, *Advocate*, 12
> December 1963)

Among at least the Catholic working classes during the Australian
career of Daniel Mannix, there was a belief that he was one of the
four cleverest men in the world. 'Men', then, meant naturally 'also
women' and two of the other three were 'Professor' Albert Einstein
and the Pope (i.e. whichever Pope happened to be then gloriously
reigning). I was never sure who the fourth was but the voices of my
diocesan scholarship education (by grace of Irish Brothers) say it
could have been Chesterton (who was so intelligent he had to
become a convert) or, especially after G.K.C. died in 1936, that
misguided sage whom he piqued with amiable barbs of wit and
'truth' — George Bernard Shaw. These voices were confirmed
recently when I picked up a now forgotten book on Australia,
written in 1939 by Halliday Sutherland, a noted English Catholic
doctor, anti-birth controller, adventurer, travel writer and highly
successful autobiographer. The 'mind of Mannix', he wrote,

is the most alert and disciplined I have ever encountered. He never prepares a speech, yet never makes a dull one; and in my opinion is capable of defeating G.B. Shaw in debate.[1]

Sutherland even believed that the expressive word 'wowser', which he defined as a person who adhered 'to the Manichean [no pun intended] heresy in its modern form', was coined by none other than Mannix (*pace* John Norton).[2]

Moreover — my memory assures me — there were grounds for hope that Shaw, who was often sympathetic to dissenting Catholicism because he was iconoclastic about everything else, would also, like Chesterton, convert, and I seem to recall the Melbourne diocesan *Advocate* being gratified that, towards the end of his life, the nonagenarian Shaw wrote letters to an Irish Mother Superior which suggested he nearly did — but just ran out of time. So a potential three out of four top places in the world intellectual stakes generated just the right balance of certitude, modesty and scope for Providence that dogma-ridden but socially insecure and lowly Irish-Australian Catholics living in a sanguine, open society needed. With so many apparently rational, certainly no more credulous, and generally better-educated people among their non- and anti-Catholic compatriots; with the ancient sectarian and racial insults of disloyalty, superstition, drunkenness and incontinence not only surviving but still flourishing; with, in the wake of the conscription and Irish independence struggles, Catholics being told publicly they need not apply for certain jobs or even lodgings, a compensatory legend was needed, especially as its subject was the ostensible cause of so many lost jobs and ruptured friendships in the otherwise genial air of Australia. There was, after all, a need to erase the suspicion that Mannix warranted the sort of indignation so ardently voiced by the loyalist Catholic doctor, intellectual and sportsman, Herbert Moran, against the Archbishop's role in the conscription plebiscites of 1916–17:

In one speech before a great assembly of people he pointed out that he had become the lightning conductor for all the abuse in Victoria, but he added, humorously, that in a thunderstorm the lightning rod usually escaped damage. Nothing was ever truer in his own case. Every time the clerical orator went forth to speak a frenzied mob of admiring partisans followed him. The speech over, the Archbishop returned to the serenity and the simple amenities of 'Raheen' and retired to sleep with the applause of thousands ringing in his ears. He himself suffered no personal injury or discomfort. But after every such display of eloquence in every State humble Catholics were discharged from their jobs . . . throughout the whole Commonwealth.[3]

Even for one more or less nurtured on the Mannix legend, it was startling, during a recent attempt to write a biographical portrait, to contemplate in cold print not only the hyperboles lavished on him but, more particularly, the accounts of the mass demonstrations with which he was invested. I believe that overall they would exceed anything accorded to any other personality in Australian history. Cyril Bryan, Mannix's first biographical publicist (a more apt term than 'biographer') entitled him in 1919 'The Champion of Australian Democracy'.[4] In 1934, E.J. Brady, after comparing Mannix to a mythical round tower with its 'clear steady vision' as well as to Socrates in suffering and Euripides in banishment, thought that 'in the twentieth century, he stands on the highest historical plane'. Happily this did not prevent Brady from also seeing Mannix as 'a dinkum Aussie'.[5]

Effulgent tributes, however, did not come only from fellow tribesmen. On his episcopal silver jubilee in 1937 his erstwhile arch-antagonist, the Melbourne *Argus*, devoted to Mannix two full pages of its weekend magazine making particular point of his arresting oratory but dubbing him

> Scholar, classical student, philosophic thinker, deeply read in the sciences and arts . . . [who never] said anything not obvious to the least literate man and woman . . . therein lies his power.[6]

Frank Murphy in the expanded second edition of his biography of Mannix commended the alertness of his then 'nonagenarian' mind for writing in 1954 'a long and learned article' in the Catholic quarterly, *Twentieth Century*, where he called for a constitutional convention and amendments 'to ease. . . relations between Commonwealth and States'.[7] Fr James Murtagh, the noted historian of Catholicism in Australia, had been similarly laudatory in his obituary of Mannix in 1963.[8] However, it would have been remarkable if Murtagh and Murphy, a feature writer for the diocesan *Advocate*, had not known[9] that this article (4000 words)[10] was, in fact, drafted by B.A. Santamaria for the joint episcopal Social Justice Statement of 1954, that it was rejected by other bishops as being too 'political' and that Mannix then allowed it, in slightly amended form, to be published under his name.[11] Certainly Murtagh knew this in 1970 and was aware that Mannix's insistence on the principle of 'subsidiarity' in the article sat at odds with his position on the Commonwealth 'Powers Referendum' of 1944.[12] Murphy, however, as did Murtagh in 1963, went on to say:

> As Archbishop Mannix seldom wrote anything, the article, afterwards published in pamphlet form, was a work of uncommon interest; it was a reminder, too, that he was a Doctor of Laws. Subsequently another Doctorate of Law [sic] was bestowed upon him by the National University of Ireland.[13]

In fact, Mannix had no legal or constitutional law training and only a first degree in divinity called a 'doctorate', which was awarded by his seminary some years after completing his post-seminary studies at the Dunboyne Establishment.[14] He was awarded a doctorate of Laws *honoris causa* in 1907 by the moribund Royal University of Ireland for his services on its Senate and probably for raising Maynooth standards to a level where affiliation of seminary to University could be made.[15] However, it was generally believed — indeed, 'put about' — in Melbourne that Mannix had legal/constitutional expertise, the article has been republished a number of times[16] under his name, commended fulsomely and, in spite of Gerard Henderson's confirmation of Santamaria's authorship,[17] Santamaria in his biography of Mannix, perpetuates the story.[18] No other biographer, however, quite matches Fr Walter Ebsworth's hero-worship, even after he had appropriated the delving and shrewdly appraising research that Fr Murtagh, after Mannix died, carried out in Ireland, as well as in Australia, for a biography that was unfortunately aborted by Murtagh's death in 1971. Ebsworth begins:

> At the time when Halley's comet was filling half the sky there flashed across the Australian firmament the name of Daniel Mannix. It was to linger high in the heavens for over half a century.[19]

By the end of the book, however, this slow-coach comet has been solidified and apotheosised into Ayers Rock, 'the greatest monolith in the world', and the magnifico whose prose was said to be more

Swift than Newman has become the greatest bishop since Athanasius:

> A fantastic claim! Yet who in fact was greater? An overseas Archbishop styled him 'the greatest churchman since Innocent III, the Pope at the time of Magna Carta'.

And just to pile the *Summa* on Ayer's Rock Mannix is best compared to 'St Thomas Aquin [sic], the acknowledged giant of the Christian ages'.[20]

These paeans are not quirkish aberrations; they were backed by the vulgar faithful throng. One hundred thousand were alleged to have crowded John Wren's Richmond racecourse on Melbourne Cup Eve, 5 November 1917, a working day, to hear Mannix — with neither a microphone nor a robust voice — tell them that they were there 'for Ireland's sake' but also 'for the sake of the Empire, of which Ireland, fortunately or unfortunately, is a part', and that Australians too were really Sinn Feiners, although they did not call themselves by that name.[21]

The crowd was said to be much greater at the 1920 St Patrick's Day procession when

> behind the Archbishop's car marched eight abreast 10,000 returned soldiers in full military uniform and detachments of nurses and sailors; but, even more remarkable, preceding the Archbishop at the head of the procession were fourteen Victoria Cross winners on white chargers.[22]

The VCs were nearly all non-Catholics and were fed and watered (not quite the right word) by courtesy of the gambler and sportsman tycoon John Wren, who also made a film of the event which was shown at the Princess Theatre where Mannix attended and spoke the night before he left[23] on the greatest adventure of his life: his voyage to the USA (where he shared platforms with de Valera), Britain (by courtesy of the Royal Navy) and Rome (where he was supposed to account for himself to Pope Benedict XV).[24] Wren,[25] in addition to composing words for a song 'Come Back to Australia' (formerly 'Erin') appears to have organised the surging farewell demonstration that caused Mannix to miss his train to Sydney though the Victoria Railways held it up for 15 minutes. 'It was', said Mannix, a unique demonstration which touched me to the heart. . . . It took me fifty minutes to cover a five-minute journey from St Patrick's to Spencer St Station. No one is to blame . . . the police did all that was possible. . . . I have no words to convey my gratitude for such an outpouring of esteem and affection, but I am truly grateful. People have suggested difficulties about my return to Australia. I think it will be much easier to return than it is to get away![26]

Mannix eluded further demonstrations by allowing the railway authorities to post notices that he would join the train at Essendon, but the train stopped especially for him at North Melbourne, half a dozen stations before. His earlier train ticket was then raffled as a souvenir.[27] One wonders if Wren influenced the Lord Mayoral reception for Mannix in Sydney, the mobilisation of exuberant crowds or paid for the green-accoutred float plane that looped over the S.S. *Ventura* as she passed out of the Heads.[28] In 1921 the Lord Mayor of Sydney presented Mannix in Melbourne with 'an oil painting' of Wren on behalf of some Melbourne Catholics[29] and it hung in a room at Raheen until Mannix's death.[30] No wonder Hughes could not seriously try to prevent Mannix's return to Australia even after he had 'criminally', in Hughes' opinion, tried to cause strife between USA and Great Britain by declaring at Plattsburg, N.Y. that England had been, was and always would be America's enemy;[31] or even after the British government itself had set an example by apprehending him on the high seas and keeping him from his native land.[32]

His Holiness, Pope Benedict, who was thought to wish Mannix 'at the bottom of the sea'[33] also would have had second thoughts about transferring Mannix from Australia both before and certainly after his reception at the Collegium De Propaganda Fide during his *ad limina* in April 1921. Twenty-three 'nations' besides Australians and Irish were represented among the students who participated in the address. As Mannix entered the refectory with their superiors, the students burst into 'a thunderclap of applause . . . from every portico'. When the address ended,

The sentiments . . . were suddenly caught up by the whole house and in the time-honoured canticle of Propaganda they were sent rising and falling like an ocean billow through the long aisles . . .

VIVAT, VIVAT, VIVAT, MULTOS ANNOS ET OPTIMOS,
FELIX PROSPER, VIVAT!

... and then, even as that tidal wave had crashed over the
river bank and come thundering down in torrents upon the open
plain below, so all their pent-up admiration burst forth in a
deafening roar of applause that surged onwards and onwards as
though it would o'ertop the hills of Rome itself. Through it all
the Australian coo-ee like a frightened bird above the tempest
could be heard calling its note; but the storm went raging on ...

More in this exultant vein follows from our Australian eye-witness
who then notes that Rome's 'best photographer' had been hired for
the occasion. 'Never have I known', he wrote,

that grand old face [Mannix was not yet 60] to betray such marks
of the touched heart within him as Propaganda's doorway closed
behind him .... He had sent his ringing calls for justice away
into the furthest depths of space, echoing away on and on into
the oceans of the infinity of God and, behold, the listening nations
had heard that voice amazed. 'The kings of the earth, and the
princes, the tribunes, the rich and the strong' had trembled before
his word but the nations themselves looked upon his face. They
saw there the image of Christ their liberator, and the angels who
minister around the throne of justice must surely have leant down
to hear the cry of admiration that broke forth from the hearts of
the people in answer to that mighty Christ-like voice denouncing
iniquity and upholding justice.[34]

I can only note here Mannix's princely progress during his return
to Australia in August 1921: the aeroplanes that swooped over the
train north of Sydney (who paid?); the civic reception in that
city (but not in anti-Labor Melbourne); the tributes of even non-
Catholics like Henry Boote, editor of *The Worker* and a more
effective anti-conscriptionist than Mannix; the address, perhaps
significantly by a certain Sergeant O'Sullivan, on behalf of the
Returned Soldiers and Sailors Association; the *Te Deums* in the
three eastern mainland capitals;[35] and the careful coaching of school-
children, at least at St Ambrose's, Brunswick, to sing *Vivat Bonus
Pastor*.[36] In the eyes of the faithful, Mannix had justified the
opinion of such 'authorities' as Fr E.J. Keating of Collingwood who

pronounced, in front of Mannix, in January 1918, when the second Conscription Referendum figures were being finalised, that

> his Grace . . . loomed as the greatest leader in Australia and, for the matter of that, the greatest leader in the world (Prolonged cheering). It was a marvellous thing that a man who had been but four years in this country had become the leader of the whole continent of Australia (Applause).[37]

It may be difficult for people in our TV age to grasp what a boon Mannix was to makers of plaster busts, medallions, badges, 'green favours', photo reproductions and picture-frames. One recurrent advertisement taking in a third of a large page, made a

> SPECIAL OFFER of His Grace's Portrait, for a short period only, Ending March 31st, 1918. A Life-like Reproduction, Hard-finished [sic] in crayon, Framed in 4 inch Massive Frame, With Gold Slip and Glazed, The Complete Portrait, 22 inches by 19 inches, packing free.

It was

> An unique opportunity to obtain a remarkable and true portrait of his Grace. All admirers of the Archbishop of Melbourne should avail themselves of this unrepeatable offer.

It cost merely 18s 6d.[38]

W. Gallagher advertised himself in the *Advocate* as 'Opthalmic Optician, By appointment to his Grace Most Rev. Dr Mannix'. Underneath was a photocopy of a letter in the prelate's barely legible, rather calligraphic, scrawl:

> The glasses which you supplied to me have given perfect satisfaction and I continue to use them with the greatest comfort.
>
> D. Mannix

The notepaper was official from Raheen with the archbishop's coat of arms aptly inscribed OMNIA OMNIBUS.[39]

Eulogistic poems appeared in the diocesan press or were sent to Mannix personally. Fr P. Dineen in 1920 after the 'Baltic' incident produced in Irish five stanzas, *Mannix Mo Mhile Stor* (*Mannix My Thousand Loves*), of which a literal translation was provided:

> Tis now seven years since the love of my heart went away from
> me . . .
> The enemy is watching the sea by night and day,
> Waiting for the ship in which the warrior will return home,
> And inciting the knaves beyond the sea to folly and fight,
> But a feather they won't lay on Mannix, my thousand loves.
>
> There will be bonfires blazing from Galway down to Cove
> On moors and mountains and the sweet sound of music playing,
> My pulse will leap with joy when I view the soil
> That will be bringing back my Mannix, my thousand loves.[40]

Fr Dineen's memory was extraordinarily short if he did not realise how unpopular Mannix had been with nationalists over his part in the O'Hickey affair,[41] and how surprised many were at his apparently new-found aggressive patriotism after 1916.[42]

I have seen no evidence that Mannix demurred at what may seem to some of us excessive adulation, although he did forbid similar demonstrations for his return from the Chicago Eucharistic Congress in 1926.[43] I hope it will not be thought iconoclastic or impertinent to ask how far the hero-worship was simply a set of spontaneous responses to his magnificently hieratic personality apparently mastering the woes and upholding the aspirations of Hibernians in Ireland and Australia, and how much it was nurtured by himself and his zealots, both clerical and lay. He did, after all, coerce the Winter family to sell him the leading diocesan paper, the *Advocate*, in 1919, threatening them that he would start an opposition paper and that church sales could be withdrawn, and then paying them for the goodwill at his own low valuation.[44] He was also well in command of the *Tribune* except when Fr James Mangan was editor and attacked the Republican Irish envoys in 1923 and praised the 'nineteen out of twenty' Australian bishops who had 'followed their brother prelates in Ireland' in upholding the legitimacy of the Irish Free State.[45] Mannix did personally 'sub' his own reported speeches, allegedly made off the cuff, but, as Murtagh came to know, carefully prepared,[46] and, as Murphy knew, altered as expedient, after they were submitted to him by an expert shorthand reporter, Frank Kelly.[47] It is also interesting to note a few items I did not find in those weeklies, such as the inflammatory Plattsburg speech on which Melbourne's dailies ran outraged editorials. After all, most Australians, including Irish-Australians, were quite content within the Empire, as Mannix acknowledged and he did claim to be an 'Australian' when he was not being purely 'Irish'.[48]

When Mannix was in Ireland in 1925 he was snubbed by the hierarchy and the Free State government — he was not received at Maynooth — though, of course, he was lionised by Republicans.[49] This was not reported in the *Advocate*, instead, that paper editorialised (26 November 1925):

> A new and powerful factor has come into the Irish political situation. The presence of Archbishop Mannix upon Irish soil, his personal contact with the leaders, and the magnetic influence of his speeches have done much to moderate party differences. His Grace has missed no opportunity of stressing two main points, or rather two aspects of the same point — the absolute necessity for unity among Irishmen and the iniquity and impossibility of a partitioned Ireland.

The lofty banality of these views is, I suggest, a measure of Mannix's political sophistication and his quest for publicity. Who sent the despatch from Ireland on which the editorial was based? According to one informant, formerly on the *Advocate* staff, Mannix provided even the advance publicity about himself before arriving in Australia in 1913 and had at that time some arrangement with the *Irish Press*.[50] On his triumphal return in 1925 he reported to his flock:

> When we went to Ireland we were warmly welcomed [as a group and as individuals]. The Australian pilgrims were met in the streets of Dublin 'by 100,000 people' and by almost as many in Cork. He went personally to the cities of Southern Ireland, 'And there was not one of these places in which I did not receive the freedom of the city.'[51]

Mannix said nothing of his treatment by the official Church and state. Mannix also spared this Melbourne audience the scathing remarks he made about the 'stepping-stones' approach to independence, his support for a republican 'no-compromise' approach, his attacks on the Cosgrave economic policy, his insinuations that the Cosgrave government was just a British puppet and, above all, that

Republicans in Ireland were better Catholics than Free Staters.[52] It would hardly have gone down well with Irish-Australians mainly bewildered and disgusted by the civil war. Yet with the years, great prescience, insight and influence were attributed to Mannix about Ireland and de Valera's future achievements.[53] De Valera and Frank Aiken said in Australia in 1948 that Mannix had not influenced the signing of the Oath in 1927.[54] His personal influence on events in Ireland seems to me — and I am not an historian of Ireland — to be limited first, as Herbert Moran put it, to impressing 'on the British the urgent necessity for "liquidating" the Irish difficulty'[55] if Great Britain's reputation in Australia and America was not to be further sullied; secondly, perhaps, to the assuaging of some Republican consciences which harboured qualms about ignoring the Irish hierarchy's strictures; and, thirdly, again perhaps, to absolving de Valera of the charge of 'perjury' in signing the Oath.[56] His reputation as a former Professor of Moral Theology stood, and he was a bishop, albeit the only one in Ireland or Australia to support de Valera. But would he have broken ranks if he had had an Irish see? Would he have said so wryly, as he did at the Rotunda in Dublin, that he was not infallible, meaning that the Irish bishops were not?[57] His clericalist mother is reported as saying that Dan did not understand Ireland and would have had a different approach if he had been allowed to land in Ireland in 1920.[58] As for Daniel himself, he told a relative at the end of his stay in 1925 that he would never visit Ireland again, and he did not,[59] not even for the Irish Eucharistic Congress of 1932 when de Valera was in power,[60] and although he was to live nearly 40 years more.

The diocesan papers revealed nothing of this. As in 1920–21 they were extravagant in their layouts of portraits, achievements, eulogies. Reception committees for Mannix were planned weeks in advance, parishes were allotted strong posts through the city to Eastern Hill to be manned by the faithful. In 1925 a Monster Catholic Excursion to the Moonee Valley racecourse was advertised for St Stephen's (Boxing) Day. The occasion was to be a 'Big Welcome to our Leader on his first public appearance subsequent to his homecoming'. There were to be horse events, cycling, basketball, Irish dancing. Alietti's orchestra from the Palais de Danse and St Vincent de Paul's Orphanage band would play. Hedley and Bartlett, musical clowns, would perform, as would O'Donnell, the handcuff king, the Irish Houdini. His Grace would arrive at 2.45 p.m. and had 'kindly consented to deliver an address at 3.45'.[61]

After 1925, leaving aside the annual St Patrick's Day procession, the Mannix extravaganzas were generally purely religious in character, although aiming at such a display of solidarity that the 'injustice' of no state aid to Catholic schools would be manifest. And although there were lay Catholic opinions to the contrary such as those of James Scullin (Labor Prime Minister), E.J. Hogan (Victorian Premier), Joseph Lyons (non-Labor Prime Minister), Arthur Calwell (Leader of Federal Opposition and Papal Knight) and others, state aid was deemed a 'religious' issue;[62] parish life revolved around the needs of the Catholic school until anti-communist threat expertise created some diversionary paranoia[63] in the mid-1940s.

One rally, not narrowly 'religious' in character, was initiated by Mannix in May 1939 through a Central Catholic Peace Committee as a result of a request from Pope Pius XII for some corporate action for peace. It was attended by Mannix and his suffragans of Ballarat, Bendigo and Sale as well as the then Prime Minister, R.G. Menzies, the state Premier, Sir Albert Dunstan and the president and secretary of the Victorian branch of the Returned Servicemen's League. It was, says B.A. Santamaria in his autobiography, 'the most extraordinary single event with which I have ever been personally connected'.[64] Unfortunately, Santamaria does not quote the even-handed, universalist approach he then took to generating peace between the nations, his 'certainty that there is no nation in the world which is sufficiently criminal in its mentality to desire war', and his condemnation of 'the bombing plane' which 'can guarantee universal defeat and spread the work of destruction among victors and vanquished alike'.[65] There can be no doubt these sentiments were also those of Mannix who said: 'We are not pacifists, or rather we are the only real pacifists. Our people will never be guilty of aggression but they are prepared, if attacked, to defend themselves.'[66] Quite consistently, in 1945 Mannix condemned the bombing of Hiroshima as 'immoral and indefensible'[67] but in 1954 he would laud General Macarthur as one of the great men of the epoch and complain that he had been sent to Korea to make war but was strictly forbidden to win it.[68] Can one doubt that his mind already pointed towards sanctioning the 'forward-defence' strategy which sent conscripts to Vietnam? Would he, like Santamaria, have been prepared to countenance even nuclear bombing of North Vietnam?[69] Had he really meant what he said in 1917: 'I am absolutely opposed to conscription in any shape or form.'[70] He did not publicly oppose it in 1942.

My problem is that, on the evidence, Mannix can hardly be regarded as a politically sophisticated or even consistent mind let alone an erudite one, if one looks not so much through the emperor's assumed clothing as simply under the prince-bishop's regalia. However, he did have charisma, to such an extent that few searching questions have been asked about him, and little checking and juxtaposing of what he said, or seemed to know, has been done. His biographers have been victims of the cult of personality, and have contributed to it. So they have not brought to attention the difficulty of finding out what Mannix actually did say in those Olympian speeches which he allegedly did not need to prepare.

For example, in September 1943 Mannix patronised a rally in Fitzroy 'to launch a relief fund for Italy and to explain the duties of Catholics in the existing political situation'. To people who had been pro-Fascist, Mannix was independently reported as saying:

> I say that Mussolini is the greatest man living today. His will go down in history as the greatest government Italy has ever had. The cultural, educational civilisation created by him, Italy and the world will always hold . . . as the greatest in the history of the globe.[71]

This statement was not reported in the *Advocate* of the following week, although a brief mention was made of the rally. The week after that, however, Mannix was reported as having said at that same rally:

> At this distance it is impossible to know . . . who is responsible for the removal of Mussolini. I was never a wholehearted supporter of his policy or his principles. I am the more free to say, therefore, that in my opinion history will call him one of the big men of the century. Like many big men he seems to have failed. But Italy will never again, I hope, fall back into the state in which Mussolini found her. We can only pray God to save any good thing that he has achieved for his country and his people.[72]

One can only marvel at the self-assurance, predicated on ignorance, with which the revised version of Mannix's speech was written and published — only 15 months after the Axis forces took Tobruk and 10 months after El Alamein where Australians died. The cult of personality affected Mannix as well as his flock.

But perhaps I should return to the mass demonstrations. Whatever may have been the highlight for Santamaria, for Mannix I do not doubt that the Melbourne National Eucharistic Congress of 1934 gave him the most profound satisfaction when half a million people knelt for the benediction and 80,000 took part in the procession 'rolling on and on', said the left-wing journalist, Clive Turnbull, 'like a great river of faith . . ... We were astonished, for none of us knew that there were so many Catholics in our State, or so many men who would walk for an end that is not of this earth.'[73] The Congress was non-political aside from the Bishop of Liverpool's plea for disarmament and, aside from the inevitable and proper 'Tribute to the Irish Priesthood' and the presence of Cardinal MacRory, the Irish primate, Ireland no longer provided a theme.[74] It is fitting if somewhat ironical that this should have been Mannix's proudest moment because in this homage to his episcopacy there was the acknowledgement that his primary interest was the Catholic Church. This he personified in his gaunt, magisterial carriage and a life-style that was at once personally monastic and of unblemished chastity and poverty if not, as at least two Popes might have thought, of obedience.[75]

Would the response of the faithful have been less if Mannix had kept out of politics? One Saturday morning during his visit in 1939, Halliday Sutherland 'received a semi-official message that Dr Mannix would be disappointed if . . . [Sutherland were] not present . . . that night' at a Catholic Action pageant at the Melbourne Cricket Ground. Sutherland had to pass over a lively dinner engagement with 'Cabinet ministers, judges, bankers and industrialists' at the Brighton Club in order to attend *Credo — A Scenic Play in which all the people of the land have their part*. There were 4000 performers and 60,000 turned up as audience.

The first scene dealt with 'Babylon the Godless' whose evil orgiastic citizens crucify the prophets who call for penitence thus trying the patience of the Angel of Destruction who razes the city. The second scene was called 'Building' where, in 'light and joy' Youth and the Guardian Angel of the Lord lead the citizens in constructing the City of God. The final scene, 'The City of God', saw the stage,

crowded with actors, . . . a blaze of light: the arena in darkness. In front of the altar, high above the city, appears The Guardian Angel of the Land —

My beloved people,
to your knees!
Here is your God
In the Most Blessed Sacrament.

Spotlights pick out a gateway opening from the stand on to the arena opposite the stage. Through the gateway there comes, amid the silence of thousands on their knees, the Most Blessed Sacrament under a canopy of white and gold: followed in procession by Dr Mannix; the Hierarchy of Australia; and hundreds of priests. The procession crosses the arena and enters the city. The play has become reality. Bishops and priests mingle with the citizens in the city. Only the Blessed Sacrament followed [not 'carried'! — J.G.] by Dr Mannix and two priests ascend the steep hill to the altar high overhead, and the service of Benediction begins. From the darkness of the Stands comes the voice of thousands singing those glorious Latin hymns . . . and then in English the Divine Praises that begin — 'Blessed be God'.[76]

This is Mannix *in excelsis* and no prelate was ever more fitted by innate dignity for such a numinous role. But his calculation is also interesting. Not only would his diocesan press extol the pageant but an eminent author would be beckoned to record it for the world and posterity. Perhaps because, as Bishop Farrelly of Lismore pointed out to Murtagh, Mannix never effectually followed up these demonstrations,[77] the Archbishop had generally become by World War II a venerable, respected figure in the Australian community, and the presence of Menzies and Dunstan at the papal peace rally symbolises greater integration of Catholics. Perhaps Mannix's Keynesian spending on buildings during the Depression helped, as the *Age*'s tribute to the Archbishop in 1937 suggested:[78] he finally crowned Eastern Hill with St Patrick's Cathedral spires in 1939 to coincide with the centenary of the first mass in Victoria and the pageant *Credo* celebrated the fact. During the ensuing war only rabid sectarians would have doubted Catholic 'loyalty', although Mannix defended the neutrality of Ireland, using, however, such grounds as that she would otherwise have been overrun by Germany.[79] With Australians preferring to be ruled during World War II by a Labor government containing a high percentage of practising and lapsed Catholics,[80] sectarian attacks became fringe activities and with the post-war European as well as British immigration programme, the Anglo-Saxon 'establishment' was becoming Anglo-Celtic. This was in part what Mannix had surely hoped his education programme would achieve.[81] (Among the 'Celts' to join the 'establishment' there were, of course, ex-Catholics and non-Catholics as well as Catholics.)

This inevitable development suffered one serious if sectoral setback: the débâcle of Santamaria's Catholic Social Studies Movement. The 'Movement' would hardly have been possible, I would maintain, without the Mannix cult of personality, without the deference allegedly due to 'the mind of the Archbishop' and without his dominant role in Australian episcopal councils.[82] It was this reverence for the Archbishop — and the paradox was that he had encouraged autonomous lay action — which prevented the members of the *Catholic Worker* monthly from publicly pointing out that the 'Movement' violated the crucial distinction between 'Action of Catholics' and 'Catholic Action' about which they (and Santamaria) had been carefully instructed by the clergy[83] and which was reaffirmed by the Vatican in 1957.

I believe that as well as justifiably looking for a mild Popish plot, particularly on Santamaria's part,[84] a future biographer must also ask whether Mannix really understood what he was doing and whether he was not only intellectually sloppy but, to a degree, self-intoxicated. He had never shown any capacity to distinguish between his ecclesial and civil roles; he simply ignored the time-worn dichotomy except through the symbolism of not making political statements from the pulpit. In 1916–17 he maintained that what a parson said in a pulpit he (Mannix) could justifiably say in a paddock.[85] He could not understand that if, as the parson believed, conscription was a moral issue, then the parson ought to speak on it from the pulpit but, if it were a political issue, as Mannix said he believed (and the Apostolic Delegate declared it to be),[86] then he might be wiser to say nothing, particularly in locations which were certainly not 'paddocks' but church functions on church premises where he wore not his top-hat but his biretta. Of course, he could rightly have discussed in his pulpit whether the parson was correct in calling conscription a moral issue but I have found no evidence that Mannix was interested enough to explore rigorously such an issue at length.

Mannix has been greatly indulged by biographers and commentators, few of whom have shown any zest for a critical analysis of his ideas or career. Hagiography has been aided by the fact that Mannix was secretive about himself[87] and deliberately destroyed papers and letters to prevent, as he said, posterity from analysing his soul.[88] It is remarkable how little was known in Melbourne about the first half of Mannix's life in Ireland in spite of his being 'the greatest leader in the world' (see above). Cyril Bryan, who wrote the first book on Mannix, went to Ireland and visited the Archbishop's mother but bequeathed, it seems, no family history. Even in its obituary issue the *Advocate* says that the Archbishop was the third of twelve children.[89] The *Tribune* said he was the third of five;[90] Niall Brennan has him as the second;[91] another reports Mannix having said he was one of 'a baker's dozen'.[92] In fact he was the eldest son.[93] So much then was known of Mannix personally 50 years after he had joined his not incurious flock. The clerical underground, however, knew better and this included priests who had been with Mannix at Maynooth and disliked him intensely. Naturally, with the solidarity of their profession they did not say openly, for example, that Mannix's nearest sibling, Patrick, became an apostate and rationalist[94] — perhaps one reason for the secrecy. Nor was it appropriate to make anything of his unpopularity at Maynooth although the story went the rounds that Cardinal MacRory, a former Vice-President, said in an unguarded moment at the 1934 Eucharistic Congress: 'Look at Mannix, strutting like a peacock, just as he always did at Maynooth.'[95] When he arrived in Australia he was alleged to be one of the Church's foremost theologians and an innovator in education,[96] neither of which claims is sustainable. Nothing seems to have been said of his role in the O'Hickey case, which must have influenced his translation to Melbourne,[97] and I would doubt that Walter McDonald's *Reminiscences of a Maynooth Professor*, where he is called the 'Mephistopheles' of the affair,[98] was reviewed in the diocesan press.[99] In his biography of Mannix, Santamaria disposes of McDonald by having Mannix regard that courageous theologian as his 'enemy', although the evidence in the book suggests only that he was sharply (and justifiably) critical of Mannix's behaviour. Similarly his receptions of royalty at Maynooth in 1903 and 1911 and subsequent criticisms of him in regard to this and the O'Hickey case by nationalist spokesmen have been glossed over.[100]

Santamaria, on Mannix's personal testimony, calls the story that Mannix displayed the Union Jack at Maynooth a 'canard'.[101] Readers of Colm Kiernan's *Daniel Mannix and Ireland* will think otherwise[102] and, again, the Melbourne clerical underground knew better. Mannix also maintained that no verbal expressions of loyalty to the monarchs were used. This needs investigation particularly in view of a letter from Mannix (12 July 1903) to the Archbishop of Dublin (which Mannix could not destroy) which says in a postscript that his President, Dr Gargan, 'may be counted on also to be' at Maynooth 'to receive his King loyally'.[103] For his biography, Santamaria did not bother to consult the material that exists at the Melbourne Diocesan Historical Commission.[104] Why bother when a 'cult of personality' has operated since before Mannix landed in Australia, operated during his life and can be used today to provide an icon for the 'Movement's successor, the National Civic Council?

Biographers have been so overawed by the Mannix charisma that no one seems to have thought it useful to analyse his speeches. Those on conscription, for example, I believe to be by turns confused, opportunistic, of 'wilful ambiguity', as K.S. Inglis says,[105] and devoid of any clear statement of principle. Mannix was, in fact, a master of the undistributed middle. During the O'Hickey case he wrote to the bishops, carefully pointing out that anti-clericalists were ranged on O'Hickey's side,[106] ergo . . . On Ireland in the 1920s he liked to draw attention to the fact that Ireland's enemies were ranged on the side of the Treaty, ergo . . . (although on one occasion, at least, he did point out that this was not in itself a convincing argument but he still thought it had its own weight).[107] In the post-Labor split elections of 1955 he was fond of saying that communists were giving their preferences to the Labor Party,[108] ergo . . . Mannix was a canny but not a subtle man.

I know of no convincing evidence that Mannix was a learned or particularly well-read man although he had an impressive-looking library and a journal subscription list.[109] He never seems to have engaged anyone in close debate; his pronouncements were delivered from protected public platforms with no question time; he would listen attentively to interlocutors and give counsel and brief opinions but he never deigned to argue. Those who have written about interviews with the Archbishop have invariably been deeply impressed but seem unable to remember anything of real substance he said, apart from humorous or wry anecdotes. All that Halliday Sutherland recorded from that 'most alert and disciplined mind' was the oft-told story of the man who wanted to call his racehorse 'Mannix'. 'But what if he should be beaten by a head', said His Grace referring to Frederick Head, then the Anglican Archbishop of Melbourne.[110] Mannix told Vincent Buckley the same story 16 years later and Buckley refers to its origin in the USA in 1920 before 'head' had replaced 'whisker'.[111] Mannix 'needed a Boswell', said Frank Murphy[112] and most acquaintances of Mannix appear to have agreed, but Boswell would have become very restive with the 'repeats' from the small repertoire that has gone the rounds. Actually Murtagh noted that in April 1970 a horse called Mannix, owned by Lady Petersham, did win the Irish Court Town Plate of two miles at 100/7. Its breeding was amusing: by Mazarin out of Nominate.[113] It would, however, be unfair to attempt to tease a trope from that because just as Mannix was a fully committed priest so he was also a political dilettante and not even the achievement of State Aid in 1963,[114] let alone the defeat of Conscription in 1916–17,[115] can be fairly laid at his door. He was neither Mercier, Mazarin nor Makarios.

There may be people who, while conceding much of what I am saying here, will still maintain that Mannix's policy of 'confrontation' and refusal to compromise (or associate) with the so-called 'establishment' gave Catholics new dignity and confidence and inspired them to make sacrifices for their faith.[116] This needs careful appraisal. It would be temerarious to suggest that Catholics were somehow worse off under Archbishop Duhig (Brisbane), Kelly (Sydney), Clune (Perth) and Delany (Hobart), to name just those contemporaries of Mannix whose careers can be consulted in recent volumes of the *Australian Dictionary of Biography*. In fact, in view of the state of diocesan administration at Mannix's death — he took little direct interest in it[117] — the question might better be: Were Victorian Catholics worse off for having such a cultic archbishop? No doubt there were gains and losses. However, some observers who have deplored the damage done to Australian political life — including the exclusion of many Catholics from parliaments[118] — through the 23-year non-Labor regime in Canberra and its almost 30-year counterpart in Victoria, have thought that not only Catholics but the mass of Australians have suffered from Mannix's interventions in politics. On hearing of Mannix's death, Archbishop Sir James Duhig, who witnessed the 50 years of Mannix rule and was his senior in the episcopacy, is said to have remarked: 'Mannix would have been a great archbishop, if only he hadn't led that rabble down Collins Street.' Without agreeing with it, this is the sort of remark that should be explored through an analytical biography.

Notes and References

1. Halliday Sutherland, *Southward Journey* (Geoffrey Bles, London, 1942), p.111.
2. Sidney J. Baker, *The Australian Language* (The Currawong Press, Milson's Point, NSW, 1978), pp.136–8.
3. Herbert M. Moran, *Viewless Winds* (Peter Davis, London, 1939), pp.157–8.
4. Cyril Bryan, *Archbishop Mannix: Champion of Democracy* (Advocate Press, Melbourne, 1918).
5. E.J. Brady, *Doctor Mannix, Archbishop of Melbourne* (The Library of National Biography, Melbourne, 1934), pp.6, 176, 227.
6. Melbourne *Argus*, 18 December 1937, typed extract in Murtagh papers. These papers in the Melbourne Diocesan Historical Commission (MDHC) are unsorted and very miscellaneous.
7. Frank Murphy, *Daniel Mannix, Archbishop of Melbourne*, new enlarged edn (The Polding Press, Melbourne, 1972), p.228.
8. Melbourne *Advocate*, 14 November 1963.
9. This writer and some members of the *Catholic Worker* editorial committee certainly knew it in 1954.
10. Most Rev. Daniel Mannix, 'The Australian Commonwealth and the States', *Twentieth Century*, vol.8, no. 3 (1954), pp.5–15.
11. Gerard Henderson, *Mr Santamaria and the Bishops* (Hale and Iremonger, Sydney, 1982), p.88.
12. Murtagh papers; and Don Watson, *Brian Fitzpatrick: a Radical Life* (Hale and Iremonger, Sydney, 1978), pp.157–8.
13. Murphy, *Mannix*, p.228.
14. Colm Kiernan, *Daniel Mannix and Ireland* (Alella Books, Morwell, Victoria, 1984), p.13.
15. Ibid., pp.36–9; Murtagh papers.
16. Issued also as a pamphlet by Advocate Press, Melbourne (n.d.), and reproduced in Melbourne *News Weekly* (organ of the National Civic Council of which B.A. Santamaria is Chairman) at least on 27 June 1973 but, I believe, more frequently.
17. Henderson, *Santamaria and Bishops*, p.88, and confirmed personally to this writer, 19 March 1985.
18. B.A. Santamaria, *Daniel Mannix: The Quality of Leadership*, (Melbourne UP, Melbourne, 1984), pp.21, 193.
19. Rev. Walter A. Ebsworth, *Archbishop Mannix* (H.H. Stephenson, Melbourne, 1977), p.1. Fr Ebsworth would have meant 1912 but Halley's comet appeared in 1910!
20. Ibid., pp.433–6.
21. Quoted in ibid., p.190.
22. Ibid., p.216.
23. *Advocate*, 20 May 1920.
24. See Michael Gilchrist, *Daniel Mannix, Priest and Patriot* (Dove Communications, Melbourne, 1982), pp.77–101; Santamaria, *Mannix*, pp.103–23.
25. No satisfactory study of John Wren (1871–1953) exists, and probably will never exist. But see Hugh Buggy, *The Real John Wren* (Widescope, Melbourne, 1977); and Niall Brennan, *John Wren, Gambler, His Life and Times* (Hill of Content, Melbourne, 1971).
26. *Advocate*, 27 May 1920.
27. Ibid.
28. Ibid.
29. *Sydney Morning Herald*, 28 September 1921 (kindly supplied by Dr B. Nairn, ANU).
30. Mr L. McCarthy, MDHC, personal communication.

31. *Argus*, 19 July 1920, quoted in Gilchrist, *Mannix*, p.88; Melbourne *Herald*, 28 July 1920.

32. Gilchrist, *Mannix*, pp.90–4.

33. Transcript of statements by Count de Salis, British representative at Vatican, 8 August 1920, Murtagh papers.

34. Typescript of MS by an anonymous priest sent by Ballarat Diocese Historical Commission to MDHC with note that 'copy received at Propaganda 1921'.

35. See *Advocate*, *Tribune*, issues of August 1921.

36. Gerard Heffey (former chairman, *Catholic Worker* editorial committee), personal communication, 25 January 1984.

37. *Advocate*, 5 January 1918.

38. Ibid., 9 March 1918.

39. E.g. ibid., 16 April 1925.

40. Murtagh papers.

41. Kiernan, *Mannix and Ireland*, pp.39–52; Ruth Dudley-Edwards, *Patrick Pearse, The Triumph of Failure* (Victor Gollancz, London, 1977), pp.74–8.

42. Walter McDonald, *Reminiscences of a Maynooth Professor* (Jonathan Cape, London, 1925), p.372.

43. Gilchrist, *Mannix*, p.126.

44. *Advocate*, supplement, '100 years of the *Advocate* 1868–1968', February 1968.

45. Gilchrist, *Mannix*, pp.110–13.

46. Murtagh papers.

47. Frank Murphy, 'Archbishop Mannix Needed a Boswell', *Advocate*, 27 November 1963.

48. The Sun and New York Herald, *2 July 1920*, reported Mannix as saying 'I know of only one national anthem and that is *God Save Ireland* ', clipping, Murtagh papers; but in *Advocate*, 16 March 1918, 'I consider myself a loyal Australian and I put Australia first, now and always (Cheers).'

49. Murtagh papers; Kiernan, *Mannix and Ireland*, pp.185–202.

50. F.D. Minogue, personal communication, 27 August 1985.

51. *Tribune*, 24 December 1925.

52. Broadsheet, *An Phoblacht*, Archbishop Mannix's speech in Dublin Rotunda, 29 October 1925, Murtagh papers; in Sligo on 7 October 1925 he said, 'I boldly make the assertion that the best Catholics of Sligo are within this hall', Murtagh papers.

53. E.g. Murphy, *Mannix*, pp.147–8; Ebsworth, *Mannix*, pp.313–15 refers to his 'overwhelmingly superior knowledge and logic'.

54. Murtagh papers; Mannix in welcoming de Valera in Melbourne in 1948 said, 'Mr de Valera had never faltered or compromised . . . his dream had come true', *Advocate*, 20 May 1948.

55. Moran, *Viewless Winds*, p.159.

56. Santamaria, *Mannix*, pp.140–1.

57. *An Phoblacht*, 29 October 1925 (see note 52 above).

58. Michael Cagney, Gibbings Grove, Ireland to Fr Murtagh, 14 June 1970, Murtagh papers. Cagney was a cousin of Mannix.

59. Ibid.

60. Various explanations have been suggested besides Mannix's personal chagrin, e.g. not wishing to politicise the religious congress or even to 'overshadow Pope's Legate not to mention the Bishops who ostracised him in 1925'. Notes by Fr Murtagh, 10 April 1971, Murtagh papers.

61. *Tribune*, 10, 17 December 1925.

62. *Advocate*, 13 and 20 May 1916 for controversy between Scullin and *Advocate* over the attitudes of Catholic Labor politicians to State Aid; on Scullin's approach

to religion and politics, see John Robertson, *J.H. Scullin, A Political Biography* (University of Western Australia Press, Perth, 1974), pp.118–19, 210.

63. See Paul Ormonde, *The Movement* (Nelson, Melbourne, 1972).

64. B.A. Santamaria, *Against the Tide* (Oxford UP, Melbourne, 1981), p.41.

65. Quoted in Ormonde, *Movement*, p.8.

66. Quoted in Santamaria, *Against the Tide*, p.41.

67. Quoted in Murphy, *Mannix*, p.196.

68. *Advocate*, 28 July 1954.

69. See Santamaria's weekly feature, 'Point of View', in *News Weekly*, 1966–72 for his attitude to the Vietnam war.

70. *Advocate*, 1 December 1917.

71. Gianfrancesco Cresciani, *Fascism, Anti-Fascism and Italians in Australia, 1922–1945* (Australian National UP, Canberra, 1980), p.210.

72. Ibid., p.219.

73. Quoted in Gilchrist, *Mannix*, p.152.

74. See J. Murphy and F. Moynihan (eds), *The National Eucharistic Congress, Melbourne, Australia, December 2nd–9th 1934* (Advocate Press, Melbourne, 1936).

75. Mannix was obliged in 1918 at an archbishops' conference to move *in camera* 'that the bishops and clergy should use prudence and caution in dealing with public questions'. It made little difference to his conduct. See Michael McKernan, *Australian Churches at War, Attitudes and Activities of the Major Churches 1914–1918* (Catholic Theological Faculty, Sydney, 1980), pp.157–8. See also reprimand by the Apostolic Delegate in 1933 and Mannix's response in Santamaria, *Mannix*, pp.142–5; and on the Melbourne response to Vatican rulings against Mannix's policy towards the Movement, see Ormonde, *The Movement*, pp.103–19; and Henderson, *Mr Santamaria and Bishops*, pp.134–5.

76. Sutherland, *Southward Journey*, pp.173–9.

77. Farrelly to Murtagh, 3 July 1968, Murtagh papers, MDHC.

78. Melbourne *Age*, 5 October 1937, referred to 'millions of pounds [spent] on bricks and mortar . . . No one person in Victoria responsible for a greater amount of employment', typed extract in Murtagh papers.

79. Murtagh papers.

80. '. . . half of the Labor Cabinet and more than half the ALP executive positions were filled by Catholics', Watson, *Brian Fitzpatrick*, p.157.

81. See B. Greening, 'The Mannix Thesis in Catholic Secondary Education in Victoria', in E.L. French (ed.), *Melbourne Studies in Education 1961–1962* (Melbourne UP, Melbourne, 1963), pp.285–301.

82. See *Catholic Worker*, July 1959; and Henderson, *Santamaria and Bishops*, passim.

83. See ibid., bibliography, pp.191–222. Numerous publications spelt out the distinction, e.g. Fr William Hackett S.J., *Why Catholic Action?* (Australian Catholic Truth Society, 1949), in which Hackett lists official Catholic Action organisations but makes no mention of the 'Movement'. Hackett was Mannix's clerical confidant, a founder of Australian Catholic Action and later Superior of the Melbourne Institute of Social Order. Henderson, pp.27–8, points out the anomaly of the bishops deciding that the 'Movement' 'was *not* a mandated movement of specialised Catholic Action. And yet they ruled that [an episcopal committee with Mannix as president] would control it "in policy and finance". There was an inherent contradiction here.'

84. Mr Santamaria's justification for organising so that Catholics can occupy key positions in major political parties has been recently restated in 'The "Catholic" Absence from Australian Politics', *Annals Australia*, April 1985, pp.5–11 (reprint from *Social Survey*, February 1985).

85. *Tribune*, 23 November 1916, quoted in Gilchrist, *Mannix*, p.38.

86. McKernan, *Churches and War*, pp.119–20.

87. Bishop L. Moran, formerly Cathedral Administrator and Vicar-General, Melbourne, interviewed by Murtagh, 17 January 1970, Murtagh Papers.

88. F.D. Minogue, *Footprints*, vol.3, no. 3 (1978).

89. *Advocate*, 14 November 1963.

90. *Tribune*, 14 November 1963.

91. Niall Brennan, *Dr Mannix* (Rigby, Adelaide, 1964), p.41.

92. F.D. Minogue to Murtagh, Murtagh papers.

93. Ebsworth, *Mannix*, pp.6–10, provides authoritative information on the Mannix family.

94. Ibid., p.7a; Murtagh papers.

95. Personal information. Murtagh records that in 1925 he was referred to as 'a turkey-cock' in the London *Tablet* but no date is given, Murtagh papers.

96. Fred Johns, *Fred Johns's Annual, Mainly a Biographical Record of Australasia's Prominent People* (Pitman, London, 1914), p.139; Ebsworth, *Mannix*, p.5.

97. Murtagh papers; Kiernan, *Mannix and Ireland*, pp.51–2.

98. McDonald, *Reminiscences*, p.259.

99. Nor would Moran's *Viewless Winds* have been reviewed, I believe, in what was a carefully controlled press. At least no informant can recollect it.

100. Santamaria, *Mannix*, pp.35, 169.

101. Ibid., p.142: 'The old canard was as untrue in fact as it was useful as a piece of propaganda.'

102. Kiernan, *Mannix and Ireland*, pp.55–8.

103. Photocopy in Murtagh papers; also reproduced in Ebsworth, *Mannix*, p.102; see also address read by Mannix on behalf of hierarchy and staff of Maynooth to King George V in July 1911, typescript reprinted from Appendix 3, Maynooth College Calendar 1911, pp.163–9, Murtagh papers.

104. See Introduction, pp.ix–xi, of Santamaria's *Mannix* with its acknowledgements. I am informed that Mr Santamaria consulted MDHC only for photographs and then by proxy. He also gives the impression (p.xi) that much oral testimony has been collected from Mannix before his death: 'Brenda Niall spent many days in personal interviews with Archbishop Mannix recording his recollections'. Ms Niall has informed me as follows (personal communication 22 December 1984): 'I really don't think I got much: in a way I think he interviewed me. There was a great deal of silence — enigmatic on his part, blank on mine . . .. My notes must still exist, but they would be very scrappy. When I read the first part of the biography a few weeks ago, the only bit I could remember clearly was [one anecdote].'

105. K.S. Inglis, 'Conscription in Peace and War, 1911–1945', in Roy Forward and Bob Reece, *Conscription in Australia* (University of Queensland Press, St Lucia, Queensland, 1968), p.37.

106. Kiernan, *Mannix and Ireland*, p.49.

107. *An Phoblacht*, 29 October 1925 (see note 52).

108. E.g. *Advocate*, 30 October 1955.

109. Murtagh records visitors who were impressed by Mannix's library (e.g. Mgr Fulton Sheen). However, a calculation of how Mannix spent his time suggests he could not have had time for omnivorous reading and there is little trace of it in his utterances.

110. Sutherland, *Southward Journey*, p.112. Cf. also Fred Alexander, *Australia Since Federation* (Nelson, Melbourne, 1967), p.305.

111. Vincent Buckley, *Cutting Green Hay* (Penguin Books, Ringwood, Victoria, 1983), p.136.

112. Murphy, *Mannix*, p.272; *Advocate*, 21 November 1963. Murphy actually wrote: 'Had someone close to Archbishop Mannix noted down his day-to-day conversation, his *obiter dicta*, Boswell's famous huge work on Dr Johnson could easily have been eclipsed.'

113. Murtagh papers.

114. There is no space here to demonstrate that this development was inevitable, but see Brother Ronald Fogarty, F.M.S., *Catholic Education in Australia 1806–1950, Vol. II., Catholic Education under the Religious Orders* (Melbourne UP, Melbourne, 1959) pp.457–79. Cf. P.N. Gill, 'The Federal Science Grants Scheme: An Episode in Church–State Relations in Australia 1963–1964', in E.L. French (ed.) *Melbourne Studies in Education 1964* (Melbourne UP, Melbourne, 1965), pp.271–354.

115. See H.V. Evatt, *Australian Labour Leader, The Story of W.A. Holman and the Labour Movement* (Angus and Robertson, Sydney, 1942), pp.409–11; F.B. Smith, *The Conscription Plebiscites in Australia 1916–17*, revised edn (Vic. Historical Association, Melbourne, 1974), pp.18–21; Ian Turner, *Industrial Labour and Politics: The Dynamics of the Labour Movement in Eastern Australia, 1900–1921* (Australian National UP, Canberra, 1965), p. 115.

116. E.g. Patrick O'Farrell, *The Catholic Church and Community in Australia. A History* (Nelson, Melbourne, 1977), Chs. 5–6.

117. Various commentators to Fr Murtagh, Murtagh papers, and to this writer.

118. On this point see B.A. Santamaria, 'The "Catholic" Absence from Australian Politics'.

8 Father Mathew's Statue: The Making of a Monument in Cork[1]

Ken Inglis

For historians as for other people the word 'monument' in Ireland suggests antiquity: but for the student, serious or casual, of modern Ireland, too, monuments may reward examination. Some studies of monuments elsewhere are instructive. Marvin Trachtenberg's book, *The Statue of Liberty* (Allen Lane, London, 1976), illuminates the history of both the USA and France's Third Republic, and shows vividly how a monument can change meaning: a statue conceived as emissary of the French liberal republican tradition turns into a symbol of America's welcome to the huddled poor. Likewise modern London's great monumental space Trafalgar Square 'became transformed', as Rodney Mace tells it, 'from an esplanade peopled with figures of national heroes, into the country's foremost *place politique*'.[2] George Mosse uses national monuments erected in Europe since 1870, and the ceremonies staged at them, to interpret a range of political hopes, fears and failures.[3] Richard Bosworth inspects the Victor Emmanuel II monument in Rome as artefact and symbol of the vulnerable new Italian state.[4] Outside the European world, Benedict Anderson and Robin Jeffrey scan monuments in Indonesia and India to gain otherwise elusive understandings. Anderson, dissatisfied with accounts of Indonesian politics based on printed matter, argues that the monuments put up by Sukarno and his successors are 'a type of *speech*', and he sets them alongside films, cartoons and other forms of political communication whose meanings he deciphers.[5] Jeffrey tells the story of an Indian state before and after independence in terms of the making, removal and replacement of statues, concluding that the study of such effigies can be 'a tool for revealing the divisions, preoccupations and politics of the people whose heroes the men and women of stone and bronze are supposed to be'.[6]

A comparative history of colonies could well be hung on the fate of imperial statues. Consider Dublin. During the eighteenth century the statue of King William III in College Green used to be adorned with lilies by Orangemen and defaced by other people. After Emmet's rising in 1803 he was painted black. He was blown up in 1836, restored, and blown up conclusively in 1929, to be replaced by Thomas Davis. King George II in St Stephen's Green was blown up in 1937 to celebrate the coronation of King George VI. Retaliatory raids were made on the statue of Wolfe Tone and the monument to Daniel O'Connell. The Queen Victoria Memorial installed in front of Leinster House a few years after her death was removed to the Royal Hospital, Kilmainham, in 1948. A cartoon had Nelson shinning down his pillar in O'Connell Street at this news and saying: 'Good lord, I must have a word with Dan O'Connell immediately.' Little did Nelson know what history had in store for *him* as an agent of the Crown. He was severely damaged in 1966 and later dismantled. Among other imperial figures Field Marshal Lord Gough in Phoenix Park was blown up in 1957, but the great obelisk to Wellington remains, perhaps because it emits no loud imperial message, or because its subject was Irish, and Prince Albert survives outside Leinster House, perhaps because he is round the back.

The modern monument most prominent in the Irish landscape is the one in Dublin dedicated to O'Connell. Homan Potterton has chronicled its creation and unveiling.[7] Peter Alter has written more analytically about it; he notes among much else that the Irish government was not represented at the unveiling in 1882, which was connected with the opening of a National Exhibition dedicated to the 'encouragement of Irish, in preference to British and foreign manufacture'.[8] In Alter's perception the making of the O'Connell monument was 'the expression of an attempt to place new symbols at the service of a certain national idea'. Alter proposes a study of Dublin's monument to Parnell. Elsewhere in Dublin and over the rest of the country it may be worth while for scholars to interrogate statues, columns, obelisks and other objects raised in honour of men and women and their causes. Here I want to ask questions about the statue in Cork of the Rev. Theobald Mathew, the Apostle of Temperance as he was known through and beyond Ireland before he died in 1856, aged 66. The statue was unveiled on 10 October 1864, the 74th anniversary of Mathew's birth in Thomastown, County Tipperary.

Father Mathew was not much more than a name to me before I visited Cork late in 1982 to teach a little Australian history and inhale Irish air. Soon he was filling my personal landscape. I walked past his effigy in Patrick Street. I saw his church whenever I turned into Father Mathew Street on my way to the Everyman Playhouse. Lorries parked outside my window in Crosses Green said on their doors: 'Southern Mills. Father Mathew Quay'. At Hallowe'en, Dr John O'Brien showed me the statue put up in Thomastown to celebrate the centenary of his launching as a temperance reformer in 1838. And when we visited that weekend in the country the house of Dr O'Brien's in-laws the Cookes, there to greet us inside the front door was a marble bust of Father Mathew by the famous Irish sculptor of the mid-nineteenth century, John Hogan, bought at auction for £10. I sensed an invitation from providence to study him a little; and it was a pleasure to sit in the Cork City Library and elsewhere, exploring the ceremony 118 years earlier when that monument to him was erected.

The crowd that gathered within sight of the ceremony was esti-mated at 100,000: 40,000 or so in Patrick Street and the rest along the quays on both sides of the Lee and north up St Patrick's Hill, a natural grandstand. As the population of Cork city in 1864 was about 80,000, we may wonder whether that 100,000 can be accurate. But the figure does come from an eloquent source: not the *Cork Examiner*, the Catholic and Liberal evening paper, but the *Consti-tution*, the Protestant and Tory morning paper which did not give the occasion whole-hearted blessing, and was unlikely to inflate the attendance. 10 October was a Monday. Employers had been urged to close for at least six hours to let their workers participate; shopkeepers had been exhorted to shut so that they and their assistants and customers could go. Special trains with low fares ran from Bandon, Queenstown, Youghal and as far as Limerick; special steamships from Queenstown and elsewhere. The arrangements remind us that in the mid-nineteenth century, public transport could deliver crowds on a scale never before possible.

Thousands of people, all men, took part in a procession to the site. Carriages at the head bore the High Sheriff of the city, members of the committee which had created the monument, the Mayor and Corporation, and speakers who would share the platform with the Mayor; behind them walked members of temperance societies and friendly societies and representatives of the trades, those bodies of skilled artisans which Maura Murphy has described as the most characteristic industrial organisation of nineteenth-century Cork: stone masons, cabinet makers, coach makers, tailors, sawyers.[9] 'To the trades of the country', the *Cork Examiner* wrote of Father Mathew,

> he principally looked for support, and the trades nobly rallied round him. In all the great temperance processions they bore a prominent part . . . The vice against which Father Mathew struggled had been the bane of this great body of people. It had . . . reduced many of their members to the lowest and most degraded position. Influenced by Father Mathew the trades rose to a man to maintain the great principle he advocated, and to take up the high position they were intended to occupy in the commonwealth.[10]

The *Examiner* judged of today's procession that 'In numbers and respectability it had never been surpassed in Cork since the days of the O'Connell agitations.' The tradesmen marched behind banners, many of which had been made for the day and displayed in shops during the previous week, such as the stone cutters' emblem showing Moses expounding the tablets of the law to the Israelites. This occasion was among other things a show, a popular entertainment.

The event was civic, not sectarian. Its themes were Cork and temperance; and they could be embraced by people of any class, party or faith. The trades had Protestant as well as Catholic members: coopers and shoemakers, Murphy finds, had Protestant minorities sometimes as large as 40 per cent. The Mayor, John Francis Maguire, struck the civic note in his unveiling speech, and said to great applause: 'We citizens of Cork, rejoice this day . . . that it was in Cork that the lowly, modest Friar rose into the sublime dignity of the greatest moral reformer of the age.' The statue would 'stand henceforward in your city as an enduring memorial of its best and greatest citizen'. Cork was a city in decline: the 85,000 inhabitants of 1851 had fallen to 80,000 within ten years; and we can hear in the speeches on 10 October 1864 a municipal concern, a sense that this city needs to make the most of its claims to pride and fame. The Mayor dwelt on Father Mathew's special place as the common property of all Corkonians, and indeed of all Irish people. 'Under his banner, all parties and all creeds united in harmony, and Irishmen long estranged learned to know and appreciate each other's virtue.

Would to God that that knowledge and that sympathy were universal throughout Ireland.'

John Francis Maguire was a Catholic, as nearly all mayors of Cork had been since the Municipal Corporation Act 1840 created an electorate which in O'Brien's words 'resulted in an overwhelming defeat of the hitherto dominant Protestant establishment'.[11] This was his fourth annual term as mayor. He was also a member of Parliament, for Dungarvan since 1852 and soon to represent Cork, from 1865 until his death in 1872. Maguire had been born in 1815, into one of the mercantile families who had given the city of Cork its prosperity. He was one of that group of Irish members at Westminster who had pledged themselves to vote together and independent of the British parties on major questions of policy towards Ireland, and he had been one of the most steadfast in keeping that pledge. He was deeply pious, and had written a book defending the temporal power of the papacy; but he was at ease with adherents to other faiths. In both politics and religion Maguire was a man of what we might now call ecumenical disposition. At the unveiling he spoke as a lover of harmony, and he shared the platform with nobody who could appear to be a partisan of any divisive cause. The three other speakers were Irish and English campaigners against alcohol.

Maguire pulled away a drape, and people close enough could see the bronze figure of Mathew, bare-headed and cloaked. The left hand gathered up the folds of the cloak, and the right was extended in a gesture of blessing. On the chest was the temperance medal worn by people who had taken a pledge to abstain from alcohol. Behind him, supporting the figure, was a Celtic cross (see frontispiece). The effigy 'bears a striking resemblance to Father Mathew', wrote the *Constitution*'s reporter. That was worth noting because the sculptor, John Foley, had never seen his subject.

The statue had been started by the eminent Cork-born sculptor John Hogan, who had been working in Dublin since he left Rome after the revolution of 1848. Hogan had already done the bust of Father Mathew that greeted me in the Cooke family's hallway. The committee had sounded Hogan out on the appropriate size and likely cost of a statue; he answered eight feet high and £1200.[12] He was keen to do the job, just as soon as his bronze figure of Daniel O'Connell was on its way from the foundry in Paris to the plinth in Limerick, where he was certain, he told the Cork committee, that it would 'place the puny efforts of the English sculptors in the shade',

and 'stand for ever not only as a monument to the Liberator but
as a satisfying specimen of Irish sculpture'. On 1 October 1857
Hogan wrote: 'I am glad to find that your Committee are eager to
commence the Mathew statue shortly, without going to sleep on it
like many things in Ireland of daily occurrence.' He would catch
the next excursion train to Cork. The committee talked Hogan down
from £1200 to £1000 and gave him £200 to go on with; but a few
months later he died. Negotiations began with John Foley, Hogan's
successor as Ireland's and later England's leading creator of monumental sculpture, whose commissions would include the figure of
the Prince Consort in the Albert Memorial. Foley quoted £1100,
which he reduced to £900 by the time the job was finished.[13]

The statue which the crowd now began to inspect was a singular
object. It was the first statue of a Catholic in a public place in
Cork — though it may be misleading to say so, for it was also the
first statue of *any* private citizen in a thoroughly public place. Behind
rails at the river end of the Grand Parade had been installed a
leaden King George II on horseback, unveiled by the Corporation
in 1861 and removed in 1862 after both horse and rider had tilted
so badly that they were given crutches, one 'under His Majesty's
right arm', as a chronicler observed in 1859, 'and another beneath
the belly of the charger, to prevent them from toppling over'.[14]
Even so, bits of the King had fallen off, possibly with help from
passers-by. On surviving evidence it is not easy to decide whether
the removal of King George II in 1862 counts as assassination or
euthanasia. Outside the Mansion House had once stood a marble
King William III and Earl of Chatham, though they were removed
after Chatham, as the chronicler of 1859 put it, 'underwent some
vicissitudes, having been mutilated, and subsequently painted in all
the colours of a harlequin'.[15] By now, indeed, the Mansion House
itself had been transformed, sold by the new masters of the munici-
pality who differed from the displaced Protestant establishment
about the character of the mayoralty: these days the building was
a hospital run by the Sisters of Mercy. There was one statue of a
Protestant citizen, the brewer William Crawford, done in 1841-2 by
Hogan, in a semi-public place, inside the Cork Savings Bank (and
now in the Crawford Municipal Art Gallery). Crawford's partner
William Beamish was also the subject of a monument by Hogan,
but that was still less public and it was not a statue: a memorial in
St Michael's Church of Ireland, Blackrock, commissioned by the

Beamish family, showed the naked brewer rising neo-classically from his grave on the day of resurrection.

The statue in Patrick Street, then, was the first of a Catholic; the first fully public one of any private citizen; and the first monument raised as the result of an appeal to the people of Cork. There was already one other monument to Father Mathew near the city: a tower a few miles down the River Lee, at Glanmire, opposite Blackrock Castle; but that had been put up privately, by the merchant tailor William O'Connor, to celebrate Father Mathew's invasion of England on behalf of temperance in 1843. When the tower was opened on Mathew's 56th birthday in 1846, the priest himself planted an oak, and Master Delacour Beamish of the brewing family planted another.[16] There was also a cross honouring Mathew in the burial ground to the west of the city known in the twentieth century as St Joseph's cemetery but called in 1864 Father Mathew's cemetery. He had bought the site so that poor people could be buried cheaply and Catholics could be buried without the threat of Protestant clergymen censoring what the priest said at the graveside. The cross commemorated Mathew's opening this cemetery in 1830. It was just in time for the cholera epidemic of 1832; and in 1846–47 the bodies of more than 10,000 famine victims were laid into that piece of ground. Father Mathew's own body was interred beside the cross, at his request, in December 1856.[17]

The movement to put up the statue began a few weeks after Mathew's death. Catholic and Protestant men of eminence in Cork, both clergy and laity, met on 19 January 1857 and resolved on Maguire's motion to mark the 'national loss' by commemorating their 'fellow citizen' with 'some enduring monument', and to put it in Cork because that city was not only the seat of his labours as a clergyman but also the 'centre of the great moral movement which under his leadership spread its blessings to the . . . civilised world'. The committee was formed, and the sum of £275 was subscribed in a few minutes.[18]

The statue was commissioned by an alliance of the old Protestant and the new Catholic civic leadership in Cork. Liberals of both faiths had already made common cause in support of Daniel O'Connell. The Protestant brewer F.B. Beamish was on the Statue Committee, even though Mathew's apostolate at the height of its popularity damaged the brewing industry. The trade was more profitable by the time Mathew died, and Beamish and Crawford, like Guinness, were benefiting by takeover of smaller competitors. A Protestant need not be a Liberal in order to approve of Mathew's crusade. Protestant Dissenters had first recruited the popular priest to the cause of teetotalism, knowing that if *he* carried its message to the Catholic masses of Cork, it would be heard with a reverence *they* could not command. When the Inspector-General of the Irish Constabulary asked inspectors in the south during 1840 to answer a questionnaire about Mathew's movement, an officer in County Limerick replied that he could detect no sectarian or political object in the enterprise: 'The motive seems to me to be a sincere desire to overcome the great cause which has long obstructed their improvement and moral and physical advancement.'[19]

Mathew was an unflinching defender of the political and social order. 'He respected rank', declared the *Cork Examiner* on 8 October 1864, 'he honoured worth, he rendered obedience to authority; but he loved the poor'. In the last ten years of his life he accepted a pension of £300 a year from Queen Victoria. He made the remarkable claim that his crusade was responsible for the failure of insurrection in the summer of 1848. Five days after the scuffle at Ballingarry in County Tipperary that was to enter one version of history as Ireland's revolution of 1848, Mathew wrote to the Unitarian philanthropist and literary man Richard Dowden (one of the three Dissenters who had enlisted him for temperance):

> The Teetotallers everywhere remained faithful — You can easily imagine what the position of Cork would be, were it not for this dragchain. — If the People of Ireland were, as in former days, Slaves to drunken habits, our greenest fields would have been deluged with blood.[20]

Daniel O'Connell was never comfortable with Mathew's vision of a people historically depraved by alcohol until the temperance crusade arrived. O'Connell judged it prudent in 1842 to forge an alliance between Repeal and Temperance. Even when delivering an oration in praise of the priest, however, he made a distinction that detached him from Mathew's view of the past: 'Father Mathew did not redeem a drunken people; but he did redeem a people who were predisposed to his mission.'[21] Mathew, for his part, was fearful that association with O'Connell and Repeal would endanger the purity of his own cause. He had to simulate delight when O'Connell, Lord Mayor of Dublin, announced that he would join a great temperance procession in Cork on Easter Monday 1842. Whether the cause either of temperance or Repeal was retarded or advanced by the connection O'Connell had contrived between them, it benefited Mathew's reputation for respectability when people could say, as Maguire did later: 'It was to Father Mathew that O'Connell was mainly indebted for the peace and good order which so signally marked those great gatherings.'[22] That was a less extravagant claim for the apostle of temperance in 1843 than his own boast about averting bloodshed in 1848. It was recognised well beyond the circle of Mathew's close admirers. A Protestant correspondent in the *Constitution* just after Mathew's death, wondering on what terms she could subscribe to a memorial fund, acknowledged: 'We are bound to consider our obligations to the late Mr. Mathew. To teetotalism, under providence, we are chiefly indebted for having escaped riot, bloodshed and perhaps rebellion, in 1843, at the time of the monster meetings.'[23]

Still, a priest was a priest; and the Protestant Tory conductors of the *Constitution* could give only conditional support to the campaign for a statue of this one. When talk of a memorial was in the air, after Mathew's death and before the meeting that yielded the statue committee, the paper declared that it would not lend itself 'to any project by which the Roman faith was likely to be instilled'.[24] The *Constitution* distinguished firmly between Mathew the moral reformer and Mathew the Catholic clergyman. A leading article the day after the unveiling paid respect to him 'as a benefactor, not as a priest'. The paper niggled about the statue. It was in the wrong place. It faced the wrong way. And the *Constitution* found graver cause to complain about what was written on the pedestal. When the statue was unwrapped it had only a temporary inscription, as the bronze lettering for a permanent one had not arrived from London in time. It said MATHEW and APOSTLE OF TEMPER-ANCE. But next month it emerged that the Statue Committee was to name the figure FATHER MATHEW. 'Did they forget', asked the *Constitution*, 'that there was but *one* Mathew, as there was but one Grattan, Nelson or Wellington? . . . Were they afraid that strangers would not take him for an ecclesiastic? And what if they didn't?'[25] The protest went unheeded. Mathew became Father Mathew, Apostle of Temperance but also priest; and he remains so to this day; presiding benignly over the river end of Patrick Street, ERECTED BY A GRATEFUL PEOPLE and UNVEILED IN THE MAYORALTY OF J. F. MAGUIRE. Why the temporary inscription omitted the word FATHER is a puzzle, for an engraving of the statue published in 1863, the year before it was finished, shows the words FATHER MATHEW on the pedestal. Perhaps some difference of judgement arose in the committee late in the day. If so it was resolved in favour of identifying the figure as a priest.

That engraving appears in a biography of Father Mathew by John Francis Maguire. It is a big book — 557 pages — and depicts a more interesting person than the figure of monotonous virtue — as the saying goes, a plaster saint — celebrated by Maguire and others in platform and editorial rhetoric. He resigns from Maynooth anticipating expulsion after holding a forbidden party, and that is how this well-born young man comes to join the humble Capuchins. He has enough ambition to be deeply disappointed when Rome does not make him Bishop of Cork in 1847 after all the clergy in the diocese vote to have him. He appears not to notice that a manservant is offensive to poor visitors and deeply, as it turns out fatally, addicted to alcohol. He is prone to dark despondency. A complex personality glints through Maguire's pages.[26]

The author knew his subject well. Indeed, Maguire made Mathew a personal cause. He had been close to the priest since boyhood; he himself had taken the pledge of total abstinence, and he believed that many fellow citizens had been saved from drunkenness and thus from poverty by Mathew's apostolate. 'I know parties in this city', he said at the meeting to consider a memorial, 'who, pointing to their well-filled store and their prosperous business, would not be ashamed to acknowledge that they owed it to the advice of Father Mathew.'[27] Maguire was sad that the crusade for temperance had gone into a decline during the 1840s. The famine, as Maguire saw it, broke up the organisation of the movement by scattering its adherents. Mathew himself was paralysed by a stroke in 1848, set off for the USA next year hoping to elevate his emigrant countrymen, returned in 1851 and was a prematurely helpless old man before he died five years later at the age of 66.

Maguire seems to have hoped that the statue might induce a posthumous revival of his hero's apostleship. The statue as educator, even evangelist: this was a common theme at unveilings in the later nineteenth century. If we smile at such a perception of a piece of metal or stone, if we find it quaintly superstitious to expect that so inanimate a medium could instruct or inspire, that shows how electricity has transformed our notions of indoctrination. Protestant as well as Catholic could hope that the statue of Father Mathew would do good. 'If the multitudes that assembled yesterday would raise a monument worthy of their benefactor', said the *Constitution* in its John Bull prose, 'let them refrain from the vice against which he warned them . . . To every backslider that statue every time he passes it will be a reproach.'

The *Constitution*'s mild reserve towards the monument may have derived in part from sheer journalistic rivalry. For Maguire was not only MP and Mayor, but proprietor of the *Examiner*, which he had founded in 1841 as an O'Connellite organ. Readers were given full reports of the campaign for the statue, and the editions of 10 and 11 October carried column after column describing the unveiling in words which were reprinted as a pamphlet. The account in Maguire's paper dwells on the good humour and orderliness of the day. So does the report in the *Constitution*, but the Protestant paper's story does not have, as the Catholic paper's does, an air of vindication.

In the weeks before the ceremony the *Examiner* had been expressing a serious concern about order, an apprehension that the day might go awry. On 1 September the *Examiner* defends the decision to have a public procession; but the committee, readers are told, 'are naturally anxious that the demonstration of the 10th of October should be of the very same character as that of which Father Mathew himself would have approved, were he still amongst us — that is, unpolitical and unsectarian'. Were he a great party leader like O'Connell, the exhibition of political emblems and banners might be in keeping; but Mathew, though an Irishman, belonged to no party. Moreover,

> there are special reasons why there should be the utmost caution — one may say the most delicate generosity of sentiment, at a moment like this, when unhappily there is too much excitement in the public mind of the country, the result of a melancholy state of things to which we have no desire now to refer.

On 6 September appears another warning against making the event a political demonstration, and a gratified report: 'The Trades of Cork . . . resolve that nothing shall interfere to mar the effect of the procession on the 10th of October.' On 8 October the paper declares: '*on the people* the Committee rely for the *preservation* of public order on Monday'; and the people are exhorted to carry no provocative banners or other emblems, and to leave green ribbons home.

The wearing and waving of the green, since 1798 a symbolic gesture of national protest, had been an issue within the temperance movement during Mathew's lifetime. H.F. Kearney notices an episode at Bruff, in Co. Limerick, when green ribbons were proposed for a procession and the parish priest, described 'by the police as 'a most excellent man', persuaded the participants to wear black.[28] The *Examiner* was relieved to notice in the crowd on 10 October 1864 a great deal of white, emblematic both of peace and of Father Mathew's purity, and very little green, which might have given offence, the paper said, 'to those who morbidly regard the national colour as a provocation to hostility, or the emblem of party'.[29]

Why had Maguire and his fellow committee members been so anxious? What did the *Examiner* mean when it spoke of 'too much excitement in the public mind' and 'a melancholy state of things to which we have no desire now to refer'? For answers we must look at two other Irish cities, at another monument and another ceremony.

On 8 August 1864 in Dublin the foundation was laid of a monument dedicated to the memory of Daniel O'Connell. Maguire was there at the Mansion House before the ceremony and in the procession to the point in Sackville Street which had been reserved for the monument by the Dublin Corporation. He was a guest at the banquet after the ceremony, and delivered a tribute to O'Connell as the Liberator of Catholics. Neither Maguire nor any other of the day's speakers mentioned O'Connell's unfulfilled vision of Repeal. John Hogan, making a marble figure of O'Connell for the Corn Exchange in 1845, put a scroll in his hand labelled REPEAL THE UNION. But within three years of O'Connell's death in 1847, writes Oliver MacDonagh, even the O'Connellites admitted that Repeal was a dead issue.[30] In O'Connell's last years the Irish clergy had orders from Rome to stay out of agitation for Repeal, and in the early 1860s only the fractious Archbishop MacHale spoke out against the policy, as he put it, of 'honouring the Emancipator only and ignoring the Repealer'.[31] The O'Connell Monument Committee was formally committed to commemorating only the Emancipator. Nobody on the platforms of 8 August said a word that could have been construed as disloyal.

Among the 60,000 or so people who joined the procession, however, and the much larger crowd — a Protestant estimate made it close to 200,000 — who watched them go by, there were many less inhibited. 'Every one wore green in some shape or other', a Protestant newspaper reported: street arabs wore green ribbons and olive leaves on their heads; cab horses were decorated with green ribbons and leaves and boughs; girls wore green dresses and bonnets and ribbons and streamers; men wore green sashes and rosettes, and women on horseback were dressed in green, 'like resuscitated Robin Hoods'. Worse still: 'Seditious emblems and mottoes stared you in the face wherever you turned.' Some Protestants even saw pikes, which they called by a name that had lately gained a new and fearsome meaning: Fenian.[32]

The *Belfast News-Letter* called for a monumental rejoinder.

A statue of the great and good King William, the true Liberator, not of Ireland alone, but of this Protestant realm, shall be raised in our streets to tell future generations of his deeds and of our loyalty to the Crown and constitution. The heart of Ulster throbs to the idea. The purpose of Protestants will be open to realize it.[33]

That statue was not to appear, but in Belfast some Protestants made a speedier and cheaper ceremonial response to the provocation in the streets of Dublin: they burned O'Connell in effigy. Reports of what happened next are confused, but day after day the headlines said: RIOTING IN BELFAST. Protestant papers savoured the rampaging on 15 August by Catholic navvies who were not at work that day because their Church was celebrating the Assumption of the Blessed Virgin. After 18 days of violence some people were dead — seven according to Norman, twelve according to Lyons — and 100 to 150 injured, in the earliest riots described by historians of modern Ireland as urban.[34]

These were the events Maguire's *Cork Examiner* had in mind when it counselled people not to wear green in honour of Father Mathew. It was a relief, even a triumph, for Maguire and people like him when the paper could report that the spirit of peace had presided over Cork on 10 October. The morning after, 22 men were charged with drunkenness — fewer than normal on a Tuesday.

Later in the week Maguire as mayor received a letter from a citizen of Cork saying that it was now time for the city to put up a companion for Mathew, a statue of 'the greatest Irishman that ever lived', O'Connell.[35] I wonder why it never did. Part of the answer is that some people preferred Catholic resources to be directed to a different monument, Saints Peter and Paul's Church. This building, and others like it — new, grand, central, designed by famous architects — were significant affirmations of Catholic wealth and confidence. 'Such a structure is a glorious monument to our city', said the *Examiner*, 'and a majestic monument of the piety and liberality of its Catholic inhabitants.'[36] Meanwhile Cork Protestants were canvassed for a kind of counter-monument, the soaring new Gothic building of St Finn Barre's Cathedral, signalling what the Protestant minority could still do in an age of Catholic Emancipation and imminent disestablishment.

Meanwhile Father Mathew became a landmark. His statue was recognised as defining the centre of the city. Buses would say simply STATUE. Folklore encrusted it. In a late nineteenth-century rhyme about sanitation:

> The stink at Patrick's bridge is wicked
> How does Father Mathew stick it?

In a joke about the Cork accent, 'statue' and 'Mathew' are made to rhyme. There have been jokes too about his apostolate, genial rejections of his exhortation to the passer-by to give up alcohol: footprints painted from the pedestal to and from a nearby pub; a bottle stuck in the outstretched right hand; the story that his outstretched hand says: 'I've been drinking since I was *so* high.' These jokes may be interpreted as devices whose purpose is to defuse the monument, to reduce its capacity to inspire awe, to turn off its power. They are possibly no longer necessary.

As a modern monument the statue was surpassed in 1906 by what was known officially as the National Monument and informally, at least for a while, as the Manchester Martyrs Memorial. The Father Mathew Temperance Society was represented in the procession on St Patrick's Day 1906 to the site of the monument, at the southern end of the Grand Parade, close to where once George II had sat on his horse; and so were the trades, as in 1864. But this ceremony was partisan as the day of unveiling Father Mathew had not been: the *Constitution*, mellower but still Tory and Protestant, reported that the speeches were made by 'prominent spirits in the more advanced sections of Nationalists'.[37] This was a project begun in 1898, the centenary year of insurrection, and delayed, like similar enterprises elsewhere in the country, by factional conflicts over the custody of historic heroes.

One living hero honoured in the ceremony was O'Donovan Rossa, the old Fenian, born in Co. Cork, whose funeral in 1915 Padraic Pearse would turn into a prologue to the Easter Rising. Two priests took part. One rejoiced that the time had passed when timorous Irishmen discountenanced celebrations in honour of Irish heroes. Certainly a lot of water had flowed down the Lee in the 40 years since John Francis Maguire exhorted patriots not to provoke Anglo-Protestant anger by wearing green on the day Father Mathew was honoured. The other priest unveiled the monument to reveal figures representing the dates now sacred to new nationalists: 1798, 1803, 1848, 1867. Wolfe Tone stood for 1798, Michael Dwyer for 1803, Thomas Davis for 1848, O'Neill Crowley for 1867. Scholars who know more than I do about the Irish invention of revolutionary tradition may like to explain why those four are there and not certain other candidates (Robert Emmet, Smith O'Brien) for the national pantheon.

The four men surround and protect a canopied woman, eight feet high, stroking her long hair with the left hand and resting her right hand on a Celtic cross, beside which is a harp. She wears a coronet. She is Erin. She appears also on the 1798 memorial at Bandon, unveiled in 1898. As a visual symbol for Ireland Hayes-McCoy says she goes back to harps made in the seventeenth century.[38] In the nineteenth century she is shaped both by the Celtic revival and by a European fashion in iconography. Intermittently in France, continuously in the USA, painters and sculptors found a market for a female figure to represent a nation which has abandoned monarchy: in France, Liberty or Marianne; in America, Liberty or Columbia. Bartholdi's figure for New York harbour I mentioned as coming out of France and being embraced by Americans. John Hogan liked to incorporate a female representation of Ireland in a variety of his sculptures, both sacred and secular. On the O'Connell monument in Dublin, begun by Foley and completed by Thomas Brock, 'Erin', in Potterton's description, 'standing by her harp, her hair wreathed in shamrocks, is the central figure of the frieze. Towards her hasten Irishmen of all classes to hear proclaimed their newly attained liberty.'[39] She adorns hotels and banks. She is put to both imperial and revolutionary uses: that Queen Victoria Memorial in Dublin includes the figure of Erin, holding the laurel for an Irish soldier dead in the Boer War; and on Limerick's memorial to the Easter Rising she is being unshackled by two fighters.

She is always significantly different from the French or American Liberty. They wear the Phrygian cap of freedom. They are republican figures. She, in Cork and elsewhere, wears a coronet. From behind, in Cork, she looks like the young Queen Victoria; and the priest unveiling her and her four servants says that the patriots gave all 'to replace the crown of nationhood upon the brow of the discrowned Queen'.[40] I am reminded of Professor F.X. Martin's observation that Pearse hoped in 1916 not for a republic but another monarchy, whose throne might be occupied by a German.

You may well wonder why I have strolled all the way along Patrick Street from the statue of Father Mathew and down Grand Parade to the National Monument and figure of Erin. I do so in hope that somebody may bring Erin to the next of these gatherings.

David Fitzpatrick's paper prompts me to go still further, turning left at the end of Grand Parade and proceeding a few paces down river from the National Monument. Here stands self-effacingly a small obelisk to honour men of the Munster Fusiliers who died in the war of 1914–18.

In 1904 a public memorial to Cork men killed while fighting Boers, erected by subscription, could say that they had lost their lives in the service of the Empire. But Cork's monument to men who went from the region to the Great War does not mention Empire, or country, or God; it says that they were 'fighting for the freedom of small nations'. In just these terms had the Irish revolutionaries tried to justify the Easter Rising to people in England and America, identifying their cause with that of the Belgians. There could be an interesting comparative study of Irish memorials for the Great War, the Easter Rising, the War of Independence and the Civil War. It would make a more complex and poignant story than that of the statue of Father Mathew.

Notes and References

1. For help in preparing this paper I am grateful to Ann Barry, John O'Brien, and people who commented on earlier versions read at the Institute of Irish Studies, Queen's University of Belfast, and the Historical Society, University College, Cork.

2. R. Mace, *Trafalgar Square: Emblem of Empire* (Lawrence and Wishart, London, 1976), p.15.

3. G.L. Mosse, *The Nationalization of the Masses* (H. Fertig, New York, 1975).

4. R.J.B. Bosworth, 'The Opening of the Victor Emmanuel Monument', *Italian Quarterly*, vol.18 (1975), p.79.

5. B. Anderson, 'Notes on Contemporary Indonesian Political Communication', *Indonesia*, vol.16 (1973), pp.39–80.

6. R. Jeffrey, 'What the Statues Tell: The Politics of Choosing Symbols in Trivandrum', *Pacific Affairs*, vol.53, no.3 (1980), pp.484–502.

7. H. Potterton, *The O'Connell Monument* (Gifford and Craven, [Dublin]. 1973).

8. P. Alter, 'Symbols of Irish Nationalism', *Studia Hibernica*, no.14 (1974), pp.104–23.

9. M. Murphy, 'The Economic and Social Structure of Nineteenth Century Cork', in D. Harkness and M. O'Dowd (eds), *The Town in Ireland* (Appletree Press, Belfast, 1981), pp.125–54.

10. 10 October 1864.

11. J.B. O'Brien, *The Catholic Middle Classes in Pre-Famine Cork* (O'Donnell Lecture, Cork, 1979), p.3.

12. Hogan to the committee is in Richard Dowden Richard correspondence, Cork Archives Institute, U.140, C.240, 241, 247.

13. *Cork Examiner*, 10 and 15 October 1864.

14. B.A. Cody, *The River Lee, Cork, and the Corkonians* (Cork, 1974, first published 1859), p.93.

15. Ibid.

16. Ibid., p.128; Michael O'Brien in *Evening Echo* (Cork, 26 September 1972).

17. J.F. Maguire, *Father Mathew: A Biography* (London, 1863), pp.74–5, 229.

18. *Constitution*, 20 January 1857.

19. Quoted in H.F. Kearney, 'Fr. Mathew: Apostle of Modernization', in A. Cosgrove and D. McCartney (eds), *Studies in Irish History presented to R. Dudley Edwards* (University College, Dublin, 1979), p.172.

20. Richard Dowden Richard correspondence, Cork Archives Institute, U.140, C.156.

21. Quoted in Maguire, *Father Mathew*, p.270.

22. Ibid., p.232.

23. 1 January 1857.

24. Ibid.

25. 18 November 1864.

26. Much in Maguire's work is revised in P. Rogers, *Theobald Mathew. Apostle of Temperance* (Browne and Nolan, Dublin, 1943) and Rev. Fr Augustine, *Footprints of Father Theobald Mathew, O.F.M. Cap., Apostle of Temperance* (M.H. Gill and Son, Dublin, 1947). For a recent scholarly perception, see E. Malcolm, 'Temperance and Irish Nationalism', in F.S.L. Lyons and R.A.J. Hawkins, *Ireland Under the Union. Varieties of Tension* (Clarendon Press, Oxford, 1980), esp. pp.74–83.

27. Quoted in *Constitution*, 20 January 1857.

28. Kearney, 'Fr. Mathew: Apostle of Modernization', pp.174–5.

29. On the history of green as 'the national colour', see G.A. Hayes-McCoy, *A History of Irish Flags from Earliest Times* (Academy Press, Dublin, 1979), esp. pp.44, 109, 121, 125–6; B. O Cuiv, 'The Wearing of the Green', *Studia Hibernica*, nos 17 and 18 (1977–78), pp.107–19.

30. O. MacDonagh, *Ireland: the Union and its Aftermath* (George Allen and Unwin, London, 1977), p.56.

31. Quoted in Alter, 'Symbols of Irish Nationalism', p.114.

32. *Daily Express*, Dublin, quoted in *Constitution*, 10 and 11 August 1864.

33. 9 August 1864.

34. E.R. Norman, *A History of Modern Ireland* (Allen Lane, London, 1971), pp.19–20; F.S.L. Lyons, *Culture and Anarchy in Ireland 1890–1939* (Clarendon Press, Oxford, 1982, first published 1979), p.137.

35. *Cork Examiner*, 14 October 1864.

36. 30 September 1864.

37. 19 March 1906.

38. Hayes-McCoy, *A History of Irish Flags*, p.46. See also J. Sheehy, *The Rediscovery of Ireland's Past. The Celtic Revival 1830–1930* (Thames and Hudson, London, 1980).

39. Potterton, *The O'Connell Monument*, p.11.

40. Quoted in *Constitution*, 19 March 1906.

9 Violence Transported: Aspects of Irish Peasant Society

Edith Mary Johnston

Ireland has a history of rural violence which is not only long but stereotyped. This is to be expected in a relatively undynamic society and, as cycles of activity recur, the historian becomes acutely conscious of a sense of *déjà vu*. The centuries may change, the players' faces may alter, but the cast, even the scenery, remain the same. As the play unfolds in all its traditional horror, the same grievances are rehearsed, the same punishments meted out and the same terror is let loose upon innocent and guilty alike. Familiar groups and individuals vie to impose their own varieties of social control. Officials representing state, Church and conventional factions compete with martyrs, real or pseudo, with traitors, bandits and a multitude of sacrificial victims of varying significance. Old speeches are made on old cues and the nightmare is reproduced once more.

Could this model have been imported in the baggage of the early Irish migrants to Australia? Certainly the early Governors of NSW, fearful that this might be the case, regarded the Irish convicts as an unwelcome, dangerous and alien complication. In 1801 Governor King wrote that:

> it is on this account that I respectfully submit the propriety of any more of those violent Republican characters being sent here for some time. . . . I am well aware, my Lord, that this colony was formed for the reception of such characters as could not with safety be kept in Ireland or England; yet, being now in an infant state, what may not be expected if their numbers are allowed to increase to so great a degree as to encourage them in making those attacks, which must ultimately subvert good government.[1]

Three years later the Castle Hill Rising gave substance to his warning, and later still the Eureka stockade confirmed the Irishman's conventional hostility to authority and violent reaction to social

137

pressures.[2] In both cases the use of 'Vinegar Hill', as a place name in the first rising and a password in the second, is a conscious recall of the final stand of the 1898 rebellion in Co. Wexford.

The fears of the authorities are perhaps most clearly enunciated by the Rev. Samuel Marsden who wrote in 1807 that:

> the number of Catholic convicts is very great in the settlement; and those in general composed of the lowest class of the Irish nation . . . they are very dangerous members of society. . . . They are extremely superstitious, artful and treacherous. . . . They have no true concern whatever for any religion . . . but are fond of riot drunkenness and cabals; and was the Catholic religion tolerated they would assemble together from every quarter not so much from a desire of celebrating mass, as to recite the miseries and injustice of their punishment, the hardship they suffer and to enflame one another's mind with some wild scheme of revenge.[3]

Thus from the moment of their arrival the Irish were considered an alien and potentially dangerous element for the future development of the new colony.

Professor Shaw found that less than 600 were specifically political prisoners, but he distinguished a further group of 4000 to 5000 as social rebels. Professor O'Farrell agreed that 'about four-fifths of Irish convicts can be properly described as ordinary criminals, mostly thieves' and this assessment was shared by John Polding, the first Catholic bishop and archbishop in Australia, who concluded that there was 'sufficient reason for supposing that the great majority were persons of wicked life'.[4] Yet, although the Irish convicts may not have differed greatly from their British counterparts in their criminality, in other respects the differences were substantial and significant. In particular their backgrounds were rural rather than urban, they included a greater proportion of women, thus exerting an influence on the development of family life disproportionate to the number of Irish migrants as a whole. Finally, in the words of the great nineteenth-century historian, W.E.H. Lecky, himself an Irish landlord, 'they were educated through long generations of oppression into an inveterate hostility to the law, and were taught to look for redress in illegal violence and secret combination.[5] By 1840, when transportation to NSW ended, the Irish component of the population was approximately one quarter[6] — earlier it had been probably nearer one-third. The difficulties presented by absorbing such a large group of alienated citizens into any society, let alone a frontier one, are daunting and the fears of successive authorities are easily comprehended.

The reasons for this alienation and its potential impact on the development of Australian society during its first century lie in the long and complex history of Ireland and particularly in the state of Ireland at the time when the migrants left it. The social structure of eighteenth-century Ireland was, like the legal system, similar to that of England.[7] In both countries political power was vested in the hands of the land-owning classes. In both countries the Anglican Church was the Church 'by law established', and membership of it was essential for those who wished to hold civil or military office. Nevertheless, in three of the four Irish provinces, Leinster, Munster and Connaught the majority of the people were Catholic and Gaelic, while the remaining province, Ulster, was strongly Presbyterian and Scottish. Thus the Irish social pyramid was flawed for the majority in all four provinces were alienated from the governing class by the penal laws[8] from which all who were not Anglicans suffered in varying degrees. However, once they had migrated, they reacted to their alienation differently. The Gaelic Irish remembered their grievances, which were undoubtedly greater, for much longer and they retained their separate identity probably, but not entirely, because of their Catholicism. The Scots-Irish, determinedly searching for a better future, tended to forget their wrongs as they merged and prospered with their Scottish co-religionists.

Irish justice, like English justice, was based on trial by jury: a system which can only operate successfully with the disinterested participation of the overwhelming majority of the nation. In 1777 Dr Hotham, Bishop of Clogher, commented that 'I believe there is no country in the world where real justice is so seldom done by the determination of a jury'.[9] A few years later the reforming landlord, R.L. Edgeworth, expressed his concern at the casual attitude of the Irish to taking oaths, 'that great bond of civil society, which rests on religion';[10] and it is noteworthy that the sampling techniques used by Dr Robson in *The Convict Settlers of Australia* highlighted perjury as a crime for which only the Irish were transported.[11] This reluctance to accept the sacred and binding obligation of an oath negated a fundamental part of the legal system. Indeed, the Rev. Samuel Marsden, obviously baffled and exasperated, commented: 'They are an unaccountable set of beings. It is difficult to prevail

upon any of them who are accused to say a single word.'[12] Nevertheless, this resistance was not entirely confined to the courtrooms of
a rejected judiciary, as is illustrated by the statement of Peter
Macanna to the tribunal inquiring into the nebulous Irish conspiracy
in 1800 when: 'he asked if Oaths were tendered and was answered
No — because no person was to be trusted but who had been tried
before and whom they knew to be true.'[13] Nearly 80 years later
Ned Kelly wrote that 'any man knows it is possible to swear a lie'.[14]

Thus in the late 1770s, the agronomist, Arthur Young, commented
that:

> The criminal law of Ireland is the same as that of England but
> the execution of it is so different as scarcely to be known and
> another circumstance, which has the effect of screening all sorts
> of offenders, is men of fortune protecting them, and making an
> interest for their acquittal, which is attended with a variety of
> evil consequences.[15]

Maintenance was not the only medieval legal custom which survived
in Ireland. William Carleton records that the popular Sir William
Richardson of Augher Castle, Co. Tyrone, devised a system of trial
by combat: sturdy disputants, who appealed to him in his magisterial
capacity, were armed with cudgels and dispatched to the backyard
of the castle to fight it out.[16] Maria Edgeworth summed up the
situation in the glossary to her novel *Castle Rackrent*, where she
remarked: '"I'll have the law on you, so I will" is the saying of an
Englishman who expects justice; "I'll have you before His Honour"
is the threat of an Irishman who hopes for partiality.'[17]

Faction fighting[18] based on regional and personal loyalties was
a strongly entrenched feature of Irish rural and urban life: the
students of Dublin University from generation to generation joined
in traditional gang warfare in support of the weavers of the Coombe
against their hereditary enemies the butchers' boys from the Ormond
market.[19] Professor Galen Broeker, in *Rural Disorder and Police
Reform in Ireland 1812–36*, describes the factions as social organisations 'whose motive beyond a desire to fight were seldom important
though quarrels over the occupancy of land seem to have provided
an added incentive'.[20] Carleton describes the violence of these
fights — and their hereditary nature — in *The Party Fight and
Funeral*.[21]

Undoubtedly old feuds of half-remembered origins contributed their quota to these long-established occasions which often had a set venue such as a gathering for a fair, race meeting or saint's day, even a funeral could provide an occasion — a Donnybrook takes its name from the activities that, in 1855, finally closed the famous fair, which had existed since the beginning of the thirteenth century.[22] Although fights between established gangs could and did break out spontaneously, the faction fight was usually a formal occasion preceded by a ritual challenge, known as the wheel, which involved set conventions such as trailing your coat and taunting formalised abuse, then the factions, often composed of hundreds of men, fought with blackthorn sticks inflicting serious and frequently fatal injuries. The ensuing funerals ensured the ongoing tradition. Faction fighting, although long established, became particularly prominent in the nineteenth century and Surgeon-Superintendent Cunningham may be referring to a mild version of this when he wrote in the 1820s that:

> The Irish divide themselves into three, namely the 'Cork boys', the 'Dublin boys' and the 'North boys'; and these are so zealous in upholding their respective tribes that when two individuals of different classes quarrel, there is no possibility of arriving at the truth, since a dozen of each class will rush forward, and bawl out at once, in favour of their respective comrades, evidence of the most conflicting, contradictory nature. The 'North boys' are commonly called *Scotchmen* by the others, and indeed many spoke the Scotch dialect so broadly as almost to puzzle *me* to unravel it.[23]

This actually was not surprising as Lallans,[24] the traditional dialect of the Ulster Scots, had diverged to some extent from the Scottish dialects then being spoken in Scotland. Many of the other Irish convicts would have spoken one of the many Gaelic dialects then in common use particularly in the south and west of Ireland. Undoubtedly this linguistic difference helped to heighten the suspicion which the Irish aroused among both their fellow convicts and the authorities in New South Wales: for example, Hester Stroud in her evidence before the Rev. Samuel Marsden on the 'conspiracy' of 1800 stated that 'from what she saw of the Irishmen being in small Parties in the Camp at Toongabby and by their walking about together and talking very earnestly in Irish Deponent verily believes they were intent upon something that was improper on Saturday afternoon.'[25]

There is evidence that the administration of justice in Ireland was degenerating even before the pressures of the 1790s brought about its virtual collapse. As in England the quality of local government depended upon the social conscience and moral calibre of the gentry who were its unpaid administrators. In 1798 the Edgeworths, whose estates were in Co. Longford, considered that:

> magistracy had at that time fallen below its proper level; many of the great proprietors of this country were absentees; and for want of resident gentlemen, magistrates were made of men without education, experience or hereditary respectability. . . . Upon slight suspicion, or vague information, they took up and imprisoned many who were innocent.[26]

Under these circumstances the administration of justice was often inequitable and inefficient; certainly it was unfit for the social pressures which increasingly bore down upon it.

By the late eighteenth century the population of Ireland was rising rapidly and at approximately the same rate as the population in England. Nevertheless, Ireland remained a rural country on which, through lack of raw materials, the industrial revolution made a very limited impact. In Munster these problems were particularly acute. Cork, the second city in Ireland and the capital of Munster, depended largely upon the provision trade. This encouraged a swing from arable to pastoral farming in its extensive hinterland — stretching as far north as Sligo — which, in conjunction with other agricultural developments, reduced the amount of rural labour employed, and gave increased momentum to the enclosure movement. These circumstances combined with the rising population to create, and emphasise, a labour glut and a land shortage.[27] Agrarian unrest broke out in 1760 and continued for the remainder of the eighteenth and all of the nineteenth centuries. In 1762 Dr Curry, one of the leading Catholics, was informed that:

> In relation to the disorders of the poor in Munster, . . . papists worry papists, the rich excluding the poorer sort to make room for flocks and herds, which are easily converted into ready money and find a ready market.[28]

Religion was not the principal cause of social unrest. In fact it became a dominant issue only under circumstances where it could be used to differentiate between those joined in a common struggle for limited economic resources.

The disaffected formed themselves into societies which terrorised the country, usually at night and often in disguise — occasionally female disguise. They adopted various names, such as Whiteboys, later Rightboys and later still Rockites in Munster, Threshers in Connaught, Hearts of Steel and Hearts of Oak in Ulster. The names and the areas terrorised changed from time to time but the methods remained the same. Their activities are illustrated by the following affidavit sworn before a JP in Queen's Co. in 1774 which describes a Whiteboy outrage:

> a party of them, blowing horns, and armed with muskets, and dressed in white shirts and frocks, entered his house . . . they carried him off mounted behind one of them, with only his breeches and a loose great coat on; that in their progress, they beat, battered, and abused him with their guns, and the man behind whom he rode wounded him severely in the legs, with long nails in his heels, commonly called heel spurs. They carried him ten miles off, to a place near Ballyconra, where they held a consultation whether they should cut out his tongue, or pull out his eyes; and at last agreed to cut off his ears, which they did with circumstances of great barbarity; and after having administered to him many unlawful oaths, they buried him up to his chin, though mangled, in a grave lined with furze.[29]

Mutilation of people and animals was a traditional part of Whiteboy punishment; other variants were houghing (kneecapping), and tarring and feathering.

To continue his operations the terrorist requires money. However, it is important that he acquires that money in such a way that it will both enlarge his image and appear acceptable to his own society, for he depends upon its respect for his survival. To this end he engineers an illegal redistribution of wealth and, acting as a middleman, he ostensibly redresses what is felt to be a social injustice, by apparently robbing the rich to give to the poor. In the late 1770s Arthur Young commented that:

[they] carried off the daughters of rich farmers, ravished them into marriages, of which four instances happened in a fortnight. They levied sums of money on the middling and lower farmers, in order to support their cause, by paying attornies, &c., in defending prosecutions against them; and many of them subsisted for some years without work, supported by these contributions. Sometimes they committed several considerable robberies, breaking into houses, and taking the money under pretence of redressing grievances.[30]

The Catholic hierarchy emphatically condemned rural violence in all its forms; for instance, Bishop Troy of Ossory condemned the Rightboy oath — and ordered his condemnation to be read in all chapels in Kilkenny City — as 'contrary to the commandment of almighty God, the canons of our holy church, and [the] laws of the land';[31] and this was very mild compared to the condemnation of Bishop O'Keeffe of Kildare and Leighlin a decade earlier. In times of rural violence, the parish priest, who had almost invariably grown up in the neighbourhood and knew its problems and people intimately tended to be caught in the cross-fire. Furthermore the terrorist often had little regard for either Church or state.

Allied to the purely agrarian grievances and often inseparable from them were the problems created by the tithe system. As the Established Church, the Anglican clergy were legally entitled to the tithes and dues of the entire population regardless of their religious affiliations. Consequently, four-fifths of the nation were burdened with double religious dues. Economic stress ensured that indignation was not confined to the tithes demanded by the Established Church, but even extended to the dues required by the Catholic priests. At the 1786 assizes held at Castlebar the county town of overwhelmingly Catholic Mayo, the court was told that 'the prisoner had informed the priest that he should lower his fees, and sinking his voice had said, "if not to have his coffin convenient"'.[32]

The Irish Parliament had from time to time passed Acts aimed at controlling agrarian unrest. By the mid-1780s all legislation was clearly ineffective and shortly after these outrages Attorney-General Fitzgibbon moved for further provisions to prevent tumultuous risings and assemblies, to more effectively punish persons guilty of outrage, riot, illegal combinations, administering and taking unlawful oaths. Only one dissenting voice in the Irish Parliament was raised against his motion. Many of the early Irish convicts were to be convicted under this stringent legislation known as the Whiteboy Act and its even more stringent successor the Insurrection Act of 1796.

Thus the early Irish migrants came to Australia from a background of almost unparalleled social confusion and the overwhelming majority made a better life in their new home than they could ever have enjoyed in the land to which the majority looked back so nostalgically, although probably there were from the beginning of the Australian colonies a number sharing the views of James McNally, who stated in 1800 that he did not wish to go home 'till peaceable times'.[33] Some, however, brought with them or handed on to their children an inheritance of smouldering grievance. For the first 100 years the authorities were always watching for the rebel and the larrikin, who was usually lurking on the frontiers of the new society. Their fears were perhaps justified by the fact that many of the most celebrated bushrangers had either been born in Ireland or were the children of Irish parents.[34] For example, John Donahue, transported from Dublin in 1825 arrived in NSW, committed another robbery, escaped, and in company with a gang of similar characters, preyed upon the early settlers in the Bathurst area for two years before he was shot by the police. His sins forgiven, he became the subject of folk mythology and of a ballad which is interesting *inter alia* for its Irish cross-references:

> This bold undaunted highwayman as you may understand
> Was banished for his natural life from Erin's happy land
> Dublin, city of renown, where his first breath he drew,
> 'Twas there they christened him the brave and bold Jack Donahue,

And the final verse:

> There were Freincy, Grant, bold Robin Hood, and Brennan and O'Hare;
> With Donahue the highwayman none of them could compare.
> But now He's gone to Heaven, I hope, with saints and angels too—
> May the Lord have mercy on the soul of brave Jack Donahue.[35]

Maria Edgeworth's father, R.L. Edgeworth, was one of the Commissioners who examined the state of Irish education in 1811. He lamented the literature then in vogue in the hedge schools (the usual source of education for the poor) commenting: 'Does any rational being imagine that there is an innate or unconquerable propensity in the human mind for reading only *The Spanish Rogue*; or *The Adventures of Captain Freny?*'[36]

Captain Freny was a famous highwayman, with a reputation for gallantry. He was eventually caught, but Lord Carrick supported him and he was pardoned and given a small customs post at New Ross where he ended his days.[37] His *Memoirs* were extremely popular. His career has certain parallels with that of the flamboyant Victorian highwayman Harry Power, who was born in Waterford in 1820 and, as he managed to avoid violence in his assorted robberies, he ended his life doing odd jobs for some of his former victims. Power, like Freny, had a reputation for gallantry and politeness. However, at the height of his criminal activities, in 1870, there was a reward out for his capture. There is strong suspicion that among Power's assistants at the close of his criminal career was the juvenile Ned Kelly. Two of Ned's uncles by marriage, Jack and Tom Lloyd, were in Pentridge Jail for cattle-stealing and tempted by the reward and a promise of immediate release, if they would cooperate with the police, Jack Lloyd agreed.[38]

The Ned Kelly ballads are reminiscent of the famous Cork highwayman also mentioned in the Donahue verse whose saga is reported in the ballad, *Brennan on the Moor*:

It's of a famous highwayman a story I will tell,
His name was Willy Brennan and in Ireland he did dwell;
And on the Kilworth mountains he commenced his wild career,
And many a wealthy gentleman before him shook in fear.

Brennan on the Moor, Brennan on the Moor
A brave undaunted robber was bold Brennan on the Moor

Then Brennan being an outlaw upon the mountains high,
With soldiers, horse and foot to take him they did try;
He laughed at them with scorn, until at length, 'tis said,
By a false-hearted young man he was basely betrayed.[39]

The Kellys were a very Irish family and with their relatives the Quinns and the Lloyds they developed something of a clan infrastructure. In 1841 the Quinns had arrived in Victoria under the

Bounty System. They were a northern Catholic family and they arrived in Australia without a criminal record.[40] They came from the vicinity of Antrim town, which had seen one of the major outbreaks of the 1798 rebellion. Co. Antrim was strongly Presbyterian with enclaves of Catholics — mainly in the Glens where the land was poorer and the terrain rougher. On their first arrival the family prospered, and there is every evidence that James Quinn was anxious to succeed in his new environment. By thrift and hard work he acquired 700 acres of land at Wallan Wallan.

However, circumstances were against him. First in 1850 his daughter eloped with John 'Red' Kelly, an ex-convict from the notoriously troubled Co. Tipperary. 'Red' Kelly, who served his full sentence in Tasmania, was apparently convicted for stealing two pigs. It is not impossible, given the nature of unrest in Tipperary, that his real crime was of a more serious nature; for instance, in *Australian Son* Max Brown states that some accounts suggest that he was involved in a faction fight at a fair. This may account for the father's reluctance over the marriage.[41] On the other hand it may have been simply a *pro forma* objection to an Irish 'runaway' marriage of the type described by the folk writer Carleton in his *Autobiography*.[42] This was quite conventional and respectable in early nineteenth-century Ireland. Nevertheless, it is difficult to see how 'Red' Kelly could have avoided introducing his associates from Tasmania into the family circle particularly as shortly after the marriage the gold rushes began, and the Kellys were among those attracted to the gold fields.

Gold brought a sudden influx of people into Victoria, thereby disrupting the fragile structure of society and sharply raised the ratio of single men to women in the population.[43] As gold fever subsided, people sought alternative employment and many returned to the land where the surplus of unemployed single young men created a potential climate for criminal activity. The eldest of the Quinn brothers was soon before the law courts on a charge of cattle rustling and thereafter the clan were never out of trouble.[44] In 1873 seven men of the Kelly-Quinn clan were in prison at once, partly for cattle rustling, which was a common occurrence in an area of recent settlement where there was tension between the squatter and selector, but also because of inter-clan feuding — Jim Kelly, Ned's uncle had been jailed for setting fire to his sister-in-law's house! (He had in fact been sentenced to death but reprieved.) Then in 1876, following a series of brushes with the law, which kindled an already smouldering sense of injustice, Ned Kelly, his brother Dan and two associates effectively declared war on organised society in north-eastern Victoria. Their banditry came to a climax in 1878 when they murdered three policemen. Shortly afterwards they robbed the bank at Euroa.

The question now arises, to what extent were they simply primitive bandits operating in the classic conditions described by historians like Eric Hobsbawm and George Rudé and to what extent were they specifically Irish? In addition there are those who would like to read into the activities of the Kelly gang what Hobsbawm describes as:

> that totally uncompromising and lunatic dream . . . a world in which the moralists are also gunfighters, both because guns kill enemies and because they are the means of expression of men who cannot write the pamphlets or make the great speeches of which they dream. Propaganda by action replaces that by word.[45]

However, Ned Kelly did leave two documents specifically intended as propaganda, the *Cameron* and the *Jerilderie Letters*, and both contain a confused statement of backward rather than forward-looking thought, along with a declaration of war against specific and traditional enemies and an intention of terrorism if his demands were not met.

The historian of nineteenth-century Victoria, Geoffrey Serle, describes the Kelly gang as 'second-generation delinquents, ill-educated dead-enders in a rural slum, who having declared war on society were inevitably destroyed. . . . They were made by direct convict tradition, by traditional Irish attitudes to an alien ruling class, and by the protest of the landless against the landowner.'[46] Undoubtedly they felt that their Irish background could and did give them a social justification for their crimes. Although difficult to disentangle from the confused invective and threatened violence — possibly reminiscent of the prelude to an Irish faction fight — the Irish theme runs through the *Jerilderie Letter*. Along with it there is a hatred of Irishmen who joined the police, as many Irishmen did in the nineteenth century, where they became prominent not only in the Royal Irish Constabulary but in Britain, the United States of America and Australia.

Thus Irish society began to divide into those who supported law and order and those who continued to be alienated from it. Naturally the former were an anathema to the latter, Kelly emphasised this intense dislike writing that:

> a Policeman is a disgrace to his country . . . in the first place he is a rogue in his heart but too cowardly to follow it up without having the force to disguise it. Next he is a traitor to his country ancestors and religion.[47]

Significantly, the police most intimately involved in the Kelly affair were all Irish. Superintendent John Sadlier was in charge of the NE Police District with its headquarters at Benalla. He had emigrated from Ireland at the age of 19 and trained as a police cadet in Victoria. The men who went after the Kelly gang were:

1. Sergeant Michael Kennedy a married man with five children an excellent reputation as a fearless, firm and respected officer. A native of Co. Westmeath he had arrived in Victoria in 1859 aged 17. Kelly wounded and then killed him. Kennedy was found with his ear amputated — a traditional Whiteboy punishment.
2. Constable Thomas Lonigan who had emigrated from Sligo. He had already incurred Kelly's enmity from a previous occasion and he was the first to be shot.
3. Constable Michael Scanlon aged 36 a migrant from Killarney, Co. Kerry, also shot.
4. Constable Thomas Newman McIntyre, a northern Protestant, an Orangeman from Belfast. He escaped. Probably he was just lucky, but possibly Kelly did not regard Protestant police in the same light as Catholic police.

Not all Irish policemen enjoyed Kennedy's reputation. The activities of Constable Fitzpatrick, subsequently dismissed from the force with his papers endorsed 'a liar and a larrakin'[48] undoubtedly contributed much to Ned Kelly's alienation. Finally, there is the ambiguous position of Aaron Sherritt whose murder by Joe Byrne was the prelude to the destruction of the gang and who may have betrayed them to the police. Sherritt too was Irish, but his father, John Sherritt, was an Orangeman and had been a member of the Royal Irish Constabulary.[49]

Many of the cases involving the Kelly-Quinn clan came before Irish magistrates and Irish judges. These men[50] came mainly from the ranks of the old Irish Ascendancy and shared their background and education in Trinity College, Dublin. The Prosecutor for the Queen at Beechworth was Arthur Wolfe Chomley, his grandfather Richard Griffith sat in the old Irish Parliament and Chomley's names; Arthur Wolfe, recalled the Irish Lord Chief Justice Kilwarden. Kilwarden, who was murdered in Emmett's rebellion, declared with his dying breath: 'Murder must be punished; but let no man suffer for my death but by the laws of my country.'[51] Henry Massey Bindon, who defended Kelly, came from a similar background. Obviously uneasy with his brief and his own slender experience at the Bar to which he had been called only ten months previously, Bindon had wanted as senior counsel Hickman Molesworth, son of Sir Robert Molesworth, a Judge of the Supreme Court of Victoria, who had begun his legal career on the Munster Circuit.

Sir Redmond Barry, senior puisne judge of the Supreme Court of Victoria, also came from Co. Cork. He was the judge before whom Ned Kelly finally appeared. He also belonged to the Protestant Ascendancy and was a graduate of Dublin University. Redmond Barry was a friend and exact contemporary of Isaac Butt the founder of the Irish Home Rule movement. However, he was not a migrant who looked nostalgically over his shoulder, and from the moment of his arrival he threw all his energies into the development of the government and society of Victoria. Although neither the guilt of the defendant and, despite the anti-capital punishment lobby, the inevitability of the verdict are in dispute, it has been suggested that from Barry's previous experiences at trials of the Quinn-Kelly clan he was a hostile judge and that in the circumstances the trial should have come before another judge.[52]

At this time there were five judges of the Supreme Court of Victoria and four out of the five were Irish and had been educated at Dublin University. The Chief Justice Sir William Foster Stawell from Mallow, Co. Cork was a great-nephew of John Foster the last Speaker of the Irish Parliament and a close friend of Redmond Barry. Sir Robert Molesworth mainly presided over Equity, Insolvency and Ecclesiastical Jurisdictions. The fourth Irish judge was the Dublin-born George Higinbotham. He was also an Anglican but not of the old Ascendancy. Higinbotham's father was a merchant and he had been educated at the Royal School, Dungannon before entering Dublin University. Some of his views carry overtones of the democratic asceticism more common in the North — his mother's family were strongly Presbyterian.[53] The fifth judge was a

Cambridge-educated Englishman, James Wilberforce Stephen, who from 1877 until his death in 1881 was seriously ill.[54]

Both Stawell and Barry had grown up in a deeply divided and partly alienated society and they came from an area of traditional rural violence. Both were determined that the colony to which they were wholeheartedly devoted should not develop a similar tradition.[55] Undoubtedly they would have viewed with concern statements like that following the mass arrests at Beechworth under the Felons' Apprehension Act, when a newspaper reported that at Beechworth 'a very unhealthy sympathy with the Kellys prevails throughout the district'.[56] The veracity of this statement is proved by the fact that it took the police two years to catch the gang after they had murdered three policemen and that despite the improved communications of the telegraph and the railway, whose danger Kelly appears to have realised. The bandit's and the terrorist's survival depends upon the support of his own community for he expresses their power to protest effectively against a society by which they feel slighted and from which they feel alienated. They may fear his actions but they respect his power and admire his defiance. He retains this sometimes grudging allegiance by social declarations such as Kelly's statement in the *Jerilderie Letter*:

> I give fair warning to all those who has reason to fear me to sell out and give £10 out of every hundred towards the widow and orphan fund and do not attempt to reside in Victoria but as short a time as possible after reading this notice . . . I am a widow's son outlawed and my orders *must be obeyed*.[57]

Finally the famous challenge from the dock which Kelly gave to the trial judge 'I will see you where I am going', has overtones of the words of Emmet at the conclusion of his trial before Lord Norbury in 1803: 'we must appear on the great day at one common tribunal'.[58] The story of Emmet was, and still is, very well known to Irish lawyers in Australia and it is indisputably part of the Irish rebel inheritance. Despite their origins, the Australian colonies, have been since their foundation remarkably peaceful[59] and perhaps this has been in no small measure due to a genuine fear that the least desirable aspects of Irish society might have been transported. In passing sentence in *Regina v. Kelly* Mr Justice Barry emphasised that:

Violence Transported

In new communities where the bonds of society are not so well linked together as in older countries, there is unfortunately a class which disregards the evil consequences of crime. Foolish, inconsiderate, ill-conducted, unprincipled youths unfortunately abound, and, unless they are made to consider the consequences of crime, they are led to imitate notorious felons whom they regard as self-made heros.[60]

Nineteenth-century Victoria was, in many ways, a very Irish state — Melbourne's wide streets and public buildings are reminiscent of the Irish capital. However, unlike Ireland, the society was a dynamic one and the men who planned it were determined that it would not be 'the same under another sky'.[61]

Notes and References

1. *Historical Records of Australia*, series I, vol. 3, p.9.

2. Quoted in P. O'Farrell, 'The Irish in Australia: Some Aspects of the Period 1791–1850', *Descent*, vol.7, part 2 (1975), p.49.

3. See T. McClaughlin, *From Shamrock To Wattle* (Collins, Sydney, 1985) p.6.

4. A.G.L. Shaw, 'Transportation from Ireland', *Historical Studies*, vol.7, no.25 (1955), p.83; A.G.L. Shaw, *Convicts and the Colonies: a Study of Penal Transportation from Great Britain and Ireland to Australia and Other Parts of the British Empire* (Faber, London, 1966), pp.182–3; P. O'Farrell, 'The Irish in Australia', p.43; L. Evans and P. Nicholls (eds), *Convicts and Colonial Society 1788–1853* (Cassell, Stanmore, NSW, 1976), p.134.

5. W.E.H. Lecky, *A History of Ireland in the Eighteenth Century* (5 vols, Longmans, London, 1892) vol.1, p.148.

6. Shaw, *Convicts and the Colonies*, p.166. A number of Irish convicts were also transported for crimes committed in England.

7. See E.M. Johnston, *Great Britain and Ireland 1760–1800* (Oliver and Boyd, Edinburgh and London, 1963), pp.17–52.

8. See M. Wall, *The Penal Laws, 1691–1760* (Irish History Series no.1, W. Tempest, Dundalk, 1961) for a full discussion of this complex topic.

9. Historical Manuscripts Commission, Stopford Sackville, I, p.248.

10. *Memoirs of R.L. Edgeworth* (London, 1820) p.275.

11. L.L. Robson, *The Convict Settlers of Australia* (Melbourne UP, Carlton, 1965), p.58.

12. *Historical Records of Australia*, series I, vol.2, p.637.

13. Ibid., p.579.

14. *Jerilderie Letter*, printed in M. Brown, *Australian Son. The Story of Ned Kelly* (Phoenix House, London, 1949), p.279.

15. *Arthur Young's Tour in Ireland 1776–9*, A.W. Hutton (ed.) (2 vols, 1892), vol.2, p.254.

16. W. Carleton, *Autobiography of William Carleton*, rev. edn (MacGibbon and Kee, London, 1968), p.42.

17. M. Edgeworth, *Castle Rackrent* (Oxford UP, London, 1969), author's glossary for the English reader, p.109.

18. See L.M. Cullen, *The Emergence of Modern Ireland* (New York, Holmes and Meier, 1981), p.247; P. O'Donnell, *The Irish Faction Fighters of the Nineteenth Century* (Anvil Books, Dublin, 1975).

19. C. Maxwell, *A History of Trinity College, Dublin, 1591–1892* (University Press, Dublin, 1946), p.134.

20. G. Broeker, *Rural Disorder and Police Reform in Ireland, 1812–36* (Routledge and Kegan Paul, London, 1970), p.15. For the failure of the magistracy, see ibid., p.41.

21. William Carleton, *The Party Fight and Funeral* (Mercier Press, Cork, 1973), p.18.

22. C. Maxwell, *Dublin under the Georges: 1714–1830* (G.G. Harrap, London, 1936), see p.177 for an illustration of a fight at Donnybrook Fair showing the combatants wielding the traditional blackthorn sticks.

23. Evans and Nicholls (eds), *Convicts and Colonial Society*, p.137.

24. D.H. Akenson and W. Crawford, *Local Poets and Social History: James Orr, Bard of Ballycarry* (PRO, Northern Ireland, Belfast, 1977), p.25.

25. *Historical Records of Australia*, series I, vol.2, p.641.

26. Edgeworth, *Memoirs*, p.360.

27. Cullen, *The Emergence of Modern Ireland*. For the general background see pp.83–108.

28. G.C. Lewis, *On Local Disturbances in Ireland; and on the Irish Church Question* (B. Fellowes, London, 1836), p.7.

29. Ibid., pp.11–12.

30. Ibid., p.12.

31. J. Donnelly Jr, 'The Rightboy Movement 1785–8', *Studia Hibernica*, nos.17 and 18 (1977–78), p.168; for Bishop O'Keeffe's denunciation, see p.169.

32. Lewis, *On Local Disturbances in Ireland*, p.42.

33. *Historical Records of Australia*, series I, vol.2, p.577.

34. For instance: Martin Cash (b.1809), transported from Wexford 1827, died 1877; Ben Hall (b.1837 in Australia, d. 1865) — mother from Dublin; Francis (Chistie) Gardiner (1830–?1903) had an Irish-Aboriginal mother; Thomas (1840–67) and John Clarke (1846–67) had an Irish mother. All of the Kelly gang were Irish-Australian. See also McClaughlin, *From Shamrock to Wattle*, pp.4–6.

35. J.S. Manifold, *Who Wrote the Ballads? Notes on Australian Folksong* (Australasian Book Society, Sydney, 1964), pp.36–40.

36. *Report from the Commissioners of the Board of Education in Ireland*, British Sessional Papers, 1813–14 (47) v, p.337.

37. J.J. Marshall, *Irish Tories, Rapparees and Robbers* (Tyrone Printing Co., Dungannon, 1927), pp.63–5.

38. F. Clune, *The Kelly Hunters* (Angus and Robertson, Sydney, 1954), pp.71–6.

39. Marshall, *Irish Tories, Rapparees and Robbers*, pp.65–6. See also p.46.

40. Brown, *Australian Son*, p.17.

41. Clune, *The Kelly Hunters*, p.17; C. Osborne, *Ned Kelly* (Blond, London, 1970), p.12.

42. Carleton, *Autobiography*, p.93.

43. G. Serle, *The Rush to be Rich. A History of the Colony of Victoria, 1883–1889* (Melbourne UP, Carlton, 1971), pp.1–2.

44. Osborne, *Ned Kelly*, pp.189–90, gives a consolidated list of 'arrests and convictions of the Quinns, Kellys, and Lloyds'.

45. E. Hobsbawm, *Bandits* (Penguin, Harmondsworth, 1972), p.113.

46. Serle, *The Rush to be Rich*, p.11.

47. *Jerilderie Letter*, in Brown, *Australian Son*, pp.279–80.

48. Royal Commission, Second Progress Report, Victoria, *Parliamentary Papers of Legislative Assembly*, 1881, III, p.x, quoted in L. Waller, 'Regina v. Edward Kelly', in C. Cave (ed.), *Ned Kelly: Man and Myth* (Cassell Australia, Melbourne, 1968, reprint 1980) p.143.

49. I. Jones, 'The Kellys and Beechworth', in C. Cave (ed.), *Ned Kelly*, p.64.

50. See *Australian Dictionary of Biography* and *Dictionary of National Biography*.

51. See *DNB*, vol.21, p.766. Chomley's brother, Hussey Malone Chomley, was named in the same tradition for two great Irish parliamentary families. Interestingly, Wolfe Tone also took his name from the Kilwarden family surname.

52. See Waller, 'Regina v. Edward Kelly', p.144.

53. E.E. Morris, *A Memoir of George Higinbotham, an Australian Politician* (Macmillan, London, 1895), p.5.

54. See *ADB*, vol.6, pp.188–9.

55. Quoted in Clune, *The Kelly Hunters*, p.208.

56. This concern is reflected in the detailed enquiry of the 1881 Victorian Royal Commission into the circumstances of the Kelly outbreak. Victoria, *Parliamentary Papers of the Legislative Assembly*, 1881, III, Report pp.i–xxxviii with 720 pages of evidence appended.

57. *Jerilderie Letter*, in Brown, *Australian Son*, p.282.

58. Quoted in R. Madden, *The United Irishmen, their Lives and Times*, 2nd edn (7 vols, Dublin, 1858), series III, vol.3, p.453.

59. See P. Robinson, *The Hatch and Brood of Time. A Study of the First Generation of Native-Born White Australians, 1788–1828* (Oxford UP Australia, Melbourne, 1985), vol.1, p.43.

60. Quoted in Clune, *The Kelly Hunters*, p.329.

61. I should like to thank Dr F.G. Clarke who read and commented on various drafts of this article, and I am indebted to Mr Colin Wisdom of *The History of The Irish Parliament* with whom I discussed this paper in its early stages.

10 The Irish in Australia: A General View*

Oliver MacDonagh

I

Ideally, this paper should deal with two countries, not one. If the effect of Irish emigration on Australia is still relatively neglected, its effects on Ireland are doubly so. In the case of nineteenth-century Ireland this is peculiarly striking. The general historian may be impressed by lurid phenomena such as the 'coffin ships' and stampedes of economic refugees when crops failed disastrously. But these were only the melodramatic outcrops of a vast steady movement of population: for the most part, it passed off silently. He may list some general emigration statistics; and it is true that, as James Stephen observed in 1858 of the Irish famine emigration returns,

> Here . . . you have a measure by which to judge the sufferings of the people of Ireland during the eight years of which 1847 was the first. The number of Irish emigrants in those years is estimated by the emigration commissioners to have exceeded 1,700,000 — an estimate which they consider as far below the truth. Those figures, well weighed and mediated, will reveal a tragedy which no mere words could disclose.

But the figures are not well weighed or mediated. Until very recently, even Irish demographic discussions were largely conducted in other terms — in terms, almost exclusively, of birth, marriage, fertility and death rates.

Yet, with the 15–34 age groups predominating in Irish emigration, the subtraction of so many young lives transformed all aspects of economic life, from productivity to income distribution, and from birth and marriage rates to the GDP. The force of this impact

---

* This chapter was delivered as a public lecture on 28 August 1985, and formed part of the conference proceedings.

depended of course upon its scale. Relatively, this was immense. More than 7 million people emigrated permanently from Ireland between 1801 and 1900, that is to say, many more people left than still remained there in 1900, and very many more than had lived there in 1801.

On such a scale, emigration was of first importance nationally; and its domestic consequences ramified almost into infinity. The economic and demographic effects were but part of the story. It is also quite critical in explaining nineteenth-century Irish political and social developments. Without the comparatively easy access to alternative employment in the New Worlds, which cheap and abundant ocean transport and the hunger for manpower in the regions of white settlement had created — without such an access, the internal conflicts in Irish society would have been more acute, and Irish politics very different in both kind and objective.

Let me take as a single example the predominance of agricultural labourers and cottiers in Irish emigration after 1850. Before the Great Famine, these landless and near-landless elements in Irish society constituted two-thirds of the entire population, and outnumbered the tenant and independent farmers by four to one. By 1900, the cottiers were virtually extinct as a class, and farmers actually outnumbered labourers. There were, as one might expect, many indications of incipient conflict between farmers and labourers, between the landed and the landless men, in rural Ireland in the second half of the nineteenth century. There were, naturally, many attempts to exploit this collision of interests by opponents of constitutional nationalism, whether American Fenians or British Tories. Yet the incipient conflict never developed into a large-scale or protracted struggle, and the substantial unity of the various national or agrarian movements was never really broken.

The explanation is, of course, the constant and heavy emigration of the poorest rural dwellers and of the younger children without holdings to inherit or acquire. The relative as well as the absolute numbers of the landless were being constantly diminished, while the hardship of the surviving labourers was gradually alleviated by the increase in the demand for their services. Correspondingly, the campaign for peasant proprietorship in the last two decades of the nineteenth century would not have been practicable at all — let alone generally successful — had not the ranks of the small farmers and their potential replacements been thinned repeatedly over the preceding 40 years. This is but one particular instance of the telling domestic effect of emigration. But it may suffice to bring home the obvious but neglected fact that the history of emigration is a vital part of the history of the donor as well as of the host society.

Moreover, the specific instance of Australia should have a special interest for modern Irish historians. During the period of the Act of Union, the *proportion* of Irish amongst the total population of the United Kingdom fell to approximately one-third of its original size. There may have been a corresponding, though doubtless less drastic, fall in the per capita income of the Irish element in the United Kingdom *vis-à-vis* the rest. But in Australia the case was different. In 1801 the ethnic and religious proportions in the population closely matched those in the new United Kingdom; but, in Australia, these proportions were preserved, like the fly in amber, down to 1914 and perhaps even a little longer. Correspondingly, political and civil parity were substantially established in the Australian colonies by the mid-nineteenth century, so that the comparative numerical and social strength of the Catholic and Irish elements could make themselves felt during the formative stages of the new societies. Historians cannot make controlled experiments, and they are constantly buffeted by idiosyncrasies in the phenomena with which they deal. But, even so, the student of Ireland under the Act of Union (1801–1922) may gain new insights, may find new questions gathering in his mind, as he observes the interaction of the Irish and the British cultures in conditions where the relative proportions of race and religion at the time of the Act of Union remained constant, and where moreover the slow political revolution of the nineteenth century was anticipated by 50 years or more.

This paper moves far from Irish history. The matrix from which the Irish emigrants to Australia derived will be glanced at now and then, but that is all. But the reader should be ever conscious that — as always in national emigrations — it is the fate of two societies, and not merely one, which is — or rather should be — the full concern.

II

To me has fallen the unenviable — not to say undo-able — task of providing an overview of Irish emigration to Australia. I am by no means certain where to stand, or look, to gain that stout Cortez-like vision of an almost infinite terrain. But there is one obvious device: to try to place the Irish emigration to Australia, during the century or three-quarters of a century or so of greatest Irish outflow, in the context of Irish emigration in general. This is practically to exclude the pre-1815 period and with it the great era of the Scots-Irish exodus, and conversely to concentrate on the years when Irish Catholics predominated numerically, so much so that most of what follows refers essentially to them.

Placing the main Irish emigration in the relevant years in the context of contemporary Irish emigration as a whole has, as it happens, some particular advantages. Australian emigration deviated in several significant ways from what we might term the Irish norm; and, further, these deviations, taken cumulatively and interactively, help us, I think, to specify many leading characteristics of the Irish performance and pervasion in the southern colonies. I do not mean of course that the Irish emigration to Australia was of a different genus to the rest. Substantially the same stock of people left Ireland for substantially the same reasons in every case. None the less certain of the Australian differences, as we shall see, were quite marked and deeply influential; and it is upon these that I shall concentrate, leaving it to another voice and another occasion to provide that other sort of general view which would picture the entire convulsive outpouring of a race as a single master phenomenon.

I should add some other brief preliminaries. For a variety of reasons, the statistics of Irish emigration, particularly to North America and Great Britain, can only be approximations. Correspondingly, the various immigration histories are still in, or barely emerging from, the pioneering age. Moreover, the isolation or identification of the Irish — other than the actual Irish-born — within the receiving societies is of course a difficult and even uncertain affair, although fortunately less difficult or uncertain in Australia than in almost any other area of Irish settlement — because of the character of Australian censuses and the opportunities which they furnish of correlating nationality and religion. Finally, the enforced generalisation of the overview forbids minute qualification and attempted precision. Instead it practically enjoins what we might call 'best hypothesisation' and the coarse, broad stroke in brush-work. All this will, I hope, explain — and if need be excuse — the sweeping, aggregative boldness and roughness of what follows. As Belloc pleaded in the Preface to *The Path to Rome*, 'Nor let us be too hard upon that just but very anxious fellow that sat down to paint the soul of Switzerland upon a fan'.

III

Let me begin the analysis by returning to the proposition that Irish emigration to Australia, in its main phase of outflow — that is, down to the First World War — differed markedly, in fate and character, from much of the rest of the great diaspora. The most obvious difference was in its relative importance to the host society. Irish emigration and re-emigration to the United States accounted for some 60 per cent of the total Irish exodus in the nineteenth century, but for only 10 per cent or so of the total of newcomers to America. Australia stood at the opposite end of the scale. Although, from an Irish standpoint, the Australian emigration was comparatively trivial — 5 per cent of the total overseas emigration at the very most — from an Australian standpoint it was decidedly large — little short of 25 per cent of the immigrants from 1788 down to the early twentieth century. No one needs to be persuaded that the Irish element in American culture is considerable. But even these crude figures show it to be comparatively feeble, in terms of its Australian counterpart. In fact, in no other region of settlement did the proportion of Irish among the immigrants equal — or nearly equal — Australia's during this century and a quarter.

Nor was this, by any means, the only peculiarity of the Australian emigration. For one thing, its volume was determined primarily by conditions in the new rather than the old land. This was strikingly unlike the cases of North America and Great Britain, which between them accounted for approximately four-fifths of the Irish exodus. There the Irish push factors far exceeded in importance the American or the British pulls. It was generally otherwise with Australia. The flows and ebbs of Irish emigration to the south bore comparatively little relation to the home economy. They were determined essentially by Australia's labour needs and public resources. This is more, much more, than a point of casual curiosity. For example, the Great Famine, so crucial to nineteenth-century Irish emigration in general, was almost irrelevant to that fragment of it destined for Australia. A mere 75,000 of the 2 million whom we may broadly categorise as the 'Famine emigrants' of 1846–56 went south, and none of these was in the condition of acute want which characterised much —

indeed most — of, say, the huge Irish migration to Canada of 1846–48. Conversely, Irish emigration to Australia was heaviest in the immediate post-Famine decades — essentially because this was the golden age of the assisted passage. Thus, Irish-Australia showed remarkably little of the bitter folk-memory or hereditary myth of hunger, disease, dispossession and even genocide which marked much of Irish-America for the next three-quarters of a century — and in pockets even more. On the contrary, the predominant Irish-Australian values appear to have been set in, and by, the placid — not to say the exhausted — 1850s.

Of the many other significant differences between the main body of Irish emigration and its Australian portion, three seem to me to deserve particular attention. First, the North American emigration drew more or less equally, in the end, from all parts of Ireland. There were marked short-term variations. Counties, such as Sligo and Mayo, with comparatively heavy emigration in the first Famine years fell well below the average during the last. There were also some long-term changes. For example, the later so-called Congested Districts of the south-west were generally the last to undergo massive American emigration. But over time all this was evened out to a remarkable degree. The Australian pattern, however, was one in which particular Irish counties and regions predominated. The contiguous land-mass of Kilkenny, Tipperary, east Limerick, east Clare and north Cork claimed an altogether disproportionate share of the total Irish outflow to Australia. In fact, this region together with a smaller region in the mid-north-east, that is, approximately one-fifth of the total land area of Ireland and with less than a fifth of its population, provided over half the Irish assisted emigrants. Doubtless, even within this mass particular districts and even parishes were markedly over-represented. Clonulty in Co. Tipperary is an example of what we might term an 'Australian parish'; and in Tyrone, to take another instance, one small district in the south-east corner of the county was a major recruitment ground for Australia. All this has two important implications, first, that Irish regional variations (now being seriously explored by historians) were probably of much greater significance for Australian than for American emigration; and, secondly, that the phenomenon of chain-migration can be studied at much greater depth, and in much wider ramification, for Australian than for almost any other immigration. The important work of Mr Richard Reid has made this clear already.

Next, Irish emigration to Australia was mainly financed from public funds, whereas the proportion of Irish emigration to the United States which was not paid for by emigrants' families or connections or by the emigrants themselves was — even allowing for landlord and poor law clearances — quite minute. This does not mean that the Irish emigrants to Australia were of a lower social class or more impoverished than their American counterparts. Far from it. It seems to me likely — though the matter still needs exhaustive investigation — that, relatively speaking, Australia attracted a higher proportion of Irish middle-class emigrants than the United States, partly for reasons of timing, partly because of the identical professional structures and partly perhaps — in the case of Irish Protestants particularly — because of the continuing British connection. Let us remember too that the cost of self-paid passages to Australia was four or five times higher than that of the Atlantic crossing; and although most Irish emigrants to Australia were state-assisted, a very considerable minority was self-financed.

But the most important point of all is that state assistance, with its stress upon certified respectability and stable employment, tended generally to favour what we might call the petit bourgeoisie, or upper working class, rather than the proletariat of the Irish country-side. True, specific bodies of Irish assisted immigrants were desti-tute — orphan girls, convicts' dependants, Crown tenants — and Anglo-Saxon Australia regarded these as — to put it at its most charitable — a *pis aller*. But if we placed over the Irish emigrants, *en masse*, the complex grid of Irish social gradations, we would find, I estimate, that the great majority were drawn from, say, the third, fourth and fifth rather than the sixth and seventh rankings in the scale. Moreover, the very fact of state management increased the likelihood of their arriving with some little capital, however small, as well as some small measure of assistance to disperse and of guidance towards immediate employment. In all of these respects, their circumstances upon disembarkation contrasted sharply with those of many hundreds of thousands of their compatriots in, say, Boston and New York, particularly in the years 1842–60.

A third most telling difference between the Australian and the other emigrations was the ocean passage; and this was still the case when at last, 20 years after it had happened on the Atlantic run, steam came to predominate in the Australian trade. This was of course, in part, a matter of timespan and the sense of distance. Broadly speaking, the passage to Australia took four times as long as the passage to North America. Naturally, this deepened greatly the feelings that the separation was permanent and the disruption irreversible. But, more palpable and more important still, the passage to Australia was subject to a very high degree of state regulation and intervention. This meant a level of discipline, ordered adjustment and health upon arrival which, upon the average, greatly exceeded that of the so-called voluntary emigrants to the United States. The point may seem comparatively trivial; but this is not so, especially before the later 1850s. The initial weeks or even days after disembarkation were often decisive in the entire future of the immigrant; and what happened or did not happen then was commonly determined by the character of the weeks or months at sea.

The United States, no less than Australia, was a highly mobile society even in the nineteenth century. But a very large proportion of the American-Irish, certainly of the immediately arrived, did not share in this characteristic. Instead, in the Famine years, they tended to pile and coalesce, like snow driven upon whatever constituted the first barrier or bank. This is, I believe, in no small part attributable to the circumstances and conditions of their translation: to the invariable confusion and disorder of the preliminary journey to Liverpool, Glasgow or Cork; of the embarkation; of the crowded, noisome and often diseased or hungry crossing; of the Babel of debarkation in the modern Babylon; not least perhaps, of the great rapidity with which these extraordinary and bewildering succession of wretched experiences was undergone. Whatever the tedium, discomfort and even dangers of the steerage passage to Australia, at every point, from the preliminary assemblage at the emigrant depot onwards, it was superior to the Atlantic crossing. The essential reason was the comparatively large degree of governmental management and statutory regulation; and these continued, in some measure, even after disembarkation. Herein, I think, lies one explanation of the vital *initial* and indeed continuing relative mobility of the Irish in the southern colonies.

Thus in three vital matters, the regional sources of the emigration, the distribution of its costs and the character of its physical execution, the Irish movement to Australia was unusual. Already we have to hand, I think, a few keys to understanding its collective behaviour in, and response to, the new land.

IV

So far I have been principally concerned with the idiosyncrasies of
the Irish emigration to Australia. But the immigration within Australia itself also shows interesting deviations. If the single most striking
characteristic was its very large scale, its second was surely its
relatively even diffusion, geographically, socially and even occupa-
tionally. The Irish-Americans — in their Catholic manifestation at
least — were disproportionately numerous in certain conurbations,
in particular districts within specific major cities and in the lowest
paid and most manual occupations in these places. Correspondingly,
a few of the NE coalfields excepted, the 'British Irish' so to say were
concentrated in Clydeside, Lancs., South Wales and London. By
the 1850s whole quarters of Liverpool, Manchester, Glasgow and
Cardiff, of Boston, Providence, New York and Philadelphia, had
become almost exclusively Irish. Even entire towns, such as Bridge-
port, Connecticut, had become predominantly Irish by 1855. So too
had certain workforces in certain regions, such as the construction
industry in New York City, or (at an early stage) navvying in some
parts of Britain.

The Australian pattern was very different. There the nineteenth-
century Irish were comparatively numerous throughout. There were
so to say no Milwaukees, Utahs or South Carolinas, no Norfolks,
Salisburys or Aberdeenshires in the southern colonies. There were
of course considerable variations in the relative density of Irish
settlement in Australia from place to place. Two colonies were
always below the average for the continent. In South Australia,
much the most Anglophilic of the colonies, the Irish constituted
only some 17–18 per cent of the total population. The Tasmanian
proportion was even lower — approximately 15 per cent. Tasmania
was for long primarily a convict settlement and, possibly because
of the hazy geography of the Chief Secretary's Office in Dublin, no
Irish convicts were sent there before 1836. There were also significant
regional differences within particular colonies. In New South Wales
the Irish settled much more heavily south than north of Sydney. In
Queensland they were disproportionately numerous in the rural as
against the metropolitan districts. On a smaller scale the differences
might be more dramatic. The Irish were very populous in the Clare
region of South Australia but scarcely to be found at all in nearby
Seppeltsfield; very numerous about Crookwell in New South Wales,
but not much in evidence about Moss Vale, merely 50 miles away.

But we must try to see all this in perspective. Perhaps this can be best done by examining the demography of Victoria, whose census statistics permit the vital correlation of religion and place of origin to be made throughout the years 1851–1914. These returns give us many measurements on different scales, for both constant areas of settlement and ever-varying densities of population. The general pattern which emerges is as follows: a minimum Irish proportion of 15 and a maximum Irish proportion of 35 per cent in almost every place and region in Victoria and at almost every point in time over almost three-quarters of a century. A very large number of cases are clustered around 23 per cent. This might serve as a paradigm for Australia as a whole between the onset of white settlement and the outbreak of the First World War. The Irish may not have been as evenly distributed in the other colonies as in Victoria. None the less the 15–35 per cent bracket must be generally applicable to Australia, provided always that we divide its population (as against its land area) into largish units.

I do not mean to suggest, of course, that there were no general resemblances between the British and American and the Australian phenomenon; but to me at least it is the differences which are striking. First, whereas the Irish settlement on the land was — to put it at its mildest and most anodyne — disproportionately low in the United States, and practically unknown in Britain it was at all stages fully proportionate to their numbers in Australia. The Irish was no more an urban immigration in Australia than was that of any other nationality. Nor were there Irish wards and quarters in Sydney, Melbourne, Adelaide or Perth in anything like the sense in which they developed in New York, Boston, Liverpool or Glasgow. Secondly, although the Irish in Australia were heavily over-represented in the ranks of unskilled labour and domestic service — over-represented by 50–60 per cent at a guess, or even 100 per cent in the case of female servants — these occupations never engrossed the main body of Irish immigrants in Australia even in the originating generation. Conversely, the Irish seem to have been spread in significant numbers over a larger range of occupations in Australia, and, in particular, to have been more numerous, relatively speaking, in middle-class and professional ranks than in nineteenth-century America, not to say, Great Britain.

Needless to say, such a generalisation covers considerable individual variations, occupation by occupation. The Irish, and especially the Catholic Irish, were rarely to be found in the higher mercantile employments, still less in banking, insurance, brokerage, Stock Exchanges and similar money-based activities. They lacked both capital and the entrée into fields recruited through an old world type of network. On the other hand, in the professions and semi-professions of law, politics and journalism the Irish were probably over-represented — in the second half of the nineteenth century, at least. In Victoria, for example, the first six Speakers of the Legislative Assembly were Irish-born; so too were half the membership of some of the Victorian Cabinets of these same years as well as three-quarters of the attorneys- and solicitors-general. There were more-over other meritocratic fields among the professions — medicine and engineering are two examples — in which they seem to have been close to their due proportion.

Similarly, although the Irish were at least on a par numerically with the other nationalities in Australian agriculture, they were to be found mainly — though by no means exclusively — in its poorer, small, mixed-farming sector. Conversely, there were areas of manual work where the Irish were at all stages under-represented — mining, to a comparatively small degree, and the skilled trades, to a very marked degree, are good examples. They were grossly over-rep-resented in some colonial police forces and in the liquor industries and trades, but only patchily concentrated in certain departments of the colonial public services. Just as there were particular small-farming districts with low Irish populations, so too were there quite humble areas of public employment where they were rarely to be found. Generally of course the lower the occupation in the social scale the higher the proportion of Irish Catholics among its mem-bers. But there were, as we have just seen, various exceptions to this rule.

Thus the social and occupational map of the Irish in Australia is partly one of eminences and hollows. But when we compare it to the equivalent maps of the major areas of Irish settlement, it is the comparative paucity and lowness and shallowness of these variations which is arresting. Moreover, in one highly important respect, the Irish exceeded in evenness most other nationalities in Australia down to the First World War. The Irish masculinity rate — that is, the proportion of men to women — was consistently below the Australian average, from some 30 per cent below initially to some 10 per cent below in the early twentieth century. In Victoria, for example, the Catholic (overwhelmingly Irish-derived) masculinity rate was about 125 as against a colonial average of 180 in 1875, and

91 as against 101 in 1900; the pattern in Queensland was similar. The relative abundance of females in the Irish inflow must have its own special significance in Australian history, not least, I suspect, in the *religious* history of that nation.

Let us now turn to some of the *effects* of this quality of evenness upon the course of Australian development. First, in terms of parliamentary politics, it meant that the Irish were almost everywhere a distinct but also a significant minority. In the great majority of parliamentary constituencies, particularly in the relatively populous eastern crescent of Australia, they accounted for one-sixth to one-quarter of the electorate. As we should expect from these relativities, completely independent political action by the Catholic Irish community was generally doomed to failure, and certain to fail if it produced a hostile coalescence of the other groups and interests. Conversely, it might be powerful if combined with one or more of the larger exogenous elements. Thus it was a key factor in many of the leading issues in nineteenth and early twentieth-century Australia, whether 'radical-democratic', as with land distribution or the rights of labour, or sectarian, as with formal civic equality or secular and denominational education, or constitutional, as with the character of upper houses, or colonial autonomy or separation — or even the cause of Irish Home Rule itself, considered as either an inference from, or a beckoning light for, Australia's own political advance. The type of outright political control which the Irish secured in the United States in very limited areas and for primarily local and sectional purposes, was generally impracticable in Australia. On the other hand, the southern colonies had no counterparts to the immense tracts of continental America where the Irish were virtually powerless. Similarly, the Irish Australians were nowhere so feeble politically as to be usable at most — as in Great Britain in the 1880s — as a makeweight which might tip the balance from one major party to another in a mere dozen or so of the constituencies.

A further political idiosyncrasy of the Irish immigrants in Australia, which may perhaps be added here, was the form of *Irish* politics which, predominantly, they adopted. Despite various specific Fenian associations in 1867–70, the revolutionary and republican traditions of Irish nationalism were remarkably weak in the southern colonies. Conversely, Parnellite Home Rule mobilised Irish Australia extremely effectively and completely. The explanation is not, I think, far to seek. Home Rule, though ill-defined, represented substantially the type of colonial autonomy which Australia had already secured, or was steadily securing. Moreover, the further or outer emanations of Home Rule seemed to parallel the drives towards colonial nationalism, which were becoming more and more manifest in Australia. Hence support of constitutional nationalism at home fitted most neatly into both the Irish Catholics' struggle for full political parity in Australia and their search for bridges and junctions with Australian liberals and radicals. We must not forget that from the moment of his landing in Melbourne, Sydney, Brisbane, Perth or Adelaide, an Irish-Australian was as much a special sort of Australian as a special sort of Irishman, just as an Irish-American became at once a special sort of American as well as a sea-divided Gael. Dual allegiance was therefore not merely likely but even practically a necessity, and the convergence of the consequential political urges dearly prized. In the United States, republicanism, Anglophobia and the revolutionary overthrow of British overlordship might be respectable, even hallowed traditions. But in nineteenth and early twentieth-century Australia the British connection remained the key, in native eyes, to continued physical security, not to add to the ultimate survival of white settlement upon the continent.

To return however to the peculiar distribution of the Irish, and in particular to its economic consequences: these are, I think, largely deducible from their place or places in the occupational structures. Anglo-Saxon, or more precisely, Anglo-Caledonian, Australians — looking inwards, viewing internally, so to say — tended to stress the working-class and even proletarian character of the Irish element in their society. This was reasonable enough. Not only were the Irish disproportionately numerous at these levels, but also there were no waves of new immigration — as happened repeatedly in the United States — to lift those currently at the bottom of the social scale. There was not even any equivalent to the inrush of Eastern Europeans into Britain in the decades 1890–1910. Meanwhile, the prototype 'White Australia' lobbies ensured that neither Chinese nor Kanakas would fill a similar role.

Looked on from without, however, all the emphases fall the other way. The urban working-class element among the Irish in Australia was smaller, relatively speaking, than elsewhere. The cities in which they lived were also smaller in scale, and more scattered in form, than the *major* centres of Irish settlement abroad. This in itself provided some mitigation of the poverty. Miserable as wage rates and uncertain as regular employment may have been in the colonies, each was of a different order from the deep and unremitting exploitation of Irish labour on the Atlantic seaboard, the Great Lakes, Merseyside or Clydeside. Moreover, there were weightier counterpoises among these immigrants in Australia than in America, let alone Great Britain. Rich, successful and influential Irish may have been disproportionately few, but they were none the less to be found in quite considerable numbers at or near the top of every Australian tree except the high financial. A single statistic may help to put this whole matter in perspective. Irish emigration to Australia between 1815 and 1914 was only, roughly speaking, one-thirteenth of the Irish emigration to the United States. Yet Australasian contributions to the Land League, the Evicted Tenants Fund and the Irish Nationalist Party between 1880 and 1910 almost equalled the total received from the United States. Of course this cannot be simply taken as even a crude measure of relative disposable income among the respective bodies of Irish 'exiles' — to use the favourite rhetoric of the League's collectors. Various other factors came into play. But when even the most ample allowances have been made for these, we are still left with what is surely a most arresting index of the relative affluence of the two communities. A second, oblique but none the less most suggestive indicator of the social and economic standing of the Irish in Australia at the end of the first quarter of the twentieth century is provided by the Australian Federal Census of 1933, the only pre-1960 national census to correlate income and religion. By then, Catholic was not of course crudely or simply synonymous with an Irish identification or origin. But no one who knows Australia between the wars would deny a very substantial correlation. In 1933 Catholics constituted some 19 per cent of the total Australian population.

Table 10.1: Breadwinners: Male, Female and Total.
Roman Catholic and Catholic undefined as percentage of grand total in each income category.

	No income	Under £52	£52-£103	£104-£155	£156-£207	£208-£259	£260 & over	Total
Male	22.26	19.60	18.00	17.72	18.14	17.14	14.86	18.42
Female	36.07	21.18	20.7	21.88	21.47	19.62	17.34	22.21
Total male and female	24.73	20.17	18.81	18.88	18.6	17.33	15.05	19.36

Table 10.1 lists their proportions, in terms of male Heads of House-holds, to the nearest whole percentage number and in the various income groups — the order is descending: in Group A (the highest income group), 15 per cent, in Group B 17 per cent, in Groups C, D and E 18 per cent and in Group F (the lowest income group) 20 per cent. In the additional Group designated 'Of No Income', which constituted nearly 15 per cent of the whole and represented presumably the unemployed male Heads of Households, the Cath-olic proportion was 22 per cent. The general picture which emerges is therefore one of a distinct but comparatively small under-represen-tation in the two highest income categories, and a corresponding similar minor over-representation in the lowest. Elsewhere, for the majority or middle range of incomes, they do not vary greatly from the national average. This would seem solid confirmation of our general findings from the other evidence.

One final consequence of the relatively even distribution of the Irish may be noted. I refer to religious organisation, in particular Catholic religious organisation, for Catholics were not only fully, but even over-represented in the Irish emigration to Australia (in round figures, some 83 per cent as against 73 per cent at home). A very large proportion of the Australian population was of course settled in the half-dozen colonial capitals. There, the construction of a parochial system, and all the accompanying ecclesiastical and religious outworks, was comparatively straightforward, the sole though enormous difficulty being the scarcity of man- and woman-power. Elsewhere however Australia was extraordinarily lacking in towns and even close communities of any sort. Here organised religion was perforce a missionary, unstable and peripatetic venture at the start.

We must recollect as well that the Australian population growth was phenomenally rapid, with almost unbelievable levels of multipli-cation in particular regions at particular times. Even *after* the gold rushes, Victoria, for example, more than doubled its total population in the 30 years 1861–91, rising from 540,000 to 1,140,000. The combination of vast distances, wide dispersion and explosive growth put its stamp, inevitably, upon the nascent Catholic Church. It had to be practical, pastoral, activist (with the corollary, doubtless, of non-intellectual) in emphasis. Money, buildings, movement, manage-ment, filled the horizon. If the demand for priests, resources and materials of all kinds in the cities was prodigious, the rural needs were greater still. To institutionalise and order religion in the near-empty countryside was an immense affair. All this was compounded in the 60 years before the First World War by the rising tide of secular state education, and the eventual Catholic response of attempting to construct an entire denominational educational system on their own account. Such a gigantic undertaking implied the steady importation of Irish teaching religious, superadded to the Irish supply of clergy, both secular and regular, to provide for parochial and ecclesiastical development. This constant, sedulous reinforcement — or perhaps we should say successive 're-creations' — of Hibernicity in Catholic Australia until well into the present century, through school and parish, has been variously evaluated. But at least its profound importance in both the shaping of Australian culture and the history of Ireland's spiritual imperialism in the century 1840–1940 seems beyond dispute.

V

How are we to explain the curiosities, the aberrations, if the word is not too strong, of the Australian portion of the great modern Irish diaspora? The key, it seems to me, is that the Irish were a founding people in Australia, and maintained their position in the new society, more or less, for almost a century and a half. Whether as convicts or gaolers, as common soldiers or petty officials, as administrators, lawyers, wives, labourers, servant girls or adventurers, the Irish formed a substantial element of the Australian immigration, somewhere between 20 and 30 per cent of the whole, from the very beginnings of white settlement. Despite various temporary accelerations and decelerations in the volume, the proportion of 20–30 per cent was maintained throughout the nineteenth century, and perhaps even later. These two factors, full participation in the very earliest development of a new nation, and the maintenance for so long of this participation upon a very considerable scale, render Australia unique, in Irish terms.

In the United States, and *a fortiori* in Great Britain, the *Catholic* Irish at least entered a firmly stratified society, an already elaborated class structure and an established, or more precisely a fixed economy. *En masse*, they were doomed, initially, to slotting into the bottom layers, or even layer, of the hierarchy of occupations. Their subsequent social movement depended, first, upon how they used what we might term the upward-percolation mechanisms in the American system; secondly, upon their deployment of compacted local political power; and thirdly — and most of all — upon fresh immigrations of still more exotic and vulnerable peoples.

In South Africa, not only were the numbers of Irish immigrants comparatively small, but it was also practically impossible for them to maintain a separate non-British identity in the midst of the rooinek-Afrikaans and white-black polarisations. *Mutatis mutandis*, the same may be said of Argentina, with the added complication that Hispanicisation could scarcely be avoided. In Canada, again, the Irish formed a much smaller proportion of the white population; they entered a largely-formed society; and not only were they inevitably entangled in the Franco-British internal conflicts, but they were also deeply riven among themselves because of the relative strength of the Ulster Protestant section in this particular Irish emigration and the natural alliance between this Ulster section and the powerful Scots Presbyterian element in the eastern provinces.

New Zealand was, of course, much closer to the Australian model than any of the other areas of significant Irish settlement. Indeed we may say that it conforms generally to that pattern. But it is always in a muted form. The Irish element in European emigration to New Zealand (13–14 per cent of the total) was considerably smaller — one-third smaller at the least — than in European emigration to Australia. Again, the New Zealand Irish were both more concentrated in location and more evenly divided, communally, into Irish Protestant and Catholic. Further, the indigenous Maori population of New Zealand was more numerous, more resistant, and perhaps also, in effect, more polarising in terms of white and coloured peoples, than the Australian Aborigines. Last but far from least, British identification was considerably more pervasive, enduring and powerful in New Zealand than on the far side of the Tasman Sea. Thus if Australia and New Zealand may be said to have formed a category of their own in terms of Irish settlement overseas, each of the distinguishing features of that category is much more clearly marked in the respective colonies of Australia.

Thus we return to the initial and continuing participation of the Irish in the building-up of new Australia, and the massive scale of their involvement, as the crucial factors in explaining their place and fate. Much, as we have seen, hinged upon the atypical equality of their distribution in Australia; and this hinged in turn, upon their presence in the first and most fluid phases of social and economic construction, and the constant reinforcement of their numbers through networks of kinship and connection. But a third element must be called upon to account fully for the Irish-Australian variation upon the general theme. It is vital to bear in mind that Australian immigration in the nineteenth and early twentieth centuries was largely confined to English, Scots, Welsh and Irish. The most considerable continental European immigration, the German settlements in South Australia and Queensland, was much below these in scale, as well as substantially self-contained. It made little impact immediately upon the general social and class structures. Non-European immigration, whether Chinese or Pacific Islander, was checked decisively at an early stage. Meanwhile, the Aboriginal population was in either precipitate or steady decline, depending on the stages of white expansion: it was also practically excluded from much of the white economy. Herein, I think — in this sort of counter-factual history — lies the explanation of the persistence of a disproportionately large Irish element in the Australian working class: to put it in the simplest of terms, there was no alternative labour to replace or displace them, as a mass. But there is of course another side of this particular coin. Poor and vulnerable the Irish lower order in Australia may have been *per se*; but *vis-à-vis* their American and British counterparts, they were relatively affluent and powerful, to say nothing of being but one large element (albeit very large) in a socially complex Irish community. In short, paradox upon paradox upon paradox, even inequality began as equal, and remained more or less equal, in Australia's first century and a half.

VI

But to end here would be a cold conclusion to a study of the uprooting and translation of real people. Even overviews need surely not be so stratospheric that actual human beings, with all the pain, puzzlement and hope of their experiences, can never be discerned. Let me conclude with one small attempt to offset the unavoidable depersonalisation of this paper, and describe one little body of Irish emigrants whom I stumbled across in archives in a convent in Parramatta, New South Wales, while this paper was being composed. In some respects they were wildly — though wildly is not perhaps quite the *mot juste* — atypical: all females, all young, all nuns — a party of Mercy Sisters setting out to take over an Australian parish school. But in other respects they are quite *apropos*. They emigrated in the centenary year of white settlement, at the midway point, so to say, in the blanching of Australia. They were Kilkenny emigrants drawn from Callan convent and its outworks. Not least, they symbolise the chief means by which Ireland was kept green in Australian minds — the leading mechanism by which the Irish Australian identity was preserved.

On 28 March 1888 Cardinal-Archbishop Moran of Sydney, formerly Bishop Moran of Ossory, wrote to his old friend, the Reverend Mother at Callan, 'I hope that you will be able to send me a Community before the end of the year . . . Parramatta will be I suppose the central house.' Three months later he followed this up with a letter from Rome, where he was making an *ad limine* visit, in which he asked to be informed immediately of 'your decision regarding Sydney and the numerous battalions whom we require there'. Very soon after, on 20 June, Moran's Vicar-General the celebrated Monsignor O'Haran, visited Callan to oversee the final choice. Each Sister was presented with a voting paper ruled in three columns: 'Will not go'; 'Will go if sent'; and 'Volunteer'. At least nine of the sisters volunteered. These were to constitute the first wave of Callan exiles. They would be led by Sister Mary Clare Dunphy, one of the long line of masterful pioneering religious superiors from Ireland: she was then only 30 or 31 years old, but had already organised and managed a poor law hospital in Kilkenny.

On 9 October 1888 the nuns left Callan. At Kilkenny, Carlow, Athy and Kildare stations they were met by priests or messages of goodwill from the local Sisters of Mercy. Two days later they sailed from Dublin, having, as the journal of the voyage records, 'had . . . Mass and Holy Communion for the last time on Irish soil'. So it proved to be. None of the nine ever saw Ireland again; two were dead in Australia within five years.

Sydney was reached on 29 November. To Moran's great displeasure, the nuns would not stay long with the Sisters of Charity in the city, but pressed on to Parramatta where they found their house of residence in fair dilapidation, and virtually without furniture: the best of the beds, Mother Clare wrote, had two legs only. They also discovered themselves to be unpopular and unwelcome in Parramatta because the Cardinal had removed another body of nuns to make way for his Mercy Sisters. The only immediate consolation was Moran's unvarying favour and protection, despite his initial vexation. For him, they represented the Kilkenny connection. Nothing constituted a higher claim for Moran than this local allegiance. The nuns were always, in his own phrases, his 'Ossory Branch', his 'Transplant of Ossory'. A greater consolation came on Christmas Eve with a packet of Callan letters. The lost life of Kilkenny was lived again in these accounts of small, familiar things.

The story of the Ossory Transplant is in many ways conventionally triumphalist. From a broken-down residence, and teaching in sheds protected in part only by sugar bags along the sides, grew the usual network of new schools, convents, orphanages and parish and hospital visitation. In the early decades this was fed by a succession of new arrivals from Kilkenny, although they were gradually overhauled numerically by native recruits. The sense of being an Irish derivative appears to have persisted down to the First World War: St Canice and St Kieran were faithfully remembered. This sense was fed not only by the newcomers from Callan but also by the letters detailing even the physical changes along the Nore Valley. And yet, a new conjoint identity was emerging. We can see this even in the Cardinal himself. As early as his European visit in 1888, he wrote of his homesickness for Sydney and his new distaste for the worn-out seediness and pettiness of the Old World. 'Do not fail to pray', he told the Reverend Mother at Callan, 'for dear old Australia'. Be pleased, he told her, that the works of Mercy were spreading 'not only through the home country but through the Greater Ireland all round the world'. Self-defensively, he tried to forestall criticism in Callan when his new journal, the *Australian Catholic Record*, was being launched in 1894: 'a good many things may be new in Australia which have been for a long time regarded as old in Ireland.' In short, we seem to see already, even in so strange an immigrant as one of the princes of the Church, the Janus-faces of Irish-Australia, even in its strongest day.

11 Sir Antony MacDonnell and Crime Branch Special

W.F. Mandle

On 29 October 1902, Sir Antony Patrick MacDonnell, a Catholic Irishman aged 58 with a distinguished record in India, took up his appointment as Under-Secretary for Ireland. His Chief Secretary, George Wyndham, had identified MacDonnell as the man he wanted. Having, it has been written, 'cast his eyes around the whole Empire' he fixed upon MacDonnell who apart from a record in India that was 'second to none' had the merit, not perhaps as unusual as Wyndham thought, 'of being an Irishman and having been out of Ireland all his life'.[1]

Wyndham had met him during the summer of 1902 and had been most impressed. The Prime Minister, Balfour, a man with considerable experience of Ireland, was less enthusiastic. It was not that MacDonnell was not a good man nor a good administrator, but did he not have a reputation as a Home Ruler? If so, he wrote to Wyndham, would not 'everything you did against the Orange extremists be put down to his advice; while even the most rigorous action . . . against the Nationalists . . . be regarded as mere tinkering and compromise?'[2]

Wyndham agreed to vet MacDonnell, and discovered that not only had he refused to join the Nationalists, but that he objected to an Irish Parliament, and to obstructionist tactics in the Commons. MacDonnell had indicated that he saw his mission in Ireland purely to assist in the solution of the land problem, to improve the functioning of the administration, and to settle the education question.[3] Wyndham therefore pressed for the appointment to be made, and Balfour yielded. Some four years later Balfour drafted a statement to his colleagues, then in Opposition, that dealt with the difficulties MacDonnell's appointment had caused, particularly in reference to Wyndham's resignation from the Chief Secretaryship in March 1905 over the Devolution proposals.

Much of what Balfour wrote bears upon that best-known aspect of MacDonnell's period of office, and is only tangentially relevant to the subject of this chapter. A substantial portion is also taken up with consideration of MacDonnell's views on the position of a permanent head of a department *vis-à-vis* his political masters. Again, this is not of primary importance to my subject, although it colours much of how MacDonnell saw his role and is of relevance to the style in which he went about his work. But, in one respect, one, moreover, that Balfour chose to single out as an example of MacDonnell's intentions, there is direct relevance. Balfour wrote:

> He was apparently under the impression that his predecessors in office had been entrusted chiefly with police work; and that they had in many cases been little more than the conduit-pipe between the Chief Secretary and subordinate officials. Sir Antony [sic] desired it to be made clear, and it was made clear, that this was not to be his position.[4]

There are other indications that MacDonnell was perhaps somewhat too concerned with what he called police work. Whilst Lansdowne was sounding out MacDonnell on Wyndham's behalf in September 1902 he was given the impression that MacDonnell thought that the Under-Secretary 'has little to do except police work, for which he has no special aptitude'.[5] Wyndham replied to Lansdowne that MacDonnell was mistaken — police work was largely confined in the castle to the Inspector-General, Sir Neville Chamberlain, and the law officers. It was true that Sir David Harrel, MacDonnell's predecessor, had been interested in such work, but that was because he had been at one time in charge of the Dublin Metropolitan Police.[6]

The question of MacDonnell's power as Under-Secretary was eventually settled in terms that Walter Long, Wyndham's successor, felt that a wise minister would not have accepted[7] and the two began working together on matters they both held to be important — land reform and educational reform. Wyndham had less interest in MacDonnell's other major concern, administrative reform, a fact which helped precipitate the Devolution crisis which led to Wyndham's resignation in March 1905.

There can be no doubt that MacDonnell took up his office with somewhat exalted ideas as to his position and his programme. His abhorrence of mundane routine, especially that of police work, had been noticed by Balfour, by Lansdowne and by Wyndham, and as he himself wrote to Wyndham during the height of the Devolution crisis, 'You can realise that the work of "Dublin Castle" apart from the "wider views" would have repelled not attracted me.'[8]

His 'wider views' were not solely concerned with land, administrative and educational reform. They did, in one respect, impinge upon 'police work'. He wrote to Wyndham a month before he took up his appointment: 'I am an Irishman, a Roman Catholic and a Liberal in politics. I have strong Irish sympathies . . . I think there is no likelihood of good coming from . . . a regime of Coercion.'[9]

We have, therefore, coming into the office of Under-Secretary a man with a distaste for reading police files and a dislike of coercion. For the police, and particularly for the Special Crime Branch, MacDonnell's appointment was a recipe for disaster.

The Special Crime Branch had been set up in 1882 and had undergone a number of changes in location within the Dublin Castle administrative structure. Originally under an Assistant Under-Secretary of its own, it was transferred to the control of the Inspector-General RIC in 1885 and then to the Chief Secretary's Office, Administrative Division, over the years 1887–98, where it was placed under the direction of a clerk, James H. Davies, although its reports went to the Under-Secretary by way of the Inspector-General.[10]

There were undoubted weaknesses in Crime Branch Special, particularly as an effect of the separation of the Dublin Metropolitan Police from the RIC generally, which up to the Easter Rising 1916 and beyond was never satisfactorily resolved. The DMP had its own intelligence branch, G Division, and, back in London, an official in the Home Office sifted and collated intelligence derived from Irish, American and mainland British sources.[11]

MacDonnell, in his declared pursuit of administrative rationalisation, decided to take the opportunity of Davies' retirement to place Crime Branch Special in the Judicial Division from July 1904 where it remained until that Division was amalgamated with the Administrative Division in 1918.[12]

Crime Branch Special's position in whatever division it was called upon to be, its lack of responsibility for the entire range of intelligence work, and its relations with the Irish police forces proper had not prevented its being an active and valuable agency. As a witness stated to the Royal Commission of Enquiry into the Civil Service in 1913, a commission chaired, ironically enough, by MacDonnell, the collection of police reports had resulted, since 1885, in 'what really amounts to a modern history of Ireland . . . they furnish really a most valuable and nearly complete record of the various agitations, political and agrarian which have taken place since that date'.[13]

Those who have worked through those files would agree; they would also note a marked diminution in their bulk and usefulness from MacDonnell's period of office onwards. One has only to compare the austere tabulations of the so-called 'Intelligence Notes' of the years leading up to the First World War with the Crime Branch Special files of the 1880s, 1890s and early 1900s to appreciate the change that had occurred. MacDonnell inherited a service which for the first few years continued to provide the service of information that had become customary over the previous 20 years. It soon became apparent that it was not to MacDonnell's taste.

He also inherited, as his Inspector-General, another old India hand, Colonel Sir Neville Chamberlain, who had commanded in the Khyber Pass and advised the government of Kashmir. Described just prior to his appointment as Inspector-General in 1900 as a man with 'charming manners, plenty of self-reliance, an unusual amount of common sense, and that unusual quality, tact',[14] he was to prove in need of all these qualities, particularly the tact, whilst dealing with MacDonnell. He held less sanguine views on the state of Ireland than did the new Under-Secretary, and was always prepared to take his police reports seriously.

Within a few months MacDonnell was reacting somewhat testily to what Chamberlain was telling him. He minuted the Inspector-General's February 1903 monthly report: 'The *facts* reported point to the growth of a better spirit throughout the country. The IG's *inferences* may be taken for what they are worth (his emphasis).'[15] Already MacDonnell was showing an inclination to accept only what he wanted to hear but he found in Chamberlain a man whose temper was more traditionally wary.

The following month Chamberlain was incautious enough to suggest there might be a potential danger in the Land Act that was so much a lynchpin of the Wyndham-MacDonnell policy. He wrote,

A second source of danger may be opened up, if the principle of a maximum reduction in rent by sales, as at present proposed in the Bill, should hereafter be largely extended or removed. A greater temptation would then exist to put illegal pressure upon landlords inasmuch as the result to be achieved would be not only greater, but contagious.

MacDonnell rapped Chamberlain firmly over the knuckles. He minuted: 'This is going beyond the scope of the Inspector-General's functions, and is out of place in such a Report as this.'[16]

The developing coolness towards Chamberlain, and increasing scepticism about the reality of the threat from the current Irish Nationalist movement surfaced in another minute of MacDonnell's appended to a report from Crime Branch Special itself that gave details of active use of the GAA by the IRB in order to strengthen the physical force party in Ireland. MacDonnell dismissively minuted this to Wyndham:

> I submit this because Colonel Chamberlain so requests. But I confess I am not much impressed: and the information I receive from other quarters does not invest the Gaelic movement at all [indecipherable] with malign and disloyal objects though the objects are certainly 'national'.[17]

During the year, partly in order to meet the costs of administering the Land Act, recruitment to the RIC was scaled down, evidently with the effect of reducing some of its intelligence activities, for word reached Major Gosselin at the Home Office in London in June that 'the belief is general that the Crime Special system is abolished'.[18]

One may hazard a guess that the increasing thinness of the reports indicates a decline in surveillance which in turn led those who had hitherto known themselves to be watched closely to believe that the watchdogs were now called off.

In December 1903 MacDonnell was moved to an unprecedented action. On the 15th he received the Inspector-General's monthly report for November. It contained, as usual, reports from the Chief Inspectors of the six areas into which Ireland was divided for police purposes — South West, South East, Midland, and so on — together with statistical summaries on outrages, police protection, and the like. The Inspector-General presented their report with his own assessment, derived from distillation and contemplation of them.

MacDonnell was apparently shocked by Chamberlain's summary and conclusions. By 18 December he had composed a draft memorandum, edited in pencil in his own hand, that explained to the Chief Secretary why he had asked his assistant Under-Secretary, Sir James

Dougherty, to examine the report 'minutely'. Dougherty had in fact completed his examination, and MacDonnell's memorandum was to accompany it.

Only the edited draft of that memorandum exists, providentially far more useful to the historian because it occasionally shows MacDonnell's initial anger being tempered with circumspection. For instance, he first described Chamberlain's section on landlord–tenant relations as 'coloured by prejudice'. Pencilled in above was the phrase 'much too gloomy'. Elsewhere there is an indication that MacDonnell considered asking that the report be rewritten 'by a fresh hand', but this phrase was edited out, and in fact Chamberlain, who called in to see MacDonnell on New Year's Eve, himself rewrote the report which he presented on 8 January 1904.

MacDonnell's memorandum, a note to the Chief Secretary, Dougherty's report and Chamberlain's revised edition of his November report supply us with some indication of what picture of Ireland MacDonnell wished to present, and, perhaps more importantly, wished to see. Missing is, unfortunately, Chamberlain's initial report; MacDonnell's draft memorandum speaks ominously: 'if it remains on our records . . .'. Seemingly it did not.

MacDonnell was concerned about two things. First, that the original report was out of line with all the year's previous reports which indicated Ireland to be in a satisfactorily peaceable condition. MacDonnell here recalled the exception of March and his own tart comment; now he called Chamberlain's misgivings about the possible ill-effects of land reform 'mere speculation . . . with no foundation in fact or in the local Reports'. That apart, news had been consistently good: the November departure from the improving norm was, MacDonnell wrote, 'out of harmony' with his own views and with other information.

Secondly, MacDonnell was annoyed with what he called Chamberlain's 'forebodings of evil'. Chamberlain had described the state of the country inaccurately, not merely by 'exaggerations of word or phrase' but in the entire tone of his report. MacDonnell catalogued the deficiencies: turbulence existed only in 'a very few localities of extremely limited extent'; Chamberlain's tabulation of outrages was misleading; and his view of the prospects for landlord–tenant relations was either 'prejudiced' or 'much too gloomy' (depending upon which term found its way into MacDonnell's final version).

MacDonnell concluded, sympathetically, that use of the initial report as an aid to policy-making 'would be positively mischievous'.

Much of MacDonnell's later anger with the grazing agitation in the west of Ireland, which caused him to call for sterner action, and to resign when the government refused to grant him the resources to do so, may be seen as the report of a man suffering from a variety of senses of betrayal, not all of them externally based.

That is to look ahead. In December 1903 Sir James Dougherty performed his task dutifully and shrewdly. His report, swiftly done, was forwarded to the Chief Secretary. Its acceptability to MacDonnell is a further indication of what he wanted to hear.

Chamberlain, granted in his turn the opportunity to make amends, largely echoed what Dougherty said, although from time to time one may sense, as one compares his revised version with the Dougherty memorandum, a certain stubbornness and an unwillingness wholly to follow the party line. Chamberlain possessed tact and good manners: we may observe these virtues in use for much of his final report, but occasionally note their wearing a little thin.

Dougherty, who entitled his report 'Memorandum on Reports of Chief Inspectors' began by stating that they were 'a remarkable testimony to the peaceful and satisfactory condition of Ireland'. Chamberlain, when he came to rewrite his report, began by saying that during November 'the country remained throughout in a peaceful and satisfactory condition'. Such deferential conformity to Dougherty's interpretation, indeed to his very words, continued. Dougherty pointed out that the Chief Inspectors' Reports contained indication of only three areas of trouble — Kanturk in Co. Cork, Craughwell in Co. Galway, and the Roscrea–Templemore area in Co. Tipperary.

Even of these places, argued Dougherty, no great notice should be taken. Kanturk, he claimed, hardly deserved the prominence Chamberlain had evidently given to it — it was a 'wild and remote mountain district, and does not affect the condition of the country, or even of County Cork, as a whole'. Craughwell had, Dougherty was forced to admit, 'always been a disturbed district, but currently only one man there was being given police protection', which, incidentally, he did not want, and there was 'no evidence or suggestion . . . of the formation of Secret Societies for unlawful purposes in this locality'. Similarly for the Roscrea–Templemore district: there had been no increase in the number of protected persons, no serious outrage and no evidence of secret society activity. Elsewhere, wrote Dougherty, throughout the whole of Ireland, Police Reports indicated a satisfactory or peaceable condition.

Chamberlain's revised report concurred. Since the Land Bill, he deftly noted, a 'remarkable change for the better continues to exist'. The areas he had, presumably, drawn attention to in the original were reassessed in the light of Dougherty's interpretation. 'Isolated exceptions', he wrote, 'exist in very limited areas in the Police Districts of Kanturk . . . Craughwell . . . and Roscrea and Temple-more. In these localities, however, the trouble is local, and results from causes not attributable to any general or widespread spirit of lawlessness.'

Dougherty had gone on to question Chamberlain's reading of outrages. Evidently Chamberlain had lumped together 'reported' and 'recorded' incidents, thus inflating the month's total to 217 rather than the more acceptable (if the MacDonnell view of a peaceable Ireland were to be sustained) 152. Moreover, suggested Dougherty, the 'recorded outrages' should be retermed 'indictable offences' and divided into agrarian and non-agrarian categories. Chamberlain complied, although one may suspect a wry smile as he totted up the recorded outrages in the Chief Inspectors' reports and found that they totalled 151, a number he dutifully presented.

It is apparent that the section of Chamberlain's original report presented under the heading 'Landlord–Tenant Relations' had, un-derstandably, given offence to MacDonnell. Chamberlain had, the Dougherty memorandum indicates, called them 'unsatisfactory'. Dougherty disagreed, but on somewhat convoluted grounds. He agreed that there had been a poor harvest, and he implicitly accepted that in, for example, Cos. Cork, Galway and Tipperary there had been trouble over the withholding of rents; but he agreed that years ago it would have been much worse, and Chamberlain 'might well have noticed this great change for the better'.

Chamberlain's revised report was subtly accommodating. 'Great fears', he wrote, had been entertained over the effects of the bad harvest and, indeed, it had 'to a limited extent, produced an effect upon relations between landlord and tenant.' Then, employing qualifying phrases and adjectives with some skill, Chamberlain went on, 'Refusals to pay rents were indulged in, but, as a rule, the rents were paid, or are being paid, and at present there is no indication of a serious combined strike against rents.' Furthermore, Chamberlain persisted in warning that the situation would worsen if overseas influences were brought to bear, a clear reference to reports of substantial Clan na Gael funding for the IRB and the GAA that were concurrently so alarming other officials in Dublin Castle and Major Gosselin, not a man easily perturbed, in London.

Dougherty had rejected Chamberlain's interpretation of the extent and importance of secret society activity: 'there is no evidence that the IRB is anything but the shadow of a once terrifying name, and there is testimony from many counties that the GAA has not been captured for Secret Society purposes'. Indeed, there was, but there was testimony from at least as many counties to the contrary; and the IRB was undergoing an important regeneration.

Significantly, Chamberlain refused fully to back down. He omitted all reference to the IRB as such in his revised version, although he again noted a potential for trouble over the rents issue, and he continued to maintain that the Brotherhood had 'a certain influence' with the GAA: 'Although, at present, these efforts may be dismissed as futile, yet I consider it necessary to keep a close and vigilant supervision.'[19]

It was precisely this close and vigilant supervision that was to falter under the successive administrations of Wyndham, Long, Bryce and Birrell — but the dereliction began with MacDonnell.

The affair of the rewritten Inspector-General's monthly report is more than a minor incident in administrative history; it reveals, by its indication of what MacDonnell regarded as acceptable, what it was that the new Under-Secretary thought he was achieving and hoped to achieve in Ireland.

Chamberlain's next monthly report, that for December 1903, was almost ostentatiously couched in soothing terms. For example, referring to rent trouble in Craughwell, Chamberlain was at pains to state that 'the friction . . . is due to local circumstances', and later, commenting on the figure for outrages, he noted that 'their effect on the general peace was very small'. The IRB showed 'but little signs of life', the GAA was making no 'appreciable progress', and in describing a growth in boycotting, Chamberlain noted that it was 'approaching the border-line where it is difficult to distinguish whether their position now is the result of personal unpopularity or of an active conspiracy'. Chamberlain, chastened by his November experience, stayed firmly on the right side of that particular border-line. His report did not wholly escape comment. MacDonnell brusquely minuted the section on secret society activity:

I wish to express my opinion that the danger from Secret Societies is insignificant; and the reports which reach Hd Qts on this head are ['mostly' erased] usually valueless.[20]

It is just as well that MacDonnell did not see the Reports of the prolonged investigation into the ages of Dublin newsvendors that occupied much of April 1904. Dougherty had wondered if his feeling that the number of adult newsvendors on Dublin streets had increased of late was correct. Were they, perhaps, showing a preference for newspaper selling rather than joining the army? The police, in a lengthy memorandum, begged to state that 'there does not appear to be any perceptible increase', but Dougherty was not reassured. Revealing that by 'adult' he had meant persons of 16 and upwards he enquired whether the police still wished to persevere in their opinion. Back came a supplementary report begging to state that the previous assessment had been based upon the impression that 'by "adult" was meant a person of mature years'. Even so, close watch maintained on offices and newstands had revealed only about 100 vendors over the age of 16, a half of them unemployable elsewhere, and so, presumably, unfit for recruitment into the army whose ranks would hardly have been devastated, it might be thought, by an absence of 50. Sir James did not again raise the matter.[21]

Such reports were trivial, and the cost of making them wasteful; but it was not always so, and it is ironical in the extreme that at a time when the IRB was becoming a well-organised efficient and effective revolutionary force, the GAA was developing as Ireland's largest nationalist organisation, infiltrated from head to foot by the IRB, and the Gaelic League was being made the object of comparable infiltration, police intelligence work was being scaled down.

Throughout 1904, Chamberlain gave MacDonnell bland reports on satisfactory conditions throughout Ireland. When, in honesty, he had to mention trouble, he met with MacDonnell's desire to minimise or turn a blind eye. In August there were reports of shooting incidents in Clare, Kerry and Galway: MacDonnell minuted them, 'it would be easy to exaggerate the significance of firing into houses'.[22] No wonder Chamberlain resorted, exasperated, to consistent use of the word 'peaceable' to describe the country.

As MacDonnell's wishes, Chamberlain's deference and police inaction blended to produce a picture of Ireland acceptable to the Under-Secretary, his antipathy to the work of Crime Branch Special, and his reluctance to take the landlords' side in any agrarian dispute increased.

In March 1905 he wrote:

> During $2\frac{1}{2}$ years of careful observation I have not seen a patch of substantial evidence to show that there is in Ireland any secret political activity of which the Govt need have the smallest apprehension.[23]

He suggested that he was toying with the idea of calling off Crime Branch work. C.A. Wilkins, who had replaced the wise old owl Major Gosselin at the Home Office Link desk, enjoined caution:

> It would be a great mistake to abandon all supervision . . . I still think that the withdrawal of all supervision would tend to encourage those more unscrupulous spirits; they must know they are being watched and they fear the consequences of being found out.[24]

So Crime Branch Special survived, but at times only barely. Faced in the summer of 1907 with a need to augment the number of police to meet the grazing lands crisis in the west of Ireland there was a suggestion that 'Crime Special Branch might be abolished without loss to the Government, and with benefit to the Police. The services of the men employed under it are wasted'.[25] MacDonnell minuted his approval in principle, but thought such an action in the current circumstances might be premature; but he never relaxed his contemptuous attitude to what Crime Special put before him. Nor did his assistant, Sir James Dougherty, a fact of some significance in that Dougherty succeeded MacDonnell and remained Under-Secretary until 1914. An Ulster Protestant academic (he was a Professor of Logic and Literature from Magee College, Derry) he was, if anything, more sceptical than MacDonnell of the value of Crime Special, echoing his master loyally, even, as we shall see, maintaining the anti-alarmist line after his superior had abandoned it. As MacDonnell prepared to resign, Dougherty minuted the June 1908 Report from Chamberlain, 'These S.S. reports have become a monotonous round of inactivity.'[26] It might be suggested that the sense of inactivity resulted more from inaction on the part of police intelligence than from the torpidity of the so-called secret societies. That so ardent a disciple of MacDonnell as Dougherty should have been in charge of police work during the formative period of the Irish Volunteer movement for instance was of damaging consequence to British administration in Ireland.

Despite MacDonnell's hopes, and contrary to the trend he wished to present, there was a recurrence of violent agitation, beginning in the west during 1905 and largely concerned with tenant efforts to unlock land used for extensive and casual grazing rather than for cultivation. Galway, the borders between Cork, Kerry and Limerick, and areas in west Mayo were noted as disturbed by January 1905.[27] The United Irish League led the anti-grazing campaign, which the Chief Secretary himself began to regard as 'very serious' in March, especially in Co. Galway.[28] Sporadic shootings continued throughout the year, and Chamberlain put in an apprehensive report for December 1905. MacDonnell was on leave, but his deputy, Dougherty, was as ever a loyal echo of his master, minuting the Inspector General's report as 'gloomier than the facts seem to warrant'.[29]

On his return MacDonnell, presented with evidence of increasing activity by extremist nationalists, voiced his own version of killing such agitation by kindness. Chamberlain, troubled at the growth of what was already being termed 'Sinn Fein' agitation and penetration, noted in February 1906 that 'the moderate leaders in Ireland have never hitherto been able to ignore the opinion of extreme men'. MacDonnell, unwilling to act, minuted that in the past, 'repression and persecution have changed movements of [indecipherable] unimportance if left alone into Martyrs' causes'. Later he stated his opinion even more bluntly:

> As for the 'Sinn Fein' Movement all I would say is that a policy of passive resistance in General Politics is not congenial to the Irish nature and the 'Sinn Fein' doctrine will die out if only we let it alone.[30]

Presumably it was let alone, but trouble continued throughout 1906, particularly in Counties Galway, Leitrim and Kerry, and in some areas of Limerick and Tipperary.[31] Anti-recruiting campaigns, led by the GAA, were stepped up, but MacDonnell, citing the Secretary of State for War's claim that recruiting was undiminished, minuted the Inspector-General's report for September that he deprecated prosecutions for distributing anti-recruiting leaflets, advocating instead a policy of 'contemptuous indifference'.[32] Chamberlain was clearly angered by this, and in his January 1907 Report presented figures that showed Irish recruiting dropping from 3615 in 1904 to 2695 in 1906.[33]

By January 1907 the troubles in Galway were continuing unabated, leading MacDonnell to make a revealing philosophical statement of his position. Writing of Galway, East Riding he said:

> In this part of the county landlords have not been slow to combine to uphold prices — no wonder that they should be met by efforts to reduce them . . . The Police have done their best to detect crime and protect unpopular people but if such people have come to see that they cannot hope to brave popular disapproval and subsist I do not see that the Government are to be blamed.
>
> A social revolution is going on in this part of Ireland and it is fortunate that we are keeping it a bloodless one.[34]

Later he criticised the landlords even more directly, accusing them of combining to keep land prices 'too high'.[35] A couple of months later he pooh-poohed Chamberlain's criticism of agitation that aimed at getting land below its market price, asking if there was indeed such a thing as a market price.[36]

By the middle of 1907 it was apparent that the anti-grazing movement was beginning to get out of hand. The unwritten law of the UIL was 'growing supreme' in Galway, Roscommon and Clare; indeed, Galway, East Riding was declared 'virtually under mob law' and over 100 additional police were being brought in to the disaffected counties and a couple of shell-shocked county inspectors replaced.[37] But MacDonnell persisted in playing down the extent of the troubles, minuting Chamberlain's assessment that the whole province of Connacht (other than Co. Mayo) was 'very unsettled' with, 'This is too wide. The disturbed parts are really a small part of the whole.'[38] A small part they may have been, but Chamberlain was able to fill six pages of his June report with a list of crimes and outrages.

Not even MacDonnell could continue to ignore the evidence. Whilst he was playing down Chamberlain's alarm, he was asking Cabinet for more funds to augment the RIC by 600 men,[39] although he was still reluctant to acknowledge the extent of the agitation, and the doubt it cast upon his previous assessment of both the state of Ireland and the power of agitatory organisations. Faced in

September with reports that Cos. Galway, Clare, Leitrim, Roscommon, Meath, Longford and Tipperary, King's County and Cork West Riding were 'unsettled and ready for open agitation' he turned to blaming the speech-making of the extremist nationalist and MP Laurence Ginnell for the trouble.[40]

He and Dougherty continued to whistle in the dark in November. Dougherty insisted that the areas of disturbance were limited, and in no respect in the condition of Land League days. Chamberlain saw things differently, and MacDonnell differently again. Chamberlain wrote:

> It seems questionable whether, underlying the avowed agrarian object, there is not the further design of demonstrating that the country cannot be governed by the Imperial administration contrary to the will of the Irish people.

On which MacDonnell commented:

> This is not correct. The agitation has existed for many years . . . it has this year received an enormous impetus from the unchecked proceedings of Messrs Ginnell, Sheehy, etc.[41]

Whether the cause was Ginnell, designing Sinn Fein nationalism, landlord intransigence, or even diminished police work in years leading up to 1907, the year was the worst for crime since 1893, with an increase of 54 per cent in outrages reported.[42]

MacDonnell began his final year in office having finally to acknowledge that what he had so long persuaded himself was so, was so no longer. His dutiful subordinate, Sir James Dougherty, was slow to perceive the change of mind. Bravely following the party line of the previous five years, he attempted in February 1908 to discern an improvement in Cos. Galway, Clare and Roscommon. Surprisingly, yet unsurprisingly, MacDonnell said he could not agree, and went on,

> There is a general feeling of unrest: and a sense of impending mischief in these counties. Unless the promised legislation meets expectations, or the Government assumes a very firm attitude there will be great trouble.[43]

The 'promised legislation' was presumably the Irish Council Bill, the 1904 Devolution proposals in a different guise, but ones that, the Liberals now in office and the Nationalists scenting Home Rule, thought were no longer sufficient. As for the 'very firm attitude', Birrell, the new Chief Secretary, doubted if it would do any good to clap speech-makers and agitators in jail, in effect, to restore the Crimes Act. Instead Birrell decided to press ahead with a Land Bill, finally enacted in 1909, that was intended to improve the financial rewards available for land purchase particularly in the disaffected areas. It was a curiously MacDonnellite response, but by now MacDonnell had gone over to the law and order approach and, finding Birrell and Cabinet unsympathetic, decided to resign in July 1908.[44]

His responsibility for the decline of Crime Branch Special has already been touched upon. The effects of that decline upon the Easter Rising, and upon antecedent events such as the formation and infiltration by the IRB of the Irish Volunteers and the nationalist gun-runnings are legitimate subjects of speculation.

Crime Branch Special was from MacDonnell's time starved of funds and staff. It also suffered from MacDonnell's and Dougherty's deprecatory cynicism. We may also note that MacDonnell allowed the Peace Preservation Act, the so-called Arms Act, to lapse in 1906, despite strong protest from Chamberlain.[45] Its absence from the statute book was, as the 1916 Royal Commission discovered to its annoyance, a factor in the development of private armies, crimes and gun-running in Ireland.[46]

Evidence given to both the 1916 Royal Commission and to the Civil Service Commission revealed the paltry resources devoted as a whole to the Judicial Division, to which MacDonnell had assigned Crime Special. A single principal-class clerk headed the Division, given occasional assistance by a first-class clerk. Only one second-division clerk was employed — 'we have no second clerk there at all' complained a witness, and furthermore, 'they won't allow us a first-class clerk for the police division'.[47] That was in the Castle itself. The Royal Commission into the 1916 Rebellion discovered that, on the ground throughout Ireland, merely a county inspector, a district inspector and 'a few sergeants and constables' were all that Crime Branch Special had, together with a police officer seconded to the military Special Intelligence Branch.[48] There is some indication that a number of undercover agents were employed, but little evidence that they provided much information.[49] On the contrary in fact. So diminished were its activities that rumours persisted that Crime Special had been abandoned. Captain Pollard, who served in Dublin Castle during the War of Independence, was convinced it had so been in 1910, with, he wrote, 'an unwisdom that is inexplicable', and with dire effects that he proceeded to set out:

> The Government had been able to check incipient criminal movements and had been able to gather information of a sort not likely to be within the scope of police detectives or the ordinary members of the force. It had been the custom for the authorities to have their own agents within the circles of the Brotherhood and kindred doubtful associations. The abolition of the Irish political secret service broke these connections, so that later, when urgent need arose, it was difficult to place agents within the organisation and quite impossible to get them swiftly into positions of importance such as had been attained by agents of the past who had slowly risen to eminence in the organization as time passed.[50]

There has been widespread acknowledgement that the 1916 Rising took the authorities largely by surprise. O'Broin puts it bluntly: 'of all the division in the Volunteer Executive, of all the moves and counter moves, the Government knew absolutely nothing . . . the British Intelligence system in Ireland had failed hopelessly.'[51] A member of the Supreme Council of the I.R.B. writing at the time was just as scathing:

> There is a lot more instructive evidence before the 'Rebellion Inquiry Commission' showing that they knew damn all about the condition of the country except what any schoolboy could gather from the papers. For instance, the Inspector General of the R.I.C. in tracing the progress of the Sinn Fein movement says — in 1908 they had evidence that the bond between Sinn Fein and the Irish Republican Brotherhood had become closer and the object of the two parties was practically the same. That is all *he* has to say of the I.R.B., and the Chief Commissioner D.M.P. has nothing at all to say. . . . In fact everything in the evidence was published in the papers and there is no clear grasp of the relations between any of the Irish Ireland movements. In fact the G.A.A., Sinn Fein, Citizen Army, the Irish Volunteers, etc., are all jumbled

up together and there is reference only here and there to the I.R.B. They seem to not be very certain of its existence at all.[52]

Evidence to the 1916 Commission attempted bravely to conceal differences and assure that 'friends', as they were called, were placed inside revolutionary societies and furnished information.[53] But occasionally the mask slipped, notably when the Lord Lieutenant, Lord Wimborne was asked,

> The secret must have been exceedingly well kept
> — Yes, it was, very.
> You had no friends in the other camp,
> — No.
> Are you satisfied with the existing Detective Department . . .
> — No, I am not satisfied.[54]

Nor was the Chief Secretary who replaced Birrell, H.E. Duke, submitted to Cabinet:

> there is an urgent necessity for better organisation and some development of the branch of police investigation which deals with criminal conspiracy . . . the present organisation of the CID in Ireland is entirely inadequate . . . There is a great lack . . . of ready and efficient means of information as to criminal and some criminal political plots.[55]

The Royal Commission Report was full of praise for the conduct, zeal and loyalty of the RIC and the DMP, but drew a sharp distinction between its efficiency in routine work and its failure over what it termed political crime, which was, of course, the realm in which Crime Special should have been functioning, as it had for 20 years prior to MacDonnell's coming.[56]

As Pollard pointed out, the infiltration of agents into the various revolutionary societies had been a major part of secret service work. The information provided was not at all times accurate, was on occasion alarmist, but was always plentiful. A phantom army of informers with code names witty and ponderous marched in the 1880s and 1890s in the ranks and occasionally close to the head of the IRB, the GAA, the INB, the Centenary movement and so on. Often pitifully paid, they provided information that was sifted, compared, checked and used to determine policy. Their work ensured that the authorities were confident they always knew what was afoot, confident also that they could, at will, set hares running, and use their agents as provocateurs.[57] The informer and the agent became the feared and hated bugbear of all revolutionary organisations.

That he, or indeed she, seems to have ceased to exist in the decade prior to the Rising is no accident of adventitious probity suddenly appearing among Irishmen, but must in large part be attributed to the willingness of the authorities to observe the comings and goings at, say, Tom Clarke's tobacconist's shop from the pavement rather than from within the back room.

The cost of running such surveillance was a factor. More potent was the scepticism of such men as MacDonnell. Until near the close of his term of office he saw no need to maintain vigilance, for reasons that have become apparent, reasons both temperamental and philosophical. To him, to his successor Dougherty, and to the Chief Secretaries they served, all nationalist activity seemed to be in the open. They were deluded, out of ignorance, largely wilfully induced, into accepting the public face of manifestly thriving organisations such as the Gaelic League, the GAA, Sinn Fein and even the Irish Volunteers as representing the inner reality; that substantial sections of all these organisations had been infiltrated by a revived and purposeful IRB by 1914 was neither acknowledged nor known by the authorities. The pitiful misinterpretations exposed by the Royal Commission into the Rising are a measure of administrative failure.

The restructuring of the IRB, the effects of the healing of the division in the Clan na Gael, the planned revival of the GAA, all occurring in the early years of the century, were known in detail to Dublin Castle, as they are to the historian, because of the work of Crime Branch Special. An annoying darkness descends after about 1905 lit only occasionally by a mundane observation until the scene exploded into the 1916 Rising.

MacDonnell came to Ireland in 1902 bent on reform, opposed to coercion, and with a distaste for police work. His reformist activity, over land, over devolution, and over education has been amply examined elsewhere. Neglected has been a study of his policies with regard to that which he most disliked. In their way, by their effects upon the substance, and, it may be imagined, upon the morale of what was arguably the most efficient police intelligence force in Europe, MacDonnell's actions in the realm of police work might be accounted even more consequential than those of the much vaunted 1903 Land Act.

Notes and References

1. E. Dugdale, 'The Wyndham–MacDonnell Imbroglio 1902–1906', *Quarterly Review* no.511 (January 1932), p.16.
2. Balfour to Wyndham, 26 August 1902, ibid., p.17.
3. Wyndham to Balfour, 24 September 1902, ibid., pp.18–19.
4. Ibid., p.36.
5. Lansdowne to Wyndham, 11 September 1902, in J.W. MacKail and G. Wyndham, *Life and Letters of George Wyndham* (2 vols, Hutchinson, London, n.d. [1925]), vol.2, p.754.
6. Wyndham to Lansdowne, 12 September 1902, ibid., p.756.
7. Public Record Office, London (henceforth PRO), CAB 37/75/55. Memorandum by W. Long, 'Sir A.P. MacDonnell, Under-Secretary for Ireland'.
8. MacDonnell to Wyndham, 27 December 1904, MacKail and Wyndham, *Life and Letters*, vol.2, p.776.
9. MacDonnell to Wyndham, ibid., p.761.
10. B. MacGiolla Choille, *Intelligence Notes 1913–1916* (State Paper Office, Dublin, 1966), pp.xxiii–iv.
11. R.B. McDowell, *The Irish Administration 1801–1914* (Routledge and Kegan Paul, London, 1964), pp.143–5. For the Home Office desk, and Major Gosselin, see K.R.M. Short, *The Dynamite War* (Gill and Macmillan, Dublin, 1979), pp.144–6, 237.
12. MacGiolla Choille, *Intelligence Notes*, p.xxiv.
13. Commons Papers Reports from Commissioners Royal Commission on the Civil Service, second appendix to Fourth Report, HC 1914, XVI, Cd. 7340, p.183.
14. Lord Roberts to Lord Cadogan, 5 December 1899, quoted in C. Townshend, *Political Violence in Ireland* (Oxford UP, Oxford, 1983), p.231.
15. SPO, Dublin Castle Inspector General's Monthly Report (henceforth IGMR) February 1903.
16. SPO, IGMR March 1903.
17. SPO, CBS 28288/S MacDonnell minute dated 23 March 1903 on February report of Crime Special Sergeants.
18. SPO, Divisional Inspectors Crime Special Precis 1–30 June 1903, minute by Major Gosselin.
19. The whole documentation that survives is filed in the SPO under IGMR November 1903.
20. SPO, IGMR January 1904, minuted by MacDonnell.
21. SPO, CBS 29460/S 10–24 March 1904.
22. SPO, IGMR August 1904.
23. SPO, CBS 29989/S MacDonnell minute of 20 March 1905.
24. Ibid., Wilkins minute of 25 March 1905.
25. PRO, CO 904/11, 20 August 1906.
26. SPO, IGMR June 1908.
27. SPO, IGMR January 1905 (MacDonnell minuted the report on vigorous agitation on the Collis Sanders estate, 'This is a special case').
28. Ibid., March 1905 minute of Chief Secretary, Walter Long.
29. For reports of shootings, see e.g. SPO, IGMR April 1905, and for Dougherty's minute, ibid., December 1905.

30. Ibid., February 1906.

31. See, e.g. ibid., June, August, October, November 1906.

32. Ibid., September 1906.

33. Ibid., January 1907.

34. Ibid.

35. Ibid.

36. Ibid., March 1907.

37. Ibid., April 1906. The replacements were made in Galway East Riding and Co. Roscommon.

38. Ibid., June 1907.

39. PRO, CAB 37/89/70, 16 June 1907.

40. SPO, IGMR September 1907.

41. Ibid., November 1907.

42. SPO, Intelligence Notes, Inspector General's Report for 1907.

43. SPO, IGMR February 1908.

44. L. O'Broin, *The Chief Secretary* (Chatto and Windus, London, 1969), pp.13–21, *DNB* (1922–1930), p.534.

45. Commons Papers. Reports from Commissioners Royal Commission on the Rebellion in Ireland (henceforth Rebellion Commission). Minutes of Evidence Commons Papers 1916, vol.ii, Cd. 8311, p.43.

46. Rebellion Commission, Report (Cd.8279), pp.4, 13. Minutes (Cd.8311), pp.13, 24, 26, 41.

47. Civil Service Commission Minutes of Evidence, pp.185–7.

48. Rebellion Commission, Minutes of Evidence, pp.10, 43.

49. See, e.g., Rebellion Commission, Minutes of Evidence pp.15, 22, 25, 51, 54.

50. H.B.C. Pollard, *The Secret Societies of Ireland* (Allan and Co., London, 1922), pp.123–4.

51. L. O'Broin, *Dublin Castle and the 1916 Rising* (Sidgwick and Jackson, London, rev. edn 1970), p.149.

52. F.X. Martin (ed.), 'The McCartan Documents, 1916', *Clogher Record* (1966), p.38.

53. See, e.g. Rebellion Commission, Minutes of Evidence, pp.25, 51.

54. Ibid., p.39.

55. PRO, CAB 37/154/1.

56. Rebellion Commission, Report, p.4.

57. For informers and their use by the authorities, see Ch.3 of *The Gaelic Athletic Association and Irish Politics, 1884–1924* (Croom Helm, London, forthcoming).

12 'A great battle' — Bishop James A. Goold of Melbourne (1848–1864) and the State Aid for Religion Controversy

F.X. Martin

Let me plunge directly into my subject. I intend to concentrate on the campaign for state-aided religious schools which took place in Victoria during the crucial years, 1860–72. The most persistent group in the campaign were the Catholics — the majority of whom were Irish Catholics — with their leader, Bishop Goold. We shall look at the Victorian Catholics in terms of numbers, social status, wealth and political muscle. Besides, we wonder what made Goold tick, and tick so defiantly on occasions. What went into the making of the man? What prompted him to volunteer for Australia, and why a mere ten years later was he selected as first bishop of Melbourne? These are relevant questions but which space does not here permit to answer. As a missionary bishop his activities were multifarious, but we shall fasten on the question of the religious schools which for him were an essential part of his pastoral ministry. We have to examine why these schools, hitherto favoured by Church and state, should have become the focal point of sectarian strife and political controversy. We shall see that, with the writing on the wall for religious schools, Goold and the Victorian Catholics set about preparing for the prospect they greatly feared — withdrawal of state aid and the introduction of a comprehensive educational system in which religion would play no official part. The guillotine fell with the Education Act 1872.

At this point I shall indicate some of my conclusions on the central issue of the religious schools in Victoria. Goold and the Catholics, clergy and laity, never wavered in their determination to maintain their schools, unlike the Protestants who were divided on the issue and eventually accepted what seemed inevitable. Goold, in preparation for the day of reckoning, formed in February 1860 a small high-powered Catholic Education Committee with clergy and laity equally represented. The immediate purpose of the committee was to provide primary education for all Catholic children in Victoria. However, when it came to the crunch after 1872 it was the local committees throughout Victoria, and not the central Catholic Education Committee at Melbourne, which made it possible for these schools to continue. The impetus in the local committees came largely from the laity rather than from the clergy. Goold with an eye to the near future, when the primary schools would produce their fruits, was determined to have Catholic secondary schools which would equal the established grammar schools of the Scots and Anglicans. With this in mind he campaigned vigorously from 1853 onwards by letters and visits to Europe in order to induce the Jesuits, the Christian Brothers, and various orders of nuns — Loreto, Good Shepherd, and Mercy — to join him, but it took more than ten years before he began to achieve these objects, and then only by a combination of good luck and strong-arm tactics.

Nevertheless, his success meant that the Catholics in Victoria were better prepared than were the Catholics in New South Wales to meet the onslaught of 'godless education' (so they saw it) as embodied in recent legislation of both colonies. Catholic historians have given Archbishops Polding and Vaughan of Sydney credit for initiating the introduction of the teaching religious orders to Australia.[1] The painful fact, at least for Catholics, is that the two Benedictines, Archbishop Polding and his lieutenant Abbot Gregory, were responsible for isolating the Marists at Hunters Hill, driving the Irish Christian Brothers back to Ireland and the Irish Sisters of Charity to Tasmania, as well as excluding the Jesuits from secondary and university education at Sydney. In a word, Archbishop Polding was a near disaster for the cause of Catholic education in the great crisis of the 1870s. Not so with Goold at Melbourne. He and his collaborators rose to a daunting challenge at a time of unprecedented expansion and development in Victoria. He was not yet three years installed as bishop when the gold rush began, to be followed by a tidal wave of immigration. Victoria was on its way to becoming the richest and most populous state in Australia, a position it maintained from 1881 to 1891. In the same way and at the same time it was Victoria, I would argue, and not New South Wales which set the example and the pace in the sphere of Catholic education. Let us now look at the man who supervised this effort.

James Goold was born at Cork in 1812, joined the order of Augustinian friars in 1831, received his clerical education in Italy and because of a chance meeting at Rome with Ullathorne, Vicar General for Bishop Polding, volunteered for the Australian mission. By early 1838 he was at Sydney, and after a few months was in charge of the Campbelltown district in succession to the irrepressible Archpriest Joseph Therry. Within eight years Goold had made his name and was in line for a mitre.[2]

The consecration ceremony took place at Sydney on 6 August 1848 and Goold immediately made clear that he was leader of the Catholics in the Port Phillip area (or Victoria as it became in 1851). He was not flamboyant in speech or action, but he could and did act with a calculated flourish when occasion demanded it. He set out from Sydney in a carriage and four for Melbourne, claiming later that he was the first person to have covered the 600 miles in that fashion. He made the journey in grand pastoral style, stopping regularly *en route* to gather in the Catholics, say mass, preach, and administer the sacraments of baptism and confirmation. A realist, not necessarily a cynic, might well remark that he was living in a dream world.

True, he was officially pastor of all Catholics in what was shortly to become Victoria, a territory the size of Great Britain, but how many assistants had he? What were his resources? In fact he had just four priests, no nuns, no Brothers. The diocese had two small churches, a few chapels, six schools. The number of his flock was about 2000 out of a total civil population of around 10,000. That was it. But Gould realised that it was not what he had but what he represented. He quickly made it evident that he would stand on principle, even when it meant confrontation successively with the Anglican Church, with Archbishop Polding, with the civil authorities, and later with his fellow Catholic bishops in Australia. He was not impetuous, nor was he aggressive, but when principle was involved he chose his ground or at least the moment at which to take a stand, and then he resisted. When necessary he fought back, and this in particular when it was the question of the schools and state aid. He had that rare combination — particularly rare in an Irishman — of hot heart, cool head, and a disciplined tongue.

As dean of Campbelltown he had been noted for his good relations with the Protestants, but even before he appeared at Melbourne as its Catholic bishop the pitch had been queered by Charles Perry, the recently appointed first Anglican bishop of Melbourne. Perry arrived there in January 1848, and since Goold had not yet been installed at Melbourne his vicar general, Fr Geoghegan, took the opportunity to call on Perry, welcoming him to the colony and, as Perry was not at home, left his card. Perry replied curtly in writing that since Catholic priests were perverting the Gospel they should be considered as accursed and consequently he could not recognise them in any shape or form.[3] He later used stronger language about them.[4] The Lord Bishop of Melbourne was not going to suffer the indignity of allowing a papistical prelate to use *his* title, Bishop of Melbourne. Perry's appeal to La Trobe, Superintendent of Port Phillip, and to Governor FitzRoy to have such usage declared illegal was referred to the law officers at Sydney but was found to have no force in law in the colonies, whereas it would have in Great Britain and Ireland.[5] Nevertheless, the colonial secretary advised that Goold should as an expedient forgo the title, advice which he simply disregarded without comment.

Goold likewise put his foot down when the colonial authorities in 1849 issued regulations which required that he should (a) submit for Polding's approval all clerical appointments in Victoria, (b) approach the colonial authorities through Polding, who was not averse to this regulation.[6] The colonial authorities knew that in Polding they had a man of their own race, class and mentality, but that in Goold they had a man who was Irish and cast differently, in a Roman mould. Here again, Goold simply disregarded the colonial authorities and Polding, knowing that he had the law, certainly canon law, on his side.

The colonial authorities may have thought that Goold would rest on his oars after he had checked Bishop Perry and dismissed the government regulations attempting to subject him to Polding. In fact he was about to launch into the most contentious area of all — education, education linked to religion. And in the process he was going to wrong-foot Governor FitzRoy and Superintendent La Trobe. In February 1848 the government at Sydney had established a Denominational Schools Board, 'for the temporal regulation and inspection of the respective denominational schools in the colony of Port Phillip' [Victoria]. Of the five members one, Edward Curr, was to represent the Catholics. He was English and Catholic, a prominent figure in business and politics, but Goold was not consulted about the appointment nor did Curr get in touch with him. Goold sent word that the appointment had been badly handled, that Curr did not enjoy the confidence of the Catholics and their bishop. A sharp exchange of letters followed involving Governor Gipps and La Trobe, who informed Goold that his comments were uncalled for and that he had no right to interfere 'with the province of the executive'. Obviously they found it preposterous that their authority had been challenged by a newly appointed Romish prelate, Irish, who was a mere 36 years old, and whose followers were mainly Irish.[7]

Goold brought the dispute to a head, one might say to a conclusion, with a masterly letter of 30 June 1849. He began with the indisputable observation that although he was spiritual leader of the Catholics in Victoria he had not been consulted about Curr's appointment as the Catholic representative on the Board. He added that Curr had not got in touch with him, directly or indirectly, which he should have done if he held his appointment as representative of the Catholic community, 'of which I am the spiritual superior'. Goold pointed out that he had no objection to Curr's appointment in his own right, but that the official notice in the *Gazette* did not describe him as the Catholic representative. Goold gave a final turn to the screw when he contrasted what had been done to him at Melbourne with the correct deference shown to Polding at Sydney in that same issue of representation. The outcome was reasonable and perhaps predictable. Goold wrote to his vicar general, Geoghegan, on 6 December 1849, 'Our struggle with the Denominational Board has ended favourably'. Curr resigned and was succeeded by Westby, another Catholic, 'with orders to place himself in immediate communication with me about our schools. He has strictly observed his instructions. He called on me, at the request of La Trobe, to so inform me and that he would abide by these instructions.' It was obvious to those colonial authorities, and to Polding, that in Goold they had bought a Tartar.

During Goold's long rule as bishop — 38 active years — education was to be a most prominent, some might believe the dominant, feature of his activity. It had early caught Polding's eye. One of the earliest references to Goold in the Propaganda Archive that I know of, is in a report on the Australian Mission by Polding, dated from London, 7 September 1846.[8] Polding stated that the pastor at Campbelltown was Goold and added the comment, 'There we have a beautiful church under the title of St Joseph and a big school'. A year later when Polding was recommending Goold as one of the candidates for the see of Melbourne he described him as noted for founding schools. It must be understood however that Goold's intense interest in education was not that of the academic, still less was it that of the education specialist. Goold's outlook was that of a pastor, but it was not the blinkered or one-eyed view of a religious radical. He was opposed to the separation of religious and secular education on philosophical as well as on religious grounds. He had received a broad cultural education, first at a classical academy in Cork, then in the philosophy and theology house of the Augustinians at Perugia. He read the works of his luminous contemporary, John Henry Newman, and shared his judgement that the integrated person should combine mature humanist qualities with the transformation that comes to practising christians as children of God. But translating that high ideal into reality in colonial Melbourne and in the outlying settlements of Victoria required transcendant idealism and an iron will. That is the story of Goold's struggle in the field of education, but I must insert the caution that Goold had no hope of success were he not the expression and embodiment of what was ardently desired by the people whom he represented.

The vast majority of the Irish who formed part of the first British settlement in Australia were convicts and Catholics. However, it is usually forgotten that a substantial number of the rank-and-file soldiers guarding the colony were Irish and Catholic, for example 200 of them in the 48th regiment in 1815. There was also a significant thin layer of Irish among the military officers, naval personnel and civil administration. More accurately, they were Anglo-Irish and mostly Protestants. Ironically, they too had their counterparts among the Irish convicts, of whom about one-fifth were Protestant. By and large, however, the Irish convicts were Catholics, yet it must be remembered that, for example, of the 2086 transported from Ireland between 1791 and 1803 nearly a third were convicted for riot and sedition. And that number could probably be expanded. Nowadays they would be described as political prisoners. The fact remains, to quote Professor O'Farrell, that the Catholic Church in Australia was born in a prison.[9] Understandably, the Irish convicts were regarded officially with deep suspicion, which turned to genuine fear when some 300 Irish convicts attempted an armed rebellion at Castle Hill in 1804. Governor Brisbane was to declare in the early 1820s:[10]

every murder or diabolical crime which has been committed in the colony since my arrival [in 1821] has been perpetrated by Roman Catholics. And this I ascribe entirely to their barbarous ignorance and total want of education . . . They are benighted and bereft of every advantage that can adorn the mind of man.

In a word, the Catholics — Irish of course — were infected with a double dose of original sin. The official religion in the colony was Church of England. Only in 1820 were the first official Catholic chaplains (they were Irish) allowed to minister to the Australian community. The concession was not only from a sense of British justice but as a means of pacifying the potentially unruly Irish. By this time the Catholics in the colony constituted about a third of the population. Some were free settlers, but the bulk of them were convicts and freedmen, with little or no property.

The Irish were undoubtedly an unpredictable political class, substantial in numbers. In Ireland they had been a deprived majority, in Australia they were a depressed minority. Once in the colony they had to face two unpalatable facts absent for example from Irish settlers in the United States. They were still under British rule and there was still the Protestant religion, favoured and near to being an Established Church. In addition they suffered from a decision made in Rome. The Catholics in Australia had to be placed under the care of some bishop, who would be acceptable to Whitehall and who if possible would have behind him the resources of a religious order. At that time which order could be considered more English than the Benedictines? And so an apparently admirable choice was made of John Bede Polding. Though his appointment may have irked the Irish Catholics in the colony it did give them a recognised leader in Australia, and there were some immediate benefits after his arrival in 1835. The most important was the Church Act of 1836, introduced by Governor Richard Bourke, who was Irish and a Protestant. It gave Catholics and Presbyterians, as well as Anglicans, an official place in the sun and consequently a hand in the Treasury purse. Money was one thing, religious leaders were another. In 1839 there were 32 Catholic priests in the colony, six of them (including Polding) were English; 26 were Irish. That situation contained the seeds of discontent at Sydney, but the problem was avoided at Melbourne by the appointment of an Irishman, Goold.

The generalised statements about Catholics and Irish Catholics in Australia during the first half century of settlement have to be severely qualified once we come to consider Victoria, or Port Phillip as it was then styled. The colonisation of Port Phillip and the surrounding hinterlands did not commence until 1835, only three years before Goold arrived in Australia, and almost 50 years after the first settlement in New South Wales. The Irish who came to Australia, and particularly to Victoria were, to use a perceptive description by Professor MacDonagh, a 'founding people', unlike the role of the Irish in the United States. In Australia they formed almost one-third of the first settlements, and for more than a century Irish immigration continued substantially in the same proportion.[11]

Goold arrived as bishop at Melbourne in 1848; three years later Victoria became a separate colony, the first census was taken, and by a coincidence the gold rush began in that same year, 1851. The extraordinary economic expansion and upsurge of population which were immediate results thus coincided with Goold's advent as bishop. The inevitable consequences would have broken, or at least daunted, many a religious leader but he was young, vigorous, self-confident, some might say, over-confident. Besides, by 1851 he had 13 years of pastoral experience in Australia, and knew how to deal with the colonial authorities in Sydney and Melbourne, as well as with the curial officials in Rome. He was part of a new society, with a population mostly composed of immigrants who brought major changes to the inherited political and social structures. Their challenge to colonial and oligarchic rule encouraged genuine parliamentary and therefore democratic government, which had many advantages for the Irish immigrants but also saddled Goold with a host of problems, particularly in the realm of education.

The setting-up of the colony of Victoria in 1851 gave the Irish a heaven-sent opportunity to have a voice in public affairs. They began with the advantage, compared with other immigrants, of speaking English (even if with an Irish brogue) and of knowing how to use, and manipulate, parliamentary democracy. Political parties, election campaigns, voting, parliamentary procedures, had been absorbing national pastimes in Ireland since the late 1820s. The wave of immigration to Australia brought a host of members of what Professor MacDonagh calls 'the stricken professions' — politicians, journalists, lawyers, physicians and teachers, and many went to Melbourne, perhaps a greater proportion than to other parts of the continent. Their success in Victoria in public life during the first 40 years, 1851–91, is shown in three premiers, O'Shanassy, Gavan Duffy and O'Loghlen, in the fact that six successive Speakers in the legislature were Irish. In that period three out of every four of the attorneys-general and solicitors-general were Irish-born. Not all, by any means, were Catholic, and therefore there was not an

Irish legal Mafia. Indeed the Irish Catholics had deep internal divisions — a proof perhaps of their democracy — but with men such as O'Shanassy, Gavan Duffy and O'Grady in parliament a strong voice was assured when some crucial issue for Catholics, such as state aid for education, was under discussion. Nevertheless, though the Irish Catholics were numerically a sizeable section of the voting public — during Goold's time they were consistently at least one-fifth of the population — they were not a controlling minority in parliament, though on occasions their influence was positive and successful. In contrast with the Irish in the United States their ratio in Victoria was high in the rural and agricultural areas, lower in the towns, cities, and mining settlements. Constituencies such as Villiers-Heytesbury and Dalhousie, those green-ribboned areas with an Irish-born Catholic vote over 40 per cent, were exceptional.

A benefit awaiting immigrants to Australia, during Goold's first 24 years as bishop, and not found in America, was state aid for religion and education, even for Catholics. This must have come as a surprise to most Catholics from Ireland and Great Britain. The benefit had begun with the stipend for two Catholic chaplains in 1820, was augmented when Ullathorne and further Catholic priests came out in the early 1830s, and went still further when Polding, the first bishop of any denomination in Australia, was voted an annual salary of £500. These hand-outs were given as concessions not as of right.

The great change came with Governor Bourke's Church Act of 1836 which accepted the realities of the situation in the colony and in his own words granted state support 'to every one of the three Grand Divisions of Christianity indifferently', though his hope was that in due time they would 'roll off state support like saturated leeches'. The Act was essentially a practical concession, and did not abandon the official principle of Anglican supremacy, but the state was no longer exclusively Anglican in its commitments. Bourke's real interest was in education not religion. He wanted education available for all children under his jurisdiction and believed rightly that the religious denominations could not cope with the total problem. For this reason he aimed at state control of education, but since, unlike the Education Act of 1872, he had no wish to exclude religion, he thought the solution lay in adopting what was known as the Irish National School System of 1831, which allowed for religious instruction of a general Christian kind, without clearly defined doctrines. That was the essential weakness of his proposal, as it was in the Irish National School System.[12] The Protestant Churches were almost unanimously opposed to the scheme, and though the Catholics initially favoured it, Bourke was forced to drop the proposal. The upshot was public education, provided to a limited extent only on a denominational basis, and state-aided on the pound for pound principle. It was not a generous policy but for Irish Catholics used for so long in their own country to deprivation under British rule it was half the loaf. The system was adequate for towns and well-filled populated areas but since it left large rural districts with no schools the authorities considered the situation as intolerable.

Governor FitzRoy sought a solution in 1848 by establishing some national schools, mainly for rural districts, with their own board. This meant that the administrative structure had to contain two boards, for the denominational and national schools. The compromise did not please the colonial authorities who saw it not as a healthy dual administration but as duplication, with unnecessary expense. Above all, it meant they did not fully control the situation, as government officials want to, in every century, in every country. No wonder they were dismayed when the survey in 1851, on the recognition of Victoria as a separate colony, showed that of the 111 public schools receiving state aid only 11 were National. This meant that the Christian churches had effective control of education. Why should parsons and priests, with their limited interests, dominate this crucial area which concerned all the people irrespective of their beliefs? It was a persuasive argument and it gained increasing force as Victoria, under the impact of the gold rush and massive immigration, changed out of all previous proportions.

The problems for Goold, in terms of churches and schools, multiplied to an intimidating extent in proportion to the multiplication of population. He had 10,000 Catholics to care for in 1848, 18,000 in 1851, and after three more years the number had multiplied to 45,000. It is helpful for our purposes to see the Catholic increase in the context of the population expansion of the whole state of Victoria and in comparison with New South Wales. In December 1851 the population of Victoria was 97,000, less than half that in New South Wales, but under the impetus of the gold rush which began in that same year it began to level with, and then outstrip, New South Wales. Within ten years, by December 1861, Victoria counted a population of over half a million, and by March 1886 —

within a few months of Goold's death — it had reached the 1 million mark, ahead of New South Wales. It took more than 10 years, the end of 1891, for New South Wales to surpass Victoria. The same tale can be told for the Catholic population during Goold's episcopate. It has already been mentioned that in 1851 he had 18,000 Catholics under his care, and that in 1854 they had grown to 45,000. By 1861 they were almost 110,000 Catholics in Victoria. Ten years later, in 1871, there were 170,000 registered Catholics in Victoria, while New South Wales counted 147,000.

The Catholic diocese of Melbourne, despite its growing pains, had considerable advantages in comparison with Sydney. It covered a smaller area, but it had a greater Catholic population, who at least in the mining areas had more wealth at their disposal than had their co-religionists in New South Wales. There was tension between bishop and clerics and laity in the Catholic diocese of Melbourne as in Sydney, but Melbourne had the advantage of a bishop who was Irish, treating with clergy and followers who were predominantly Irish. Goold had their measure as he proved in two major disputes. He had the further advantage that with his tight control of diocesan affairs he was able, with greater ease than Polding, to impress his stamp on a community in Victoria which was only in the second and more important stage of formation. Whereas Polding for a variety of reasons divided his New South Wales territory into a number of suffragan dioceses — Armidale (1862), Goulburn (1862), Maitland (1865) and Bathurst (1865) — Gould did not do likewise until 1874 with Sandhurst and Ballarat. I believe it is significant that it was only after the battle-lines were drawn by the Education Act 1872 that Goold felt free to subdivide his diocese.

All during those intervening years Goold was increasingly conscious that the day of reckoning for the denominational schools was approaching, and he prepared accordingly. There was an apparent contradiction in the fact that while there was a rising tide of popular and professional opinion in favour of a universal secular system of education, and with it the abolition of state aid for religion and therefore for the denominational schools, the annual grant to the Christian religion rose not steadily but dramatically. It had been stipulated as £6000 in the Constitution Act 1851, was increased to £30,000 in 1853 and to £50,000 in 1854. This was not intended as a greater favour for religion and denominational schools but as a response to the mushroom growth in population and with it the need in conscience for politicians to provide education for the rising generation. The only major educational system available was that of the denominational schools and they therefore reaped the unexpected financial harvest. But for those who had political eyes to see the storm clouds were obviously on the horizon and approaching fast.

It must have been a wry satisfaction for those of the secularist politicians who were shrewd — and many of them were — to know that the increasing golden stream was carrying the denominational schools towards a disastrous waterfall. If you establish a need for an individual or for a community by ample benefactions they quickly become dependent on those grants. Let me hasten to add that I am not suggesting that the secularist politicians — most of them with a genuine anxiety to ensure education for the young — had plotted a Machiavellian trap for the religious leaders. Circumstances in Victoria created an urgent need for universal education; the secularist politicians were prepared for a time to fund the denominational schools, but then to create a vacuum by withdrawing state aid for denominational schools. Inevitably, only the state could apparently fill the vacuum. Not many religious leaders of the different Christian denominations — Anglicans, Presbyterians, Catholics, Wesleyans, Baptists — saw or foresaw the pitfalls. Goold did. I am not presenting him as an ecclesiastical genius, pocket Napoleon, though he had a physical resemblance to the dumpy little Corsican corporal. Like Bonaparte he must have resembled a sack of potatoes on the back of a horse, which he so often used on his pastoral expeditions.

The year 1856 is a red-letter date in these events. Victoria became a separate colony by the Constitution Act 1851 but full responsible government did not come until 1856. Clause 53 of the constitution is crucial to our story. It declared that state aid to religion could not be abolished except by Act of Parliament passed by an absolute majority of both Houses. The all-important clause about an absolute majority was to give the denominational schools, in democratic terms, a hardly justified stay of execution for 15 years. Let me explain what I mean by 'hardly justified in democratic terms'.

The election of 1856 brought into Parliament a large majority committed to a programme which was 'liberal', democratic and secular. One of their agreed four main objectives was the abolition of state aid to religion, but the stumbling-block was clause 53 of the constitution, to which I have already referred. Three Bills, repealing clause 53, were passed in the Lower House by large majorities between 1857 and 1861 but were thrown out in each case by the Council. The second Bill gained a small, but not absolute, majority in the Council, and was therefore defeated. Yet, to the understandable exasperation of the secularists in their year of election triumph, 1856, over 80 per cent of state aid went to denominational schools, which received £70,000, in contrast with a mere £15,000 for the 'National Schools'. The secularists fumed at their own impotence and sought a solution in what is known as the Common Schools Act 1862.[13] It was the last attempt to compromise before the Education Act 1872 inundated the denominational schools in 1872. When the flood subsided Goold and his followers were among the few religious groups who survived, intent on maintaining their denominational schools.

The Common Schools Act established a single Board of Education, instead of the previous two. It was composed of five laymen, representing the five denominations — Anglican, Catholic, Presbyterian, Wesleyan and Jewish — and supplied limited state aid to schools which had an average daily attendance of at least 20 children, whose teachers were approved of by the Board, and which guaranteed at least four hours daily for secular instruction alone. Religion was not excluded, it was simply ignored, which meant that the denominational schools were free to maintain their religious instruction. Two main problems were not solved. There were rural areas where education was deficient or absent; there were settled and urban areas where there was duplication with denominational and national schools. Inevitably and urgently these two problems would force the authorities to formulate a new policy which would ensure equal educational opportunity for all children of the state.

The first Catholic representative on the Board was a distinguished English convert, W.H. Archer, Registrar-General of Victoria, and his successor was a prominent politician, Michael O'Grady, a Member of Parliament. Out of all the representatives they only were resolute in upholding the denominational cause. Moreover, the dice were loaded against the denominational schools. It was specified in Parliament that the Board was instructed to restrict the influence of the denominations in education. In effect this meant reducing the teaching of religion. And that is what happened. In 1866 a Royal Commission reported on 'the comparative neglect on the part of the clergy of the Protestant denominations of religious teaching in denominational as well as in other schools'. In 1869 the Inspector of the Board stated that only 42 out of 299 national schools gave religious instruction. These facts, given as information and not as criticism by the Inspector-General, are an enlightening indication of a noticeable change taking place in the social character of Victoria. Melbourne, described as being in the 1850s 'a church going town' had by the 1860s become a bustling commercial centre, beginning to compete with Sydney as the leading city in Australia, having among its professional classes, especially the lawyers and journalists, men who were anxious to be abreast of the latest European advances in science, political ideas, social development. In such a golden city men bowed the knee to Mammon rather than to God. With the majority of the population in Victoria still of rough pioneering stock, the men of Melbourne, or rather the very limited number who were rationalists and sceptics, were able to take more than full advantage of what appeared to be the ominous implications for religion from the findings of Darwin in science and in the queries of agnostics about the Bible. The Christian denominations were divided not only into different sects but in some instances into bitterly opposed groups, who had no agreed common policy about the place of religion in the schools. Goold and the Catholics had clear-cut ideas on what they wanted but that very fact triggered off the vigilant anti-Catholicism of the low church Protestantism which was manifest at Melbourne in the persons of Bishop Perry, Archdeacon Macartney, and the Reverend John Dunmore Lang.

Is it any wonder then that a succession of high-minded administrators such as Governor Bourke, Governor Gipps and Hugh Childers, the Inspector for denominational schools, took the attitude of 'a plague on all your houses' when they looked at the stark reality of a rapidly expanding Victoria and the confusing behaviour of the Christian denominations? They decided that the only constructive policy was a compulsory, secular, education, leaving it to the denominations to fend for themselves. The hard educational statistics in 1861 showed that there were more than 50,000 pupils, of whom 37,000 were in church schools and 14,000 in national schools. The devastating fact emerged that these figures still accounted for less than half of the colony's children. That conclusion was borne out by a Royal Commission in 1866, chaired by the Attorney-General, Higinbotham, an Irishman, which sharply criticised the effect of the 1862 Act and commented that 'a very large proportion of children in the colony still received no education'. The response came the following year, 1867, when he introduced a Bill with a widely accepted principle of compulsory education but harnessed it to a frank proposal for the withdrawal of state aid from 'denominational schools and every sectarian system of instruction'. He thought to quieten the expected hostile reaction in Catholic and Anglican circles by granting that religious instruction of a general kind was still to be 'encouraged and sanctioned' in the state schools, but he exposed his personal convictions when he spoke in Parliament of what he described as the 'pestilent energy' of the sects.

That energy quickly manifested itself. The Anglican *Church News* of 1 June 1867 dismissed the Bill with a lapidary comment, 'The Broad Arrow is stamped everywhere' — the government in control of the buildings, the teachers, the curriculum, the children; and with religion all but forbidden. The Catholic reaction was no less definite and was better organised, but with less effect because of the lurking fear, even among possible Anglican allies, that Rome had sinister designs on Australia, particularly since the advent to Melbourne in 1865 of the Jesuits, known to be in Goold's inner counsels. I shall speak of them shortly. The decisive intervention in 1867 was by Dr Perry, the Anglican bishop, as we know from the letter which Dr Brownless, Vice-Chancellor of Melbourne University, wrote on 27 June 1867 to Goold then in Rome. Brownless reported:[14]

> We have had great excitement, since you left, in opposition to the iniquitous Bill proposed by Higinbotham. The Catholics acted very unitedly on the occasion, and the final and extinguishing blow was given by Dr Perry in a letter which appeared in the *Argus* and evidently took the Attorney-General unawares . . . Up to [the time of] that letter appearing it was not thought improbable that the Bill would pass the Lower House, but when Dr Perry characterised it as irremediably bad, its doom was no longer doubtful.

It may well have been too expensive a victory. It helped to convince any wavering liberals that since Anglicans and Catholics would not compromise, even with government assurance of religious instruction of a general kind, that henceforth no quarter should be given and that the only realistic solution was a comprehensive system of secular education, devoid of religion. The liberals and secularists were not anti-religious, except for a vocal section of radicals, but many of them believed that religion was a spent force except as a divisive influence and that its place should, and inevitably would, be taken by a new secular humanism through the medium of education. Perfection was round the educational corner.

The secularists, convinced that they were on the rising tide, increased pressure on the denominational schools. In 1868 the Education Board began a process intended to phase out the denominational schools silently, but Goold and his Catholic Committee of Education refused to stay silent. The strategy of the secularists was to establish national schools in areas where there were already denominational schools, and as a first consequence to withdraw state aid from the denominational schools there, on the score of economy. It was an apparently commonsense policy to prevent duplication. Why pay twice in any area for teachers and resources when the money was needed urgently for areas where there were no schools? It was based immediately on the argument of economy but was motivated by the liberal ideal of making education available to all children of the state, irrespective of religious allegiance.

How did the Churches react to the stark alternatives facing them? Minor Protestant sects, such as Baptists and Presbyterians by the logic of their own religious traditions, were willing to go along with the policy of the secularists. The Anglicans were divided. Their leader, Bishop Perry, wished to retain religious instruction in the schools but did not insist on it, and was prepared to see denominational schools disappearing from the rural districts. His primary concern as head of the Anglican Church was to safeguard its vested property rights. In the Anglican tradition he did not object to state control of education, and as a conscientious member of the establishment he accepted the principle that adequate education must be provided for all the children of the state. A minority section of the Anglican Education Committee found a different voice in their outspoken secretary, Macartney, dean of Melbourne. In effect, though not in so many words, he was willing to take his stand with Goold and the Catholics, believing that Christian children should be trained in schools with a special atmosphere.

The government Education Board decided in 1868 to initiate a policy of eliminating the denominational schools by withdrawing state aid from them. To justify this deprivation a new state school, open to all, was to be set up in the same area as an existing denominational school. Since money would be made available for one school only it would go to the state school. The Education Board took a formal decision, the controversial 'Rule 63', to spell out the method being adopted, and when the Catholics objected that this would be in violation of the Common Schools Act 1862 the Board appealed to the Attorney-General, Higinbotham, who ruled in favour of the Board. The Catholics refused to admit defeat, took a test case — the withdrawal of state aid from their school at Lauriston — and brought it to the Supreme Court. There finally it was ruled on 3 September 1872 by Chief Justice Stawell that Regulation 63 'is entirely opposed to section 10 of the Common Schools Act'.[15] Thus the Lauriston school case passed into Australian legal history, but though at the time it seemed to the Catholics to be a famous victory it rang hollow. Even before the Lauriston case was initiated by the Catholics in April 1871, the liberals had decided that what they needed was a victory in Parliament, not in the law courts, and that the great obstacle to their goal — an Education Bill imposing a totally secular policy on all state schools — was clause 55 of the constitution which required an absolute majority of the Council to make such a Bill law. In 1869 the liberals campaigned again in the Assembly to have the clause repealed in favour of a simple majority, but the Council stood firm — for the last time. The following year, 1870, the Council gave way, not because of a change of heart but because of the political conviction that it was unjust and dangerous to continue resisting the resolute will of the majority of the elected members of the assembly. With the repeal of that clause — truly a famous victory for the liberals — the way was now open for the introduction of a new Education Bill.

By 1872 the Catholics, led by Bishop Goold and his Education Committee of clerics and laity, were now alone of all the denominations in the process of expanding their network of schools in proportion to the population growth. The other Churches had gradually, but in many cases reluctantly, given way to the extension of state authority. Parents were becoming used to state schools from which religion was officially excluded, where teachers had an assured higher income and where modern facilities would be provided by the government. What arguments did Goold and the Catholics advance for their refusal to join the state system and at the same time to expect state aid for their own school system? When four Catholic MPs had opposed Michie's Education Bill in October 1857, and asked that adequate provision be made for denominational and specifically Catholic schools, their arguments were presented by Patrick O'Brien under four main headings — the Catholics formed one-fifth of the population; they had proved themselves to be good and loyal subjects; they held a substantial amount of property; they contributed as much proportionately to the public purse as any other group, and they therefore had a democratic right to a full share of public money for the schools, which they needed because of their religious conscience, itself an accepted democratic principle. Goold issued a special pastoral on education, 1 January 1860, repeating O'Brien's arguments but adding what had been inferred by him, namely that the bishop's authority as pastor must be upheld. These were the basic arguments which the Catholics advanced during those turbulent years before the 1872 Educational Bill was enacted.

From the beginning of his rule as bishop, Goold had a clear conviction of his obligation as pastor. In his lengthy letter to La Trobe on 30 June 1849, on the controverted question of Curr's appointment as Catholic representative on the Denominational Schools Board, he referred at one point to the Catholic community, 'of which I am the spiritual superior', and at a later point described himself as 'the guardian of Catholic education in Port Phillip'. This continued to be his stance up to 1872 and beyond it, to his death. Finally, let us look briefly at three episodes which recapture the ideas, the drama and the passionate feelings of those involved in the education struggle. First, the coming of the religious orders, particularly the Jesuits, to Victoria; secondly, the inflammatory elections at Melbourne in June 1872 which were to have a decisive effect on the passing of the Education Bill later in the year; thirdly, the impact of the Education Bill on the Catholic community during those first ten crucial years, 1872–82.

By the time Goold founded the Catholic Education Committee in February 1860 he already had laid a solid infrastructure of primary schools in 88 places, most of them with separate boys' and girls' schools, staffed with 143 teachers and 23 assistants, all lay people.[16] Goold realised that unless the Catholic community moved promptly into secondary education, which was then getting underway in Victoria, they would continue to be gravely disadvantaged. Lay teachers were available for primary schools, but by what magical wave of the hand was he to produce qualified secondary teachers — rare specimens then in the colony? Here is where the international character of the Catholic Church was his salvation, with its religious families of priests, brothers and nuns. Goold himself was a member of a religious order, with the confidence and knowledge how to present his case. He sought assistance from France, Italy, Great Britain and Ireland, but since the majority of his flock were Irish he concentrated his efforts on the religious orders in Ireland. His efforts in the 1850s bore no fruit but as the education controversy intensified in Australia so did his pressure on certain religious orders.

Goold wanted only the best for Victoria. So, for boys' secondary education he sought the Jesuits and the Christian Brothers. For girls there was a greater variety of teaching nuns, if they could be induced to come to Australia. Goold secured what he wanted, partly because he was lucky, partly because he made his luck. He was set on having the Jesuits in his diocese even if the prospect sent spasms of alarm down the spines of Protestants in Victoria. Fortune smiled on him. The veteran archpriest J.J. Therry, who died conveniently for Goold in 1862, left the bulk of his considerable estate for the introduction of the Irish Jesuits in Australia. This eased the problem for them of financing a mission so far overseas. Once Goold had cleared permission with the Jesuit general at Rome the Irish Jesuits responded with generosity equal to Therry's. They sent as pioneers two of their best men, Joseph Lentaigne and William Kelly, who arrived in September 1865. Lentaigne had until recently been head of the Jesuits in Ireland. Kelly was a sparkling intellectual and a riveting preacher. They were followed by a succession of dedicated Jesuits who were put in charge of St Patrick's College, Melbourne, and were given pastoral care of a large district comprising Richmond, Hawthorn and Kew. Two very different public events within the first ten years of Jesuit presence at Melbourne proved what a difference the Jesuits were making for the Catholic community in Victoria.[17] When Duke Alfred of Edinburgh came on a state visit to Melbourne in 1867 and the public schools gave a display in his awesome royal presence the English ode for the occasion was composed by Fr Kelly and the Latin address was delivered by one of the pupils of St Patrick's College. The second event, and which held greater importance for the Jesuit Fathers and for the pupils of St Patrick's College, was the success of the candidates from St Patrick's College in the examinations both for the public service and for matriculation to Melbourne University in 1871. The Catholics had arrived, but only just in time.

Recognition must also be given to the Irish Christian Brothers who were forced willy-nilly, in the spirit of the Biblical wedding feast, to participate in Bishop Goold's educational activities. The Brothers, invited to Sydney by Archbishop Polding, had taught there from 1843 but withdrew to Ireland in 1847, licking their wounds. They were not agreeable to return to Australia but Goold refused to take 'No' for an answer. At his request the Cardinal

Prefect of Propaganda Fide, Barnabo, issued what was in effect an order to Brother Hoare, Superior General of the Brothers, in October 1867, that a community be sent to Melbourne. Four Brothers, led by 34-year-old Brother Ambrose Treacy, arrived there in November 1868. Their success in Australia was phenomenal. When Brother Treacy retired to the ranks in 1900 there were 130 Brothers in Australia, with 24 houses and 35 schools.[18]

The success of the nuns was even more remarkable, though it has not yet received the recognition it deserves, even from Catholic historians.[19] The Mercy nuns were the first sisterhood established in Melbourne, when Mother Ursula Frayne and two Sisters arrived there in March 1857. They were the first swallows of a Catholic summer in Victoria but space does not allow opportunity even to outline how fundamental was to be the contribution of nuns to Catholic education throughout Australia as well as in Victoria. It is a largely untold chapter of dedication to the underprivileged and in which the nuns had to suffer as much from Catholic bishops as from Protestant bigotry.[20]

The elections at Melbourne in 1872 were a landmark for Catholic education in Victoria. Goold, apparently despite advice to the contrary from his lay and clerical advisers, decided to make the state aid issue a political touchstone. He published a pastoral in 1872 on the education issue, in the expectation that he could call out a *grande armée* of Catholic voters to rout the secularists. Paradoxically Goold's achievement was to call out a Protestant vote, alarmed at the prospect of the 'huge and hideous fabric of priest craft' directed from Rome. Goold was to be defeated as thoroughly as had been Napoleon in Russia.

J.W. Stephen, the successful secularist candidate in the elections, expressed the conviction that the Education Act would 'drive a wedge' between the Catholic clergy and their people. Nevertheless the result of Goold's defeat was to force the Catholic community in Victoria to decide that they would go it alone if they wished to retain their religious identity in education.[21] This they did, not without some misgivings and with considerable sacrifices. It was only in the 1960s, and in a very different political climate, that their policy began to reap the official benefits that Goold and his people had fought for in the 1860s.

Notes and References

1. This view is expressed starkly by Monsignor C. Duffy in *Footprints*, vol.4, no. 8 (1982), p.8, 'Vaughan's name is synonymous with the climax of the education struggle — so much so that Polding's part is sometimes overlooked, yet all the great initiatives in education up to that time were taken by Polding.' R. Fogarty in his magisterial two-volume work, *Catholic Education in Australia, 1806–1950* (Melbourne UP, Melbourne, 1959), vol.2, p.475, had pointedly stated, 'The crowning of Archbishop Vaughan, therefore, as the hero of Catholic education in Australia is quite inaccurate. There were warriors in plenty before his time.' But such legends die hard.

2. The standard account of Goold is embodied in P.F. Moran, *History of the Catholic Church in Australasia* (Oceanic Publishing Co., Sydney [1896]), Ch. 17, 'The Catholic Church in Victoria'. Written in the same spirit is the version by W. Ebsworth, *Pioneer Catholic Victoria* (Polding Press, Melbourne, 1973). Critical assessments of Goold on particular issues are available in T.L. Suttor, *Hierarchy and Democracy in Australia, 1788–1870* (Melbourne UP, Melbourne, 1965); and J.N. Molony, *The Roman Mould of the Australian Catholic Church* (Melbourne UP, Melbourne, 1969). For much information and a partial view of Goold see M. Pawsey, *The Demon of Discord: Tensions in the Catholic Church in Victoria, 1853–1864* (Melbourne UP, Melbourne, 1982); M. Pawsey, *The Popish Plot: Culture Clashes in Victoria, 1860–1863* (Studies in the Christian Movement, Sydney, 1983). For an overall factual account of Goold see the notice by J.R.J. Grigsby in *Australian Dictionary of Biography*, vol.4, 1851–90, pp.265–7. Indispensable is the education setting, 1854–84, presented by P. O'Farrell, *The Catholic Church in Australia: a Short History, 1788–1967* (Geoffrey Chapman, London, 1969), Ch. 3; P. O'Farrell, *The Catholic Church and Community: an Australian History*, 2nd edn (New South Wales UP, Sydney, 1985), Ch. 3. For enlightening information on Goold in his old age, as crotchety and uncooperative, see the letters edited by Ian Waters in *Footprints*, vol.4, no. 1 (1980) and no. 2 (1981). A concentrated study of Goold has been undertaken by Frances O'Kane; the first part of her work has been published, *A Path is Set: the Catholic Church in the Port Phillip District and Victoria, 1839–1862* (Melbourne UP, Melbourne, 1976); the remainder, taking the story up to 1886, has been presented for a PhD degree to the University of Melbourne. I am heavily indebted to D.F. Bourke, who has prepared an official history of the Catholic diocese of Melbourne for publication in 1986 and generously placed the results of his research at my disposal.

3. See the letter, cited in O'Kane, *Path is Set*, pp.26–7. A. de Q. Robin, *Charles Perry, Bishop of Melbourne* (Western Australia UP, Perth, 1967), pp.46–7, skates over this incident, describing Perry's letter as 'courteous'.

4. Perry described the Church of Rome as 'apostate and idolatrous' and its members as 'victims of satanic delusion', in the January 1850 issue of *Melbourne Church of England Messenger*; see O'Kane, *Path is Set*, pp.48–50.

5. See the letter of the law officers, J.H. Plunkett and W. Foster, to the Colonial Secretary, E. Deas Thomson, 21 November 1848, in Moran, *History of the Catholic Church in Australasia*, p.745.

6. See letter of Goold to his Vicar General, F.B. Geoghegan, Melbourne, 6 December 1849, calendared by J. Keany in *Footprints*, vol.1, no. 9 (1973), p.17.

7. Ibid.

8. Polding to Propaganda, London, 7 September, 1846, in APF (Archives of the Sacred Congregation of Propaganda Fide, Rome) Scritt. rif. nei congressi, 1846–47, Oceania, vol.3, fo. 24v.

9. P. O'Farrell, 'The Church in Australia', in *Dublin Review*, no. 508 (1966), p.139.

10. Ibid., p.137.

11. O. MacDonagh, 'The Irish in Victoria, 1851–91; a Demographic Essay', in T.D. Williams (ed.), *Historical Studies*, vol.8 (Gill and Macmillan, Dublin and London, 1971), p.68.

12. For the actual effect of the National School system in Ireland see M. Daly, 'The Development of the National School System, 1831–40', in A. Cosgrove and D. McCartney (eds), *Studies in Irish History presented to R. Dudley Edwards* (University College, Dublin, 1979), pp.150–75.

13. See P.J. Pledger, 'The Common Schools Board, 1862–1872', in A.G. Austin (ed.), *Melbourne Studies in Education, 1959–60* (Melbourne UP, Melbourne, 1961), pp.95–114.

14. A.C. Brownless, 117 Collins St, Melbourne, 27 June 1867, to Goold at Santa Maria in Posterula, Rome, in Melbourne Catholic Historical Commission Archives, Group H, no. x.

15. See Fogarty, *Catholic Education in Australia*, vol.1, p.203.

16. See Catholic Education Committee Minutes and Correspondence, vol.II (7 February 1860–8 May 1872), in Melbourne Catholic Historical Commission Archives, pp.61, 63, 65, 67, for the list of schools, teachers and assistants, on 1 January 1861, in Victoria.

17. Here I acknowledge my debt to Fr Joseph Dargan, S.J., provincial of the Irish Jesuits, and to Fr Fergus O'Donoghue, S.J., archivist of the Irish Jesuit Province, for allowing me free access in 1985 to the Australian files, 1860–1930, in the archives, hitherto classified as confidential and unavailable to academic historians.

18. See K.K. O'Donoghue, *P.A. Treacy and the Christian Brothers in Australia and New Zealand* (Polding Press, Melbourne, 1963).

19. Within the last two decades a host of minor studies have been published about individual nuns and local convents in Australia. They contain much useful information but are intended to edify rather than to present in a critical spirit. More recently a new approach is evident, critical and with an overall view, e.g. the biography of the foundress of the Mercy nuns in Australia, M.X. O'Donoghue, *Mother Vincent Whitty: Woman and Educator in a Masculine Society* (Melbourne UP, Melbourne, 1972); and M.R. MacGinley, *Roads to Sion: the Presentation Sisters in Australia, 1866–1980* (Boolarong, Brisbane, 1983).

20. What Mother Mary McKillop (1842–1909), foundress of the Sisters of St Joseph, an entirely Australian order, had to endure from episcopal authorities is well known, but many of the other pioneering Sisters had similar experiences. It is relevant to note that Mary McKillop was born in Melbourne, educated by the Mercy nuns there, and had the support of Bishop Goold.

21. Two published items deserve particular attention in this context. (i) the report of the Royal Commission on Education, Melbourne, 1883. This thorough investigation of 1000 printed pages, with the final 300 pages on religion in education, presents evidence, under oath, of witnesses, Catholic and non-Catholic, from a decade of experience of the 1872 Educational Act. (ii) E. Murphy, 'The First Ten Years: Catholic Education in Victoria, 1872–1882', in *Footprints*, vol.2, no. 1 (1974), pp.6–12.

13 Writing the History of Irish-Australia

Patrick O'Farrell

In general histories of the American Irish, one may note the prevalence of dedications to, and acknowledgement of, the role of parents, affirmations of debt to family and an Irish world, and to a tradition of Irish Catholicism, however Americanised: perhaps the most engaging of these is in Andrew M. Greeley's *That Most Distressful Nation. The Taming of the American Irish*: 'To My Parents . . . from whom I learned both the joys and the anguish of being Irish. On the whole it hasn't been a bad balance.'[1] But most are much more respectful to Dad and Mum, and some even so in Gaelic. Here are works arising naturally from *pietàs*, piety in the best sense, the outgrowth of a sense of familiar belonging and continuity, however sharp the critical internal stance, however professional, or unprofessional, the historical methodology. I was going to contrast this significantly with the matter-of-fact, unsentimental, good working-class stance of Irish Australia, typified in the dedication of Vincent Buckley's *Cutting Green Hay*[2] — 'For Solidarity' — no nonsense here about dear old Dad came weeping from the mountains of Mourne, to sire me in this harsh distant land, but terse and straight from the shoulder, 'For Solidarity' — when caution took me for a dekko to P.S. Cleary's *Australia's Debt to the Irish Nation Builders*.[3] There I read:

> From the son of a little Irish mother to his compatriots who cherish a double heritage — their sunny native land, and the tradition of unswerving fidelity to spiritual and national ideals — brought from Tir na n-og, the old land that is ever young. Lest we forget.

It's all there — even the bit of Irish, and an echo of Anzac Day: Lest we forget. But that was 50 years ago, 1933, and the American dedications are now. My point stands. My own books carry no

217

dedications, and if Buckley wants to toast Solidarity in two words, good for him: it may be that he sees Ireland as his 'Imagination's home'[4] but *Memory Ireland*[5] indicates that he was by no means comfortable while living there.

This matter of dedications or their absence is not a trivial irrelevancy, but rather a symptom of contrasting styles, and differing attitudes to Irish heritage. Why is it that I am embarrassed by the fulsome sentimentality of these American declarations? Why is it that I feel no need to tie my own work in to some ancestral tradition? Basically because I do not see myself as Irish, whatever others may think, a self-assessment which, I believe, is general to a distinction between the Irish American and the Irish British-colonial experience. The colonies were too far and too British to foster or even allow the survival of a sense of debt or belonging to Ireland amongst the local born, a deficiency noted by the Sydney *Freeman's Journal* as early as 14 July 1855. I wish to example my own case, not least because it will allow me to explore why, and how, I come to be writing a history of the Irish in Australia, without seeing it as ancestor worship.

Despite the 30 years I have lived here, despite my Australian citizenship, I am not an Irish-Australian. For all my Catholicism, my authors were Maritain, Mauriac, Chesterton, and for that matter T.S. Eliot, C.S. Lewis; my New Zealand parish was founded by French Marist priests. And my father, from Tipperary, in contrast apparently with Irish fathers in America, seldom spoke about Ireland, and when he did, made clear that he was glad to have left it. He had no quaint broguish sayings, no brooding dark moods, never got drunk, was a Justice of Peace, enjoyed the races and loved New Zealand. He laughed a lot and the house was full of visitors and talk, mainly politics, for he was president of the local branch of the New Zealand Labour Party. Priests and Marist Brothers were constant visitors, for the talk, and for Dad's home brew: each year he made and bottled an 80-gallon cask. I learnt nothing, consciously at any rate, of Irish history or culture, save that it was a joke: Brother Egbert, a marvellously eccentric New Zealander, persisted in using the Latin period to teach us epic poems he had composed about incidents of ancient Irish history, Brian Boru and the like. There was a pub in town of that name, so Brian had local meaning. The poems were farce and we learnt no Latin. My first acquaintance with Irish history came in 1964, when, aged 30, I decided to read myself into it, following conversations with the then Irish Ambassador to Australia, Dr Eoin MacWhite.

I intrude this personal detail to support a point of substance which might be lost in the fog of the obvious created by my name and Catholicism. Neither, or more or less neither, is the reason for writing a history of Irish Australia, and if my case of colonial ignorance is extreme, it nevertheless illustrates a tendency to a sceptical lack of deference to the Irish tradition very different from American filio-pietism. No; my reasons were dramatic and explanatory, not sentimental or apologetic: I wished to be excited and amused, not to worship.

To plot the route to this point. In the early 1960s I became bored with the history I had been researching for the previous ten years, that of the Australian and New Zealand labour movements: in 1982 I published an article on boredom as historical motivation, which investigates that condition as a stimulus to much human behaviour — including my own.[6] Anyway, turning to Russian history I found ample revolutions, and plenty of action and agony — indeed, more agony than I bargained for in the necessity to master the language before gaining research access. Whilst researching within the boundaries of English, I came upon a British White Paper of 1918 which investigated Bolshevik dealings with Sinn Féin, of which I had never heard. It was this matter I took up with Dr MacWhite, a Russian expert, which led eventually to my introducing the teaching of Russian history at University College, Dublin in 1965, but immediately to contacts with the Irish National Association in Sydney which at that time (1964) had among its membership several veterans of the 1916 rebellion period. I remember the delight with which I was regaled by one of the Organ brothers with tales of his smuggling, as a seaman on the Australian–American run, of seditious newspapers and revolutionary messages from insurrectionary Ireland. Ah, here were my own people, my hoped-for history, not so far as I was concerned in any Irish context, but in the tradition of my boyhood magazines, the British *Champion* and American *Flying Aces* which had been my boyhood war-time New Zealand reading and re-reading. The founder of the Irish National Association, Dr Dryer, had kept everything and collected more: his widow gave me access to the lot, together with her trust and friendship. I still feel the excitement of beholding that mountain of Irish historical sources, never before used: treasure trove! And I still feel a twinge of guilt, remembering Mrs Dryer's faithful Christmas cards, with two dollars enclosed for my children, true widow's mite, both humbling and warming. Could one neglect such gentle obligations, and continue by inaction, an injustice to a people despised and neglected by the traditional purveyors of establishment history?

The answer is yes, when the competing demands were those of the Catholic Church, an historical cause I served by accident from a different sense of obligation, and to some extent in spite of itself and myself. But this too drove me back to the history of the Irish — what was Catholic, what was Irish? I wrote two books on Ireland to try to work that out,[7] but from 1972, when I discovered — or rather, had brought to my attention — in the Public Record Office of Northern Ireland, very substantial sources from an Australian Irish Protestant tradition, historically unfamiliar, but humanly very familiar from New Zealand experience, the whole matter took on new dimensions of complexity. William V. Shannon, in his standard work on *The American Irish* announces boldly 'this book discusses only the Catholic Irish'.[8] Most other writers on that subject have done the same, without Shannon's candour or reasoning. I could not see the subject of the Australian Irish as a Catholic one, not merely because I was fully aware from 1972 of a major Protestant dimension, and at least then conscious of significant Anglo-Irish one, but because I had already written a history of the Catholic Church[9] and in my headlong flight from tedium I had no intention of writing it again under another name, or of mistaking a Catholic for an Irishman, or vice versa: he was, they were, quite another thing, if not entirely.

This protracted diversion into the personal history of a 20-year project is designed to do more than deny the obvious but spurious equation: Irish Catholic Australian O'Farrell[10] equals a History of the Irish in Australia. It also seeks to draw attention to the real reasons for anyone pursuing the subject — that it is one full of human interest, vitality and colour; that it is one of central importance to the evolution of Australia's national life and character; that it is complex, subtle and intellectually demanding; that it offers the utmost professional challenges available in Australian historical writing. I have virtually no interest in genealogy, though I immediately concede the compelling interest it has for others, and the value of their specific and individual researches in making possible the building up of a real picture of the past. And I have no interest whatever in ancestor glorification; by all means let us praise famous men or women, but let us not pretend that all such persons are of our race, religion or society. I write about the Irish, because I enjoy the variety of their historical company: I write about them in Australia because someone owes them — and us all — that, and why should it not be me? The circumstances have pointed that way and so have my interests — particularly my interests in idiocy (of which more later), laughing, contradictions, heroism, sanctity and goodness, and, of course, my abiding fascination with devious politicking, and with the delights of kaleidoscopic emotions.

Given the variety of the Australian-Irish and the absence of any natural chronological organisation of their history, the major problem in writing a history of the Irish in Australia is organisation, discovering a principle of overall unity which provides both coherence and meaning relevant to the material available. J.F. Hogan's *The Irish in Australia*[11] in 1888 and P.S. Cleary's *Australia's Debt to the Irish Nation Builders* in 1933 were both built on the triumphalist 'me too' principle, claiming Irish involvement in a national enterprise constructed by great names: both are basically books of lists of more or less Irish recruits, conscripted often against their will or any reason, to serve a common Australian glory, very vaguely defined. Both books were propagandist, essentially replies to the constant assertions that the Irish were worthless peasants, and they both fell into the trap of wholesale name-dropping. They coralled into the Irish camp any Australian public figure with an Irish name, or an Irish grandmother twice removed, and paraded them as proof of Irish excellence. This gave Irish Australian readers a warm glow of vicarious pride in, for instance, Marcus Clarke, English born, never in Ireland, but with Irish family connections. Critics scoffed at this kind of compulsory Erinism, and drew acid attention to the fact that most of these allegedly 'Irish' public figures in Australia were Anglo-Irish, that is members of precisely that English garrison in Ireland that the Celts were so anxious to eject.[12] But for all the ridicule it attracted in the 1880s, it was one way of holding such a book together, and of comforting a people who felt themselves despised, and virtually the same methodology was used by Cleary in 1933.

By 1977, when I gave an ANZAAS paper on the Irish in Australia, I was still unable to think of a viable way in which to present the subject with dignity and pace. With dignity, because I see the Irish as part of a total scene and do not envisage the telling of their story as competitive; with pace, because I hold a symphonic view of the construction of books: they need movements and themes to live, and to go anywhere, and mean anything: I reject mere assemblages. The solution to my problem came under duress, as these things so often do. Al Grassby had organised an Irish Day Seminar for the Sydney Carnivale 1978 and I gave a paper on the Irish and Australian History: The Hon. Mr Justice Lionel K. Murphy presided — his father came from Tipperary. That paper advanced the proposition that the Irish were the key dynamic factor in Australian history.[13] I was convinced that here was an idea which would carry a worthwhile book, and indeed was sufficiently important and compelling to demand immediate full-scale pursuit. Not that I regarded the case as closed: the reverse, opened. History is mystery: my job is to air and test solutions. There is no point in writing history in which there is no mystery; no point either if it offers no potential solution.

But why go for broke? Why must the Irish be put forward as *the* key to Australian history? Surely a less sweeping claim might be more tenable? This kind of objection was made to the religious interpretation of Irish history made in my *Ireland's English Question*: no single interpretation of history could be valid; reality was too complex for that. My response to that was, and is, that the apparent complexity of reality is no bar to their being a single interpretation of its meaning or operation, particularly in certain given times, places and circumstances. Further, an interpretation is precisely and only that — an arguable, evidence-supported way of looking at things. That is, the question to ask of it is, does it fit the facts and is it therefore valid? As to whether it is true, that is another level of question. A commentator obviously persuaded by my *Ireland's English Question* but not prepared to be convinced, said it was 'ingenious' — a judgement which no doubt will be made on the argument of *The Irish in Australia*. Why argue at all? Because the device of argument attracts attention, because the structure of argument compels a rigorous attention to evidence, because the historical ground of Australia's evolution and character is already occupied by other specious arguments about bushmen and Anzacs masquerading as received wisdom and obvious orthodoxy, and because this is a first-rate argument.

It has been pointed out to me by learned commentators on my work,[14] as well as by ignorant and offensive ruffians, that my method of presentation of the past is dialectical; that I stress contrary viewpoints, extremes; that I see history as debate, as challenge and response, as black versus white. They have a point, but a superficial one. Like life, history (I mean the actuality of the past) is full of dull or obscure patches: things are seldom all laid out neatly. The polarising method of presenting this piebald situation has immense advantages of intelligibility and clarity. One does not set up false dichotomies where none exists, but one pursues contrasts, conflicting tendencies, differences, to their polarities, in order to reveal their essence and point up their operation. Further, I would claim that the subjects I choose are beset by conflict: they are dramatic situations requiring a dramatic format, and appropriate roles. To translate this into the chapter headings of the present book, I present the Irish in Australia as a series of persona — prisoners, immigrants, settlers and unsettlers, nationalists, rebels and Australians. All of course overlap, in time and within individuals, but the labels and their sequence, represent my view of the generality of the actual historical process, and how the historical mind can be apprised of it. That is how what happened can best be comprehended.

Obviously, this argumentative approach will need an insistent style to carry its momentum throughout the book, but this must be sharply distinguished from anything triumphal — or apologetic. Cleary offers a model to avoid: 'Upwards of thirty Irishmen have been governors or acting-governors of Australian states, and more than that number were judges . . . We have counted a hundred and thirty seven in the list of Cabinet ministers . . .'[15] And so on. To which an appropriately cynical contemporary response might be — as many successful Irish rogues as that! Quite apart from the present low estimation of judges and politicians, the whole exercise is absurd, implying as it does that success in public life, even as both Hogan and Cleary admit, frequently at a cost of repudiating Irishness, is a true estimate of Irish value: the procedure avoids the question of what 'Irish' means, and what 'success' means, as well as courting devastating contradiction. Sadly, in colonial Victoria, green stamping-ground of O'Shanassy and Gavan Duffy, from 1846 to 1900, while Scots were about 16 per cent of the population, 29 per cent of all parliamentarians were of Scots birth.[16] Gavan Duffy himself was well aware that what was important was not lists of Irish or pseudo-Irish public names, but the proportion of those names to the Irish segment in the population.[17] The brave catalogues of Hogan and Cleary mask the true situation which was, of course, that the Irish — or at least the Catholic Irish — were under-represented virtually in every public area except gaols, asylums and the Catholic Church. And this is the alternative scenario; that the Irish were the persecuted underdogs, oppressed and cheated of their fair share of political and economic power by grasping Scots and scheming Sassenachs. But through it all they clung firmly to their faith, uncorrupted by wealth or power, led by their stalwart *soggart aroons*, saying the rosary with tender piety, a credit to their holy religion — but with no credit at the local store.

This will no longer do, at least not as what purports to be history; but let me turn to something less obvious. Off Nassau St in Dublin, in the forecourt of the Taxation Department building, is a large colourful ceramic mural depicting themes from the Book of Leinster, the eighth-century prose epic of cattle-raid, warfare, heroism and treachery. An adjoining plaque reads: 'Who have copied down this story or more accurately fantasy do not credit the details of the story or fantasy. Some things in it are devilish lies and some poetical figments, some seem possible and others not, some are for the enjoyment of idiots.' The enjoyment of idiots. Any people that erect a mural for the enjoyment of idiots in the precincts of its Taxation Department poses major problems for historical comprehension, especially when at the same time it owns that its past is littered with 'devilish lies' and 'poetical figments' and warns the observer to beware. It is mockingly self-aware (sometimes) of its own illusions and self-delusions — but which are they? Chesterton's aphorism applies: 'For all their wars are merry, and all their songs are sad', but is far too simple: the contradictions and paradoxes run far deeper than that. As to the enjoyment of idiots, history is singularly bad at capturing the comic, yet the element of humour — with all the range from malice to mawkishness, wit to knockout farce — is central to the Irish experience. How to convey it in the form of history?

This is a general stylistic problem to which most Irish historians do not even advert. There are others specific to this project. To write general history one needs detailed primary studies of relevant events, persons, regions, institutions, processes. Save in the area of the Catholic religion, the situation is rudimentary: a general history in present circumstances can be little better than a sketch map. Unfortunately, this is not simply a matter of possible research tasks as yet undone. Until the 1950s it was the policy of the major Australian libraries not to preserve newspapers and other materials of Irish Catholic relevance, on the assumption that these persons were of no historical consequence. Nor was this idea that the 'establishment' made history, *was* history, confined to the establishment itself. The Irish themselves accepted it, and destroyed their vestiges accordingly: they still do — a species of irresponsible future suicide. But there was another process at work, or rather, not at work. By the late nineteenth century the American-Irish experience was sufficiently self-conscious and confident to produce a satirist of national, indeed international stature (in Australia, H.B. Higgins was among those who read him), Mr Dooley, Finley Peter Dunne. The American Irish went on to produce major novelists — Scott Fitzgerald, John O'Hara, James T. Farrell — the dramatist Eugene O'Neill, and an entire popular film world archetypically inhabited by Barry Fitzgeralds. In America, both art and entertainment affirmed that the American-Irish world was a real and important environment to belong to, sufficiently resourceful and mature both to take seriously and poke fun at. It is said that the American-Irish envy us our 'John O'Brien'; I envy them Mr Dooley, formidably nobody's fool, in cutting brogue. Such a sceptical Irish eye on the Australian scene would have offered perceptions valuable to an historian, but much more importantly, would have altered, sophisticated, the intellectual atmosphere, the cultural climate, in such a way as to make Irish-Australia a force to be reckoned with. The spectrum of Australian-Irish literature is presently too narrow to illuminate the subject widely and deeply — and history is a branch of literature: my history will be stunted not only by my own limitations, but by its sparse literary environment. Absurd as it is to complain that there are not enough Australian *Memory Ireland*s, this paucity is a fact of literary life.

Let me make short shrift of some self-imposed limitations. I have written two other related books — on Catholics, and the letters of Ulster Protestants: they are readily available and I ought not duplicate them. Economics and time dictate a book of certain length: I have far too much material, especially on 1915–21. On that period I propose to write a further book. And, like all general histories, it will be quite inadequate on the particulars which compose it.

Which brings me to the question of readers. One writes first for oneself: if I cannot convince myself I know the Irish, how can I convince others? But I know that I have here a problem: it lies in the area of claims of possession to the true Irish heritage. Reviews of my *Letters from Irish Australia*,[18] letters written mainly by Ulster Protestants, have alerted me to the fact that some critics do not regard these as 'true' Irish, but aberrant and inferior wimps and no-hopers, with a certain pathological interest as a deviant sub-species: I ought to have known this from direct experience of Ireland itself, where the claims of Ulster Protestants to be 'Irish' are violently denied. To such critics in Australia, they are 'expatriate planter stock from Scotland', mere 'squatters' in Ireland, and their Australian representatives were 'shiftless', unstable, not self-reliant, not suited to pioneering, failing to recognise the potential of the land, writing 'mawkish . . . highfalutin' epistles', afflicted with 'basic pessimism' and 'Micawberism' — which is all to say, un-Irish. 'They came from established homes whereas the *real native Irish* [emphasis mine] were mainly the dispossessed of the earth . . .'[19] — like the reviewer's parents.

To pursue this point further with another reviewer, who objected to the title, *Letters from Irish Australia*: 'this is not *Irish Australia*', these were letters from 'the men of the north'; these were 'the O'Farrell writers'. 'O'Farrell uses the term *Irish Australia* in the title of his book, yet ignores the cockies of Bungaree':[20] Bungaree is the reviewer's home town. Another reviewer doubted the validity of the whole exercise of presenting Irish immigrant letters: his grandmother was not in my index and anyhow, she did not write letters home.[21]

I cite these reviewers not to contest with them, but to note their preconceptions. Mark the prescriptive diction: 'this is not *Irish Australia*'. Not, 'this is only a part of Irish Australia', or, 'this is a part of Irish Australia I don't like or think unimportant', but, wham — straight denial of occupancy; out with them, they don't belong. Why? Because they are not *us* — 'us' being what we know from our grandmother, parents, or Bungaree. For the job of being Irish, no other Irish need apply.

The takeover bid for sole possession of the identity of being Irish by Catholic forces was a later nineteenth-century process, but its most militant Australian residuum appears to me now to be mainly, but not entirely, in ex-Catholic quarters. Those of Irish Catholic origin who have drifted from or rejected their religious creed have turned to its Irish stereotype elements as confirmation of their identity, choosing conveniently to their own life-style, those aspects which are boozy, riotous, race-going, and coarse: big, Behanesque, bog-Irishness suits their self-image. At the Marengo races on St Patrick's Day 1868, a crowd of drunken Irish diggers danced on the road, roaring at the terrified townspeople: 'We're bloody Fenians! Come on! We'd soon kill a man as look at him.'[22] A great joke a

week after the firing of shots at the Duke of Edinburgh by an alleged
Fenian in Sydney. But more than a joke, an act of deliberate
defiance, the spirit that has endeared hell-raising to subsequent
generations of Irish Australians, the tradition of rebellious non-
conformity dear to the Irish heart. The Irish heart? There are many
Irish hearts, and the makers of mayhem have long been encouraged
by Ireland's enemies to believe that they have a monopoly of
Irishness. Quiet, decency, respectability, such as evidenced in letters
from Northern Ireland Protestant immigrants, seems foreign,
though precisely those qualities were common to most Catholic
Irish, certainly those depicted by 'John O'Brien'.

In fossicking across two centuries of Irish Australian history, I
have encountered too many different and contrasting types of Irishman and Irishwoman to be willing to concede any claimant faction
the monopoly of the title of Irish. Mine is a book about kinds, ways,
and degrees of being Irish in Australia: all are welcome, and if they
do not like each other, they must settle it amongst themselves.

Notes and References

1. (Quadrangle Books, Chicago, 1972).
2. Subtitled *Friendships, movements and cultural conflicts in Australia's greatest decades* (Penguin Books, Melbourne, 1983).
3. (Angus & Robertson, Sydney, 1933).
4. See Vincent Buckley, 'Imagination's Home', *Quadrant*, vol.23, no.3 (1979); his 'Identity: Invention or Discovery', *Quadrant*, vol.24, no.8 (1980), is on the same general theme.
5. Vincent Buckley, *Memory Ireland: Insights into the Contemporary Irish Condition* (Penguin Books, Melbourne, 1985).
6. Patrick O'Farrell, 'Boredom as Historical Motivation', *Quadrant*, vol.26, nos 1–2 (1982).
7. These were: *Ireland's English Question: Anglo-Irish Relations 1534–1970* (B.T. Batsford, London, 1971); *England and Ireland since 1800* (Oxford University Press, London, 1975).
8. William V. Shannon, *The American Irish: A Political and Social Portrait* (Collier Books Edition, New York, 1974), p.vii.
9. The present edition is *The Catholic Church and Community. An Australian History*, rev. edn (New South Wales University Press, Sydney, 1985).
10. Just after writing this disclaimer, a further example of this false pigeon-holing appeared in a review of my work by Fr George Pell in the Melbourne Catholic *Advocate*, 1 August 1985. This sought to explain unpalatable judgements of mine by reference to these categories, and is an interesting translation of procedures histori-cally used from outside Irish Australian Catholicism being converted for polemical use inside the contemporary Catholic church. 'Irish Catholic', for instance in contem-porary journalistic usage, has become a dismissive pejorative label, with connotations

of clannishness and obscurantism, inferior social origins, and devious Labor politicking.

11. Australian edition (George Robertson and Co., Melbourne and Sydney, 1888).

12. For an example of such criticism, see A. Patchett Martin, *Australia and the Empire* (D. Douglas, Edinburgh, 1889), pp.135–56.

13. Patrick O'Farrell, 'The Irish and Australian History', in *The Irish Contribution to Australia*. Proceedings of the Irish Day Seminar, Carnivale '78, Sydney, 22 September 1978 (Office of the Commissioner for Community Relations, Canberra, 1979); this paper was also published in *Quadrant*, vol.22, no.12 (1978).

14. Gregory Haines, 'The History of Patrick O'Farrell', *Australasian Catholic Record*, vol.55, no.2 (1978), p.173.

15. Cleary, *Australia's Debt*, p.xiii.

16. See Malcolm D. Prentis, *The Scots in Australia: A Study of New South Wales, Victoria, and Queensland, 1788–1900* (Sydney University Press, Sydney, 1983).

17. See *Civil and Religious Liberty*. Speech of C. Gavan Duffy, Esq. at Melbourne, on the presentation of a property qualification to him 20 August 1856 (Michael T. Gason, Melbourne; William Dolman, Sydney).

18. Patrick O'Farrell, *Letters from Irish Australia 1825–1929* (New South Wales University Press, Sydney; Ulster Historical Foundation, Belfast, 1984).

19. Review by G.M. Cashman in *Footprints*, vol.5, no.7 (1985), pp.15–16.

20. John Hanrahan, 'Some Irish eyes are smiling, smiling', *Australian Book Review*, no.67, December 1984/January 1985.

21. Review by Peter Cochrane, *Sydney Morning Herald*, 20 October 1984.

22. This incident is cited in Mark Lyons, 'Aspects of Sectarianism in New South Wales circa 1865 to 1880', unpublished PhD thesis, Australian National University, 1972, p.130.

14 The Desolate Boys: Juvenile Crime and Punishment, Ireland and New South Wales

Portia Robinson

On the morning of 23 March 1799 Patrick Corrigan was 13 years old. He and four young friends were playing marbles on the steps of Parliament House in Dublin. During 'a friendly scuffle' one of the boys cried out that four golden guineas had been stolen from his pocket. His four friends were subsequently arrested, charged, convicted and sentenced to transportation to Botany Bay. Corrigan's parents, respectable citizens of Francis St, Dublin, petitioned the Lord Lieutenant of Ireland for clemency for their young lad.[1] The plea was rejected. Patrick Corrigan, pickpocket and thief, sailed for New South Wales.

Another Irish lad, Owen Carty, was more fortunate, although he had no parents to plead for him. A native of Roscommon, Carty was under sentence of transportation for sheep-stealing when his trial judge reviewed his case. The judge described Carty as 'a very young boy . . . naked and half-starved . . a miserable wretch driven to crime by necessity'. Carty and his young sister lived alone. Their father was dead, their mother 'gone begging'. They had only one possession, a lean sheep. This the boy tried to exchange for a fatter beast from a neighbour's flock. Hunger, poverty and want, the learned judge commented in his report, had driven the lad to theft. So young Owen Carty was pardoned, released from gaol and, presumably, returned to his little sister and their scraggy sheep.[2]

Both Corrigan and Carty were juvenile criminals, charged with 'normal' adult crimes, convicted and sentenced according to the law. They were part of that growing problem of increasing crime which was causing so much concern to the authorities and the respectable inhabitants of Ireland and England. How to prevent crime? How to deter the young miscreants, the thieves, the shop-lifters, the pickpockets, the vagabonds and rascals who infested the towns and cities, who roamed the countryside of Ireland?

229

To law-abiding contemporaries the answer was simple and traditional: deter by fear. Fear of a punishment so severe that terror alone would make the would-be offender draw back in horror.

Deterrence, combined with the need for retribution for a wronged society, was the basis for English criminal legislation. The traditional solution to an increase in crime was a corresponding increase in the severity of punishment.[3] Actual figures for the numbers of criminal convictions in both Ireland and England were unreliable and often non-existent.[4] The extent to which contemporaries were convinced that crime was increasing may be seen from the severity of the punishments added to the criminal law. During the reign of George IV more offences were declared capital than had been in the combined reigns of all the Plantagenets, the Tudors and the Stuarts.[5] Criminals and would-be criminals, however, were not deterred. Boys and men, girls and women, continued to appear in increasing numbers to face charges which carried the death penalty.

Was this because the statutory punishment of death had lost its deterrence, so much so that young boys would risk death every time they picked a pocket, stole from a shop or dwelling?

Social Origins

Motivation for crime is notoriously difficult to attribute, but one characteristic of most of those charged in Irish courts may offer some explanation both for the extent of crime and for the apparent lack of fear of death as a deterrent among young people. This characteristic was shared by English contemporaries: most of the convicted came from the same 'class' origins. That is, they were from that 'class which normally commit crimes, the poor and the indigent'.[6] The exceptions, mainly from what we would call 'working-class families', such as Patrick Corrigan, were still, to their contemporaries, the lower orders.

Death, and especially an ignominious death on the gallows, was the most awe-inspiring of punishments to those who made the laws and to the respectable orders of society who obeyed them. To the lower orders, to the poor, to the employed as well as the unemployed, to the destitute, to those without hope or opportunity, death was simply another of life's hazards. Disease, malnutrition, living and working conditions, as indeed, the conditions in the gaols and

Bridewells of town and county, all contributed to a short life-expectancy.[7] For the children of the poor, the children of the unemployed or the destitute, the orphans, the 'desolate boys', the opportunities of reward from honest labours were slight, if they existed at all. Where need or greed, inclination or parental example, or, as petitions for clemency claimed, simply 'high spirits' and 'boyish pranks' led to criminal charges, conviction, the death sentence and execution, these were hazards to be faced and, if possible, avoided. The incidence of crime in Ireland, as in England, was not reduced by the corresponding increase in the severity of punishment.

Juvenile Crime and Punishment

There was little significant difference in the crimes of young criminals from those of adult offenders. Were the children to receive the same statutory punishments as the adults? Was there, perhaps, a more lenient attitude towards juveniles on the part of trial judges and juries? Did petitions on their behalf to the Lord Lieutenant receive more favourable attention? Existing records do not show this. Owen Carty may have been pardoned for stealing that sheep, but Thomas Gallagher and Patrick Dougherty received seven years' transportation.[8] Dominic and Owen McAteer, two young brothers convicted of the same offence of sheep-stealing, were sentenced to death. While awaiting execution in Dundalk Gaol, the Inspector of Prisons commended them to mercy 'as they are young and may possibly become useful subjects if they are reprieved to . . . encrease [sic] the Settlement at Botany Bay'. This Grand Jury declined to recommend mercy 'because no circumstances implying any doubt of the guilt . . . in any way alleviated the offence as stated by the Judge'.[9] The young brothers were hanged.

There was no predictable pattern at all in the punishment of, or attitudes towards, juvenile criminals. Three lads, James Roche, Patrick Supple and Andrew Fehilly, sentenced to seven years' transportation were refused clemency by the trial judge after an appeal from the parents: 'I am sorry to say', declared that learned man, 'that they appeared to be of a description of young miscreants and shoplifters who infest that city [Limerick] in hordes.'[10] They belonged at Botany Bay. Was it that punishment and not reformation was the aim of transportation? Was Botany Bay viewed solely as a place of punishment?

Transportation From Ireland

Transportation was the traditional English solution to the problem of housing and maintaining felons. Major felonies carried the death penalty, but this was frequently commuted to terms of transportation. Single felonies were usually punishable by transportation, although imprisonment, whipping, the pillory or hard labour in the houses of correction could be imposed.[11] The punishment which gave the government least expense was transportation. Professor A.G.L. Shaw has estimated that 'probably about 7500 Irish convicts were transported [to the North American colonies] during the century before the American Revolution'.[12] There is no evidence, however, that, after transportation to New South Wales began, there was any conscious or unconscious 'policy' that it would be preferable to transport juvenile offenders to that convict colony. There is some evidence that the question of whether or not transportation was preferable to confinement in the home country for all criminals was discussed in Ireland at the time when transportation was recommencing after the American Revolution. In 1790, the year before the first convict transport from Ireland arrived at Port Jackson, the Lord Lieutenant of Ireland wrote to the Grand Juries of all Irish counties asking for information on the possibility of building penitentiaries in Ireland as an alternative to the traditional punishment of transportation. The Report of the Grand Jury of Donegal was typical of the replies:

> [they] appeared to think that some scheme of the kind might be necessary, but the idea was quite a new one to them and they were at a loss what opinion to form about it and seemed afraid of the expense.

This fear of expense was linked with the proposal to build new penitentiaries in the counties, with the probability that they would be maintained by the local authorities. Benefits to the criminals could be seen, such as 'a spare diet, separation and solitude', which, it was recognised, 'were best calculated to induce reflection from which real reformation can only be expected'.[13] These reformative and even humanitarian advantages, however, did not outweigh the problems of expense and administration. Nothing positive came from this Inquiry. The most usual sentence for major felonies remained transportation, either as the statutory punishment or as an alternative to the death penalty.

Transportation of Juveniles

Comparatively few young criminals were transported from Ireland during the period under consideration. Comparative, that is with numbers charged and convicted. The paucity of contemporary Irish sources makes it impossible to estimate percentages with any accuracy. An investigation into criminal cases in Ireland between 1790 and 1820, where records exist, does suggest that most of the young felons who escaped death on the gallows remained in Ireland.[14] One could generalise and add that those sentenced to transportation were mainly, in the eyes of 'respectable' society, the 'young rascals and miscreants who infest' the city streets. There are, however, so many exceptions to this generalisation that this is not a valid assumption.

It becomes clear that there was no pattern, no predictable order, theory or policy with regard to juvenile offenders. Why, for example, was Owen Carty pardoned, Gallagher and Dougherty transported and the McAteer brothers hanged all for the crime of sheep-stealing? Why was Leslie Ferguson, 'a very young lad' capitally convicted for horse-stealing[15] and Private John Whelan, convicted of 'rape upon a very young and innocent girl', excused his sentence of whipping and imprisonment and allowed to re-enlist in his regiment?[16] There appears no answer except the vagaries of judges and juries.

Juvenile Criminals: Crime and Petition

What, then, were the crimes of the Irish boys? In almost every instance, juveniles were charged with and convicted of exactly the same types of crimes as were adult offenders: shoplifting, pickpocketing, robbery, burglary, perjury, passing counterfeit coins. In most cases, it was not so much the actual crime as the circumstances surrounding it which were indicative of contemporary attitudes to juveniles. Cases, for example, which showed the extent of family or community support for a lad sentenced to death or transportation.

Family support was strong, at all levels of society, from street-sweeper Richard Gavin, to wealthy merchant James Conway. Both men were residents of Dublin City; Gavin's two sons were awaiting execution for robbery, Conway's son had been sentenced to death for stealing monies.

The street-sweeper petitioned that his boys be transported;[17] the merchant explained that his son was but 'a giddy boy . . . the money stolen by him had been recovered and returned to its owner' and the owner supported the father's plea that the son be allowed to enlist.[18] The merchant's son joined King George's army, the street-sweeper's sons were hanged.

Did the social and economic status of the parent affect judicial decision to commute sentence? Again, no pattern emerges. The main influence from the well-to-do or comparatively well-to-do fathers, appears to have been that they could influence their sons to 'pray permission to enlist', or, in a few cases, offer to provide the necessary sureties for their child to go to America.[19] This latter form of self-transportation, as it was called, meant that the offender was punished by exile, but exile at his or her own expense, and as a free settler in the United States rather than as a convict in New South Wales. This 'legal' escape from transportation to the convict colony was also invoked in 'political' cases. In August 1800, the mother of James Moore of Kilraughts in Co. Antrim, pleaded the youth of her son who had been sentenced to transportation, and added that, on account of his youth, '[he had been] seduced into Political and Criminal Conduct and prays he might be permitted to transport himself to America'.[20]

Dread of Transportation

Evidence of parental concern for children comes from the petitions sent to the Lord Lieutenant.[21] Reading beyond the expected flowery language, the distressing descriptions of immediate circumstance, these petitions show forcibly how transportation was dreaded both by the lad under sentence and his family. It was far preferable to enlist, if this could be arranged, in the navy or army. Elizabeth Burke, mother of William Burke, a lad already on the transport ship in Cork harbour, wrote to her former mistress, the Lady Louisa Cary, begging her to intercede with the judge and allow her misguided child to enlist rather than be transported to Botany Bay.[22]

Enlistment of felons under sentence of death or transportation was a common practice. Recruiting officers from both the navy and the army regularly visited gaols, hulks and even the transports lying at anchor in Cork harbour, preparing to sail for New South Wales. The young, the fit, the healthy, could be offered 'the King's shilling'. There was no certainty that this *would* happen. The Inspector of Prisons reported that the naval recruiting officer had become 'rather selective . . . refusing to take the very young men out of Newgate Prison for fear of disgracing the Navy':

> [He] refuses to accept three very fit lads. The Navy seems to be disgraced by taking them out of Newgate . . . the taking of half a bag of coal and a bottle of rum are not crimes of a very heinous nature at this time in my opinion . . . the men are able and willing to serve King and Country and are incapable of doing so.[23]

Rather than gamble their lives on the possibility of being chosen for the King's service, numbers of lads, convicted of both 'political' and traditional 'criminal' offences, petitioned the Lord Lieutenant, 'praying enlistment'. Considering the experiences, duties and dangers of soldiers and sailors in times of peace as well as war, this decided preference for enlistment rather than transportation is strong evidence for the 'horrors of transportation' during this period.[24]

Neighbours could and did petition for local boys under sentence of the law. James, Mark and John Redmond, all from Wicklow, were in Phillipstown Gaol awaiting execution when their neighbours petitioned the Lord Lieutenant for mercy. John and Mark were 'very young lads' who had come to the house of James in which they had concealed stolen goods. Because of their extreme youth, the petitioners asked that only Mark be hanged as a deterrent.[25] There was, however, no pardon for the two young lads: Mark and John were hanged together, but their elder brother was reprieved and later transported to New South Wales. It is more than probable that he owed his life to the goodwill of neighbours towards his family. What memories of that family did he take to Botany Bay?

A Criminal 'Class'?

Most of the boys sentenced to death or transportation were very clearly from the lower orders of Irish society. Some of these were, without doubt, part of that criminal underworld which existed in all the towns and cities of Western Europe, 'working' in gangs or in family groups. One of these was 16-year-old Lawrence Leonard, confined in Carlow Gaol in 1808. The Chief Justice commented that 'his father [was] transported for the same Offence, his Mother an Old Offender'.[26] This 'criminal class' also included boys who 'fell into bad company' usually as a result of coming to Dublin in search of work. Such a case was that of the young lad who left his family in Stradone in Co. Cavan 'to be put to a trade' in Dublin City. After a few months, 'He fell into bad company and was concerned in the robbery of a shop which he . . . afterwards confessed to the owner of the shop and upon his own confession was found guilty and sentenced to be hanged.' The two trial judges reconsidered the circumstances of this case and recommended that young Reilly and his accomplice, Terrence Kelly, 'another young boy', be pardoned on terms of life transportation.[27]

Juveniles As Political Criminals

Boys as well as men were convicted of breaking the ordinances and regulations imposed after the civil disturbances following the Rebellion of 1798 and sentenced to transportation. The background of these cases not only underlines the severity with which these restrictions were enforced on the population, but indicates the types of lads caught up, innocently or not, with the political problems of Ireland.

John Egan was an apprentice living in Thomas St, Dublin when he was sentenced to transportation 'for being out during curfew'. Egan petitioned the Lord Lieutenant: 'I had nothing to do with the troubles of 23 July last . . . look with an Eye of Pity on a poor Orphan . . . I had gone to meet the Tullamore Boat.' His master supported his appeal: '[the young lad] was an indentured apprentice since 1 May 1801 during which time he has behaved and conducted himself in a soberly and orderly manner and never absented himself from his business on any pretext.'[28] Did young Egan sail to Botany Bay as a 'notorious Rebel and Traitor'? His record is lost in the mists of time.

'The Desolate Boys'

One group of juveniles *were* sentenced to confinement in Ireland at the Penitentiary for Young Criminals at Smithfield.[29] An analysis of one of the remaining Quarterly Reports (ending 5 October 1812) gives some indication of the attitudes of the authorities towards boys confined indefinitely in this institution, the types of boys committed, and their 'crimes'. It does not explain why these particular boys were sent to this penitentiary rather than to a general gaol or prison, or even transported as sentenced. A possible explanation as to why these lads were more fortunate than so many of their contemporaries, lies in the crimes for which they were committed. There is, however, no consistent pattern evident, for other boys of similar ages and social origins were transported or imprisoned for identical offences. Most of the lads were committed by police or civil magistrates, a few by the Recorder of Dublin. The unanswerable question is why were they sent to the penitentiary? Especially in those cases where the boy was guilty of a major felony and originally sentenced to death or transportation.[30] Why were older lads committed? John Manning was 16 when confined for robbery and still in the penitentiary at 19; James McDanniell was committed at 18, Arthur Maguire sentenced at 21 as 'disorderly', and John Armstrong at 18 for 'rioting and disobedience'.[31] Were these offences lesser, for example, than 'being abroad before daylight'?

The October Quarterly Report lists by name some 108 boys committed since 1806. Some 13 had been discharged — to the Royal Navy, to fathers, to friends, to a master as an apprentice, to the House of Industry. The ages of the boys on entering the institution ranged from 7 to 19 years. One had been committed at the age of 5 for petty theft in 1809, and several were 9-year-old vagrants. Crimes ranged from robbery, embezzlement (of his father's money), petty theft, shop-breaking, riotous and disorderly behaviour, runaway schoolboy or apprentice, or escaped from the House of Industry, to 'artful and disobedient' and 'a desolate boy'.

What was a desolate boy? Again, remaining records offer no definition. A desolate boy was not necessarily one without friends or family. Thomas Downes, 11, was released by the governors to his friends after some five weeks' confinement. James Hughes, committed at $13\frac{1}{2}$ was released as an apprentice some 10 months later, despite his 'delicate' health. Thomas Hughes, 11, after three months during which he was at the penitentiary school, was released to his friends. Nor was a desolate boy necessarily very young, although in 1809 a 6½-year-old and a 7-year-old were committed as 'desolate boys', one employed winding, the other weaving, one 'rather sullen', the other 'good' in his behaviour. The desolate boys in the penitentiary could not be distinguished in any way, except by their 'crime', from the other young criminals with whom they shared their daily life.

The boys committed to the penitentiary were both Roman Catholic and Protestant, although the Catholics predominated. Under the column listed religious knowledge, industry, moral conduct, the individual entries scarcely varied. Most were indifferent in all three respects, a few 'middling' or 'improved'. Young Dennis Plunkett, 16, committed as a vagrant in 1812, spent his time 'cleaning the yard'; his health was bad, his religious knowledge was bad, and he was not improving either in moral conduct or industry. The health of the boys, however, was usually described as 'good', with an occasional 'delicate' or 'scrofulous' or 'scald head'. Again, there was no discernable difference among the 'desolate boys' and those committed for specific offences.

The inmates of the penitentiary were, with very few exceptions, either 'at school' or employed at shoemaking, weaving, winding or as a shoe-closer, or in a beetling yard. All basic trades which could enable them to gain honest employment on release. Only two or three were employed cleaning the prison or the yard. One of these was a 14-year-old, Patrick Collins, a petty thief who was released to the navy at his own request.

The unanswerable question is why were these 108 boys selected for this penitentiary? Two or three were sent as an alternative to transportation, as was William Griffiths, 'a quiet boy', sentenced to transportation at the age of 13. There is some evidence to show that the Inspector of Prisons could, and occasionally did, recommend that juveniles be sent to the penitentiary rather than to New South Wales. Thomas Walshe and William Coyle were in the New Prison in 1804 when they were recommended as 'Proper Objects for the Penitentiary' and their papers endorsed 'released to the Penitentiary'. Why were these two 'Proper Objects' and other lads of the same age executed, transported or confined with adult offenders?

That boys convicted of major felonies were confined at the penitentiary does indicate that there was no official reluctance to allow 'desolate boys', petty thieves and runaways to share their daily life with these convicted felons. Was there any conscious policy to segregate juveniles from adult offenders? The evidence does not suggest this. Boys and men, girls and women, shared the same prison quarters throughout the county and town gaols of Ireland, shared the same bare subsistence gaol rations, the insanitary conditions, the overcrowding, the filth; shared the same rooms of confinement as the diseased, the feeble-minded, the cripples, the babies and children of the convicted men and women. That only boys were confined together was unusual. That boys convicted of major offences were confined with the desolate boys was in keeping with the general lack of segregation of all convicts, regardless of sex, age, health or crime. The interesting feature of the Penitentiary for Young Criminals is that it existed at all, that young ruffians were given this opportunity to learn a trade, to be taught the principles of religious and moral instruction, to be given some opportunity for reformation and a new life on release. There was no care or concern when poor, ragged Owen Carty was released as to what would happen to him. The circumstances of his crime and conviction would surely justify Carty as the most desolate of desolate boys.

Evidence abounds that children from at least the age of 10 years were sentenced in the criminal courts of Ireland to terms of imprisonment, transportation or death for 'normal' adult offences. In 1800, 19 boys aged between 10 and 17 years were serving sentences for theft. These boys were removed from the *John and Ester* where they were confined with adult felons, to the New Geneva barracks.[32]

The recurring question is why were so few juveniles actually sent to New South Wales as transported felons, why did all those who received this sentence try so desperately to escape sailing for Botany Bay, why did parents and friends petition that the punishment be commuted to enlistment? In 1808 Robert Robinson, about 16, in Carrickfergus Gaol, Co. Antrim under sentence of death, was reprieved on condition of transportation. Robinson escaped from the transport ship, made his way to Belfast, was apprehended breaking into a house. At this trial he again received the death sentence, but with the added notation 'not to be reprieved'.[33] Had Robinson accepted that sentence of transportation how different would have been his experiences in New South Wales?

Transportation: Punishment or Reformation?

Was it that transportation was viewed by the Irish authorities as a sentence so severe that it would not only be appropriate punishment for wrong-doers but would act as a strong deterrent to would-be criminals? How would this affect attitudes towards juveniles? There is certainly no evidence of any belief or theory that the transportation of juveniles at this time would or could lead to their reformation. It was a sentence of punishment, not hope. This dread of life in the convict colony could explain why those lads under sentence were willing to accept as an alternative the life of soldier or sailor, why their friends and relations tried to intercede with the authorities to gain permission for the boys to enlist rather than sail to Botany Bay. The dangers, the discipline, the corporal punishment all associated with the occupations of soldier and sailor were well known. Yet this life was viewed as far more acceptable than that of a convict at Botany Bay. Was it simply fear of the distance, the unknown of that far-away settlement, sentenced to banishment, never to return? From the point of view of the authorities, the distance of the penal colony could be a decided asset, a final solution to the problem of crime by removing the wrong-doers permanently.

It is obvious that this dread of transportation was not lessened at this time by any belief or knowledge that in the convict colony the ex-felon had opportunities to gain respectability, material security, through economic independence, that the opportunities for work, for self-advancement, were far greater than the dreams of any lad in Ireland. So it was that, on the one hand, the authorities stressed the severity of the sentence of transportation and did not recognise that, for juvenile offenders, the opportunities offered at Botany Bay far surpassed even those which might result from years of confinement at the Penitentiary for Young Criminals. On the other hand, the boys themselves had no realisation that the social and economic conditions with which they were so familiar in Ireland were not the same at Botany Bay. Take, for example, the experiences of young John Hogan.

Hogan was just 17 when he was sentenced to transportation for 'being out before day'. His friends petitioned for his pardon:

A boy of seventeen years . . . an orphan and destitute of clothes . . . his mother prevailed upon him to go to Limerick where his step-father lived for the price of a coat to wear. The night being very lightsome he got up early thinking that day was approaching; on passing through the town of Adare he was taken up by the centinel [sic] and sentenced to seven years' transportation on his trial for having been out before day; he was sent to Cork where he still remains. When called for trial the first day at Limerick his witnesses attended the Court but the Court was adjourned and when re-opened a week later and he was asked whether he was ready he answered in his ignorance 'Yes' not considering his witnesses did not come to Court.

By the time the petition was heard, young Hogan could not be found. He was on his way, another 'dangerous political ruffian' sailing for Botany Bay.[34]

Botany Bay: 'A Sink of Wickedness'?

Contemporary Irish attitudes to Botany Bay were very clearly linked with the assumptions and expectations of 'respectable' society towards a convict colony. The very name, Botany Bay, was synonomous with criminality, debauchery and depravity. It was an infamous place, rivalling Sodom and Gomorrah, a place where 'convicts of both sexes became even more depraved than at the time of their arrival'. This belief was inextricably linked with the infamy associated with the word 'convict', with all the connotations the term 'convict colony' implied. As for the children and young people of that place, the 'convicts' children' as they were called, it was believed that, spawned in drink, growing up in a riotous and lawless immoral society, 'hourly forced to watch the iniquitous behaviour' of their abandoned parents, they 'imbibed vice with their mother's milk'. These assumptions as to the nature of colonial society were based on the presumed life-styles in Ireland and England of those whose infamy had led to conviction of major statutory offences. These were the assumptions of 'respectable' society. The reality of life in the colony was quite a different matter.[35]

Colonial Children

New South Wales was, unexpectedly, 'an extraordinary place for children'. By 1813 almost one quarter of the population was under

the age of 12 years — the contemporary definition of a child.[36]
Unlike contemporary Ireland, there was no problem of juvenile
crime, no problem of juvenile destitution, poverty, lack of opportunity. The so-called 'children of the convicts' were not only a
respectable and industrious generation, but remarkably honest and
law-abiding.

How was this so? Why, in the Old Country was there an ever-
present problem of juvenile crime and unemployment, but in that
country to which the outcasts, the scum, the sweepings of the gaols,
hulks and prisons, 'the refuse of Ireland', were transported, there
was none of these problems.

Two major features of colonial society were directly responsible
for this paradox. First, direct influence of parental example and
second the unique nature of labour and its rewards in the convict
colony.

The parents of the native-born Australians, far from being the
stereotyped degraded convicts, were, in most cases, industrious and
self-supporting farmers, tradesmen and workers of the colony. They
were to be found at all levels of the social and economic hierarchy
of New South Wales, whether among the minority who came free
as officials, soldiers, settlers, or the majority who came as convicts
and, after sentence was served, settled with wife/partner, taking
advantage of the opportunities offered the industrious ex-convict to
gain an economic living standard beyond any possibility in the home
country. Respectable contemporaries in both Ireland and England,
however, continued to see New South Wales as 'convict', continued
to accept without question or first-hand knowledge, that it was an
infamous, depraved and vicious society, continued to judge the
convict and the ex-convict from the same standpoint: an outcast for
ever from respectable society. Yet New South Wales was developing
unique characteristics, a place where respectability and success were
not based on the past, but upon economic achievement, on individual
success. A country where children were not exploited as cheap
labour, where work was abundant, where skilled labour was at a
premium, where land could be had for the asking, the only conditions
being an 'honest, sober and industrious character'. Honest, sober
and industrious? Ex-convicts so described? To the respectable, this
was a contradiction in terms. To the ex-convicts of Botany Bay it
was an incentive, an opportunity, to obtain for a man and his family
the security of economic independence.[37]

This is not to argue that all the inhabitants of New South Wales became industrious and sober paragons of virtue. It is not to ignore the crime and prostitution which existed, as it did in all towns and cities of Europe, nor to overlook the illicit distilling, the robberies and thefts. It is, however, to argue, on the basis of the colonial court records, that very few of the parents of the colony's children were ever charged or convicted in New South Wales. It is to state unequivocally that the children themselves, as children and as young adults, were only on very rare and isolated occasions charged in the courts with any criminal offence or misdemeanour. That the crime of 'desolate boy' did not exist at Botany Bay.

Why was this so? This remarkable honesty of the colonial-born was directly linked with the example of their parents and with the unique nature of their homeland. The boys of the first generation of white Australians normally followed the trade or occupation of their fathers. That is, the sons of farmers and landowners themselves became landowners, the sons of tradesmen became apprentices and tradesmen themselves. On the land, ownership was not simply by inheritance as in Ireland, where the elder boy was normally the only one to follow the father as landowner. In New South Wales all sons could and did petition the governor for land grants, receiving an average of 60 acres each. In this way a new type of rural family emerged, sons and fathers frequently owning land in the same districts, strengthened by inter-marrying among the landed families at all levels of social and economic hierarchy with little regard for the civil condition of the parents.

In the towns, where skilled labour was at a premium, boys were indentured by their fathers or guardians and, on completion of their apprenticeship, found that their skills were so greatly in demand that the economic rewards for labour were far higher than in contemporary Ireland and England. Those boys who became skilled or semi-skilled agricultural workers were in the same position, free labour being in demand.

As a direct result of the penal nature of the colony, there was no need to exploit child labour. In contemporary Britain and Ireland where the children of the poor were expected to work almost as soon as they could walk — after all, 'it kept their little minds from vice' — New South Wales had no need for child labour. The convicts were sentenced to terms of penal servitude. They were the workforce of the colony. Their labour was freely available under the assignment system. Who, then, had need of the inexperienced young child?

Again, there were no mills, no factories, no mines, the traditional employers of young children. This led to situations deplored by the *Sydney Gazette*, where young children were reported as playing on the wharves and roadways to the great detriment of their morals.[38] The *Gazette* admonished the parents for so neglecting their duty as to allow their children to pass their childhood in idle play.

Juvenile Convicts in New South Wales

The juvenile convicts who were transported to New South Wales shared many of the conditions of colonial life with the native-born as well as sharing the opportunities and rewards available to them on completion of their sentences. Individuals are almost impossible to trace, numbers difficult to estimate from remaining records. In 1803 Governor King wrote to Lord Hobart on the problem of juvenile convicts 'of whom I am sorry to say there are a great number'. King reported that, 'to lessen the evil as much as possible the convict boys that arrive . . . are put 'Prentices to the boat-builders or carpenters and several have made themselves very usefull [sic]'.[39] The only indication of how many 'a great number' might be, comes some 15 years later from Major Druitt who gave evidence to Commissioner Bigge on the categories of male convicts. Druitt explained that there was only one specific classification apart from 'male convicts' and this was 'the Boys, who are kept in a room to themselves from the age of 14 to 19 to the amount of fifty'.[40] These boys were apprenticed in the same way as were their predecessors, sharing instruction with the native-born apprenticed in the government lumber or dock yards or the carpenters' barracks. Bigge was told that 'at one stage there were thirteen or fourteen convict boys apprenticed . . . and some of them did very well'.[41]

Some of the convict boys were housed in the Male Orphan School. Thomas Bowden, master of that colonial institution, described the education, exercise, diet and general care of the inmates: 'They work in the garden from rising till eight. They go into school from nine to twelve. Till two they dine and play — from two till five they work at their trades of Taylor and shoemaker and some in the garden.'[42] There is no need to emphasise the difference between the life-styles, experience, opportunities and prospects for those juveniles transported to Botany Bay from those who remained in rural or urban Ireland.

The desolate boys remained in Dublin, learning their manners, their morals, their trades in the Penitentiary for Young Criminals. Equally desolate boys throughout all the counties of Ireland were charged, sentenced, hanged, imprisoned, transported or, in rare instances, pardoned to return to their lives of poverty, hunger and destitution. Throughout this period these lads and their families continued to beg that they be not transported. Had they but known it, Botany Bay, that land of convicts and kangaroos with all its evil and infamous connotations, was a place where desolate boys were unknown. It was a place where juvenile crime was almost non-existent, where opportunity replaced despair, where child labour was not exploited, where free labour, skilled or unskilled, was at a premium. It was, had all those juvenile criminals of Ireland but known it, a land not of, but for, the desolate boys of Ireland.

Notes and References

1. Petition for Patrick Corrigan, 23 March 1799, no.116; Petition for James Connor, convicted with Corrigan, 5 November 1799, no.151, *Prisoners' Petitions and Cases, 1788–1836*, State Paper Office, Dublin Castle, Dublin.
2. Report of Judge Mayne on the case of Owen Carty and other cases tried before him, 24 August 1817, no.4090, *Prisoners' Petitions and Cases*.
3. See Sir Norman Birkett (ed.), *The Newgate Calendar*, 2nd edn (The Folio Society, London, 1952), pp.6–8; see also Lord Castlereagh, *British Parliamentary Debates*, House of Commons, 1 March 1819, vol.xxxix, col.741.
4. For figures relating to the incidence and increase of crime, see excerpts from Patrick Colquhoun, *A Treatise on Indigence*, (J. Hatchard, London, 1806), pp.45–7, statistics from Home Secretary's Department from 1805 in L. Evans and P. Pledger (eds), *Contemporary Sources and Opinions in Modern British History* (2 vols, F.W. Cheshire, Melbourne, 1967), vol.2, pp.87–9.
5. F. Buxton, MP, *British Parliamentary Debates*, House of Commons, 2 March 1819, vol.xxxix, cols.808–10.
6. House of Commons, Select Committee on Police, *British Parliamentary Papers*, 1818, vol.v, p.216.
7. Gaol conditions described, for example, in the Petition of Charles Murray 'who is in the greatest distress that ever human being was in . . . I am here confined this 16 months striving to live on the Gaol Allowance which is three ['pieces'] of bread in the twenty-four hours and some water . . . I am almost famished.' 14 March 1804 (unnumbered), *Prisoners' Petitions and Cases*: also Reports of Foster Archer, Inspector of Prisons, 1812 Report, Official Papers 488/48, Report 25 November 1817, Official Papers 488/45, State Paper Office, Dublin (hereafter SPO).
8. Petition of Thomas Gallagher and Patrick Dougherty, 11 March 1812, no.4013. Note that Dougherty was permitted to enlist but Gallagher, found unfit for service, was transported (*Prisoners' Petitions and Cases*).
9. Petition of Dominick and Owen McAteer, 1 September 1809, no.3974, *Prisoners' Petitions and Cases*.

10. Petition of James Roche, Patrick Supple, Andrew Fehilly, 24 August 1817, no.4090, *Prisoners' Petitions and Cases.*

11. For crimes punishable by the Deprivation of Life, Single Felonies, Misdemeanours, etc., see Patrick Colquhoun, *A Treatise on the Police of the Metropolis* (London, 1796), pp.436–45, reprinted in Evans and Pledger (eds), *Contemporary Sources*, vol.2, pp.99–103.

12. A.G.L. Shaw, *Convicts and the Colonies*, 2nd edn (F.W. Cheshire, Melbourne, 1971), p.36.

13. Opinion respecting Penitentiary Houses, 20 May 1790, Official Papers 17/4, SPO.

14. This investigation, part of work in progress on the Irish transported to Australia, 1788–1820, is based on an analysis of all Prisoners' Petitions and Cases held in the State Paper Office and an examination of all official papers relating to Prisoners charged, confined etc. in county and town gaols during this period.

15. Petitions of Leslie Ferguson, 21 August 1817 (unnumbered), *Prisoners' Petitions and Cases*. Sentenced to death, Judge Osborne recommended life transportation.

16. Report of Judge Daly on case of Private John Whelan of the 101st Regiment, tried spring assizes 1810, held in Galway County, no.4015, *Prisoners' Petitions and Cases.*

17. Petition of Richard Gavin, sweeper of the water fountain of the south side of Dublin City, for his sons, James and Abraham, 5 November 1799, no.151, *Prisoners' Petitions and Cases.*

18. Petition of Michael Conway, merchant, of Dublin City, for his son James, 21 March 1799, no.3899, *Prisoners' Petitions and Cases.*

19. Self-transportation was also pleaded by persons 'of good character' who had the means to 'transport' themselves and families to America, as in the case of the elderly churchwarden, Hamilton Gillespie, 27 March 1812, no.4019, *Prisoners' Petitions and Cases.*

20. Petition of mother of James Moore for her son, sentenced at Ballymena, 18 August 1800, no.504, *Prisoners' Petitions and Cases.*

21. An index to the remaining petitions may be found in bound volumes in the Reading Room of the SPO.

22. Petition of Elizabeth Burke for her son William Burke to Lady Louisa Cary, endorsed 'to write to the judge . . . any objection to his serving abroad generally or to his being sent with the Rebels into the Prussian service', 29 March 1799 (unnumbered), *Prisoners' Petitions and Cases.*

23. Report on J. Pouncer, Naval Recruiting Officer, Newgate Gaol, Dublin, 20 April 1804, Official Papers 529/203 SPO.

24. For contemporary accounts of the experiences of sailors, see Henry Baynham, *From the Lower Deck, The Old Navy 1780–1840*, (Hutchinson, London, 1969).

25. Petition from the inhabitants of Clonculloye, County Wicklow on behalf of James, Mark and John Redmond, 10 October 1799, no.215, *Prisoners' Petitions and Cases*. A similar case was the 'application of very many Honest and Loyal Neighbours . . . on behalf of two unfortunate Young Men . . .', 28 November 1797 (unnumbered), *Prisoners' Petitions and Cases.*

26. 'Convicts in Gaol fit for a Penitentiary', Report of Foster Archer, comments by Chief Justice, Carlow Gaol, 26 January 1810. Leonard was sent to the penitentiary but does not appear on the 1812 Quarterly Report for the Penitentiary for Young Criminals.

27. Petition for Thomas Reilly (n.d.) no.3976, *Prisoners' Petitions and Cases.*

28. Petition of John Egan, 11 October 1803, no.812, *Prisoners' Petitions and Cases.*

29. Quarterly Report on the Penitentiary for Young Criminals at Smithfield, 5 October 1812, Official Papers 373/15, SPO.

30. William Griffiths, listed in the penitentiary, and Lawrence Leonard, Ephraim Greaves and George Ownes, selected by the Inspector of Prisons as recommended for the penitentiary despite transportation sentences. Official Papers 308/2, SPO.

31. Boys listed in the Quarterly Report.

32. Return of children sent from on board the *John and Ester* to New Geneva Barracks on the 10th February 1800. Official Paper (misc.) SPO.

33. Report on convicts fit for the penitentiary, Official Papers 308/2, SPO.

34. Petition for John Hogan of Adare County Limerick (n.d.) (unnumbered), *Prisoners' Petitions and Cases*, SPO.

35. For full discussion on the connotations of 'convict' and contemporary assumptions concerning Botany Bay and its inhabitants, see Portia Robinson, *The Hatch and Brood of Time, a Study of the First Generation of Native-Born White Australians c.1788–1828* (Oxford UP, Australia, Melbourne, 1985), vol.1, Introduction p.3 ff.

36. For detailed discussion on the colonial children, see Robinson, *The Hatch and Brood*, esp. Ch.2, 'The Observ'd'; for numbers of children, see p.23.

37. For the colonial children of landowners, see Robinson, *The Hatch and Brood*, Ch.7, p.117 ff.; for the sons of tradesmen, Ch.8, p.205 ff.; for other occupations, Ch.9 (seamen) p.235 ff., Ch.10 (unskilled, semi-skilled), p.257 ff.

38. *Sydney Gazette*, 23 May, 3 June 1804, 18 August 1805.

39. King to Hobart, 9 May 1803, *Historical Records of NSW*, vol.5, p.115.

40. Bigge Appendix, evidence of Major Druitt to Commissioner Bigge. 27 October 1819, *Bonwick Transcripts*, Box 1, pp.11–22, Mitchell Library, Sydney.

41. Bigge Appendix, evidence of T. Messling to Commissioner Bigge, *Bonwick Transcripts*, Box 1, p.531; see also Robinson, *The Hatch and Brood*, pp.132–5.

42. Evidence of Thomas Bowden to Commissioner Bigge, 27 January 1821, *Bonwick Transcripts*, Box 8, pp.3329–31, 3337–9; see also evidence of Rev. William Cowper, 23 January 1821, ibid., pp.3347–54, 3368–71.

15 Telling it Slant: Swift and the *Journal to Stella*

Peter Steele

Emily Dickinson has a poem which goes like this:

> Tell all the Truth but tell it slant—
> Success in Circuit lies
> Too bright for our infirm Delight
> The Truth's superb surprise
>
> As Lightning to the Children eased
> With explanation kind
> The Truth must dazzle gradually
> Or every man be blind—[1]

Hearing this, one catches more than a note characteristic of Dickinson herself. There is also the air associated with many a modern writer, in prose or in poetry, an air of ellipsis, of wary knowledgeability. Her epigrammatic bent is one which other ironists, from Kafka to Beckett, have found virtually inevitable: her reserve about the viability of innocently intended utterance is theirs besides. 'Tell all the truth but tell it slant — /Success in Circuit lies' might be the watchword of any of a hundred modern writers: though they might have deep reservations about the 'all' in the admonition.

Looking back at Swift's writing from such a milieu, it is possible to see an element of the same sort in it. In saying this I do not wish to do any kind of violence to its peculiar character: literary kidnapping, in whatever interest, has never seemed to me much of an activity for a grown person. Still, our own circumstances alert us to those of other times and places: if they did not do so, we should go unalerted to our graves. And in a sense it is an axiom in all attention to Swift that he is not the man ever to allow himself to be taken unawares. Commentators friendly, unfriendly or neutral

talk of his ironies, his masks, his rhetorical aggressivity, his disposition *reculer pour mieux sauter* in a dozen fashions. The worldly-
wise need not kidnap Swift: he is more likely to kidnap them.

Were I allowed to settle on only one of his works, great or small,
to illustrate this propensity, it would probably be *Gulliver's Travels*.
The alert reader will have noticed that in the commendatory letter
which prefaces it, the suppositious Richard Sympson offers in salute
to the book that 'there is an air of truth apparent' about the whole,
and may become the more rueful as he makes his way through the
whole farrago. The joke lies in the veridicality with which the *Travels*
are conducted. Clear-eyed, one is given an ever-heavier heart, as a
Gulliver for whom the Yiddish dictum 'you can't fool me — I'm
too stupid' might have been invented, leads the reader into the most
questionable territories. The Swift who jettisoned the flourished
virtuosity of *A Tale of a Tub* and embraced instead the deprecations
of *Gulliver* knew what he was about: he was Englishing us into
exoticism to a degree that the earlier, farouche performance could
never bring off. Still, the *Tale* and *Gulliver*, not to speak of much
of the poetry, are fictions indeed: and we might not expect to find
the same angularity of address in Swift's correspondence. Here too,
though, the contemporary culture of the questionable comes to our
aid, if aid it is. Modern students of autobiographical or quasi-
autobiographical writing are assiduous in urging that our seeming
franknesses are always in some measure designing — that the writer,
including the writer of letters, lays his hand not after all on his own
heart, but upon that of his reader. The pen as it were is mightier
than the sword because it is a disguised sword — and is also a two-
edged sword.

To cultivate a *frisson* of this sort indefinitely is, after a while, to
cultivate nothing at all, since the saying logically dissolves itself.
And yet, once again, we are being pointed towards something central
in Swift's letter-writing, including *The Journal to Stella*. The late
Irvin Ehrenpreis noted in an essay on *Swift's Letters* that he was 'a
reader who prefers Swift's letters to the bulk of his other works,
whether for their style, their life or their literary design'[2] and in that
essay as in his magisterial biographical and critical study of Swift,
he articulated some of the ways in which intricacy, irony, the
guarded and the give-away touch meet in those letters. My present
essay is in effect a nod in *pietàs* towards the shade of Ehrenpreis:
but I hope that it may also do some justice to the shade of Swift. I

quote Ehrenpreis's introduction to his own study of the *Journal to Stella*:

> It can hardly sound exciting to say the so-called *Journal* consists of sixty-five diary letters addressed by Swift to Mrs Johnson and Mrs Dingley from September 1710 to June 1713. Perhaps a descriptive account would be more provocative. They are, then, letters by the finest prose stylist of his time to the woman he trusted supremely, recording the most dramatic years of his life and involving the main historical figures and public events of those years. It had been standard practice for scholars to search the *Journal* for information about Swift's life or the reign of Queen Anne. Other appeals of the letters have received less appreciation.[3]

One of those 'appeals', it should be said, is the frankness with which Swift can acknowledge that it is no part of his policy to be frank to all. So, in Letter 10 (November 1710) we have:

> O Lord! does Patrick write word of my not coming till *spring*? Insolent man! he know my secrets? No; as my Lord Mayor said, No; if I thought my shirt knew, &c. Faith, I will come as soon as it is any way proper for me to come; but, to say the truth, I am at present a little involved with the present ministry in some certain things (which I tell you as a secret) and soon as ever I can clear my hands, I will stay no longer: for I hope the first-fruit business will be soon over in all its forms. But, to say the truth, the present ministry have a difficult task, and want me, &c. Perhaps they may be just as grateful as others: but, according to the best judgment I have, they are pursuing the true interest of the public; and therefore I am glad to contribute what is in my power. For God's sake, not a word of this to any alive.[4]

That last direction answers to Swift's lifelong anxiety about being out-guessed and out-flanked. In a few years he was to be beyond any help from the Tories who were, just now, soliciting his aid and offering a *quid pro quo*. He would, at that later stage, and for much of the rest of his life, find ways of generating new sources of personal power and political influence — would become the Swift of Yeats' pantheon. But whether, as now at the age of 43, or when writing the *Legion Club* at the age of 69, he was politically sanguine or politically desperate, his dread of being 'found out' went beyond an understandable fear of sanctions that might be visited upon him. It had to do above all with his fear of being made a fool of — or, if things did not go so far as that — his losing the authority which both flowed from and reinforced his capacity for devastating formulation. Sometimes the lie of the land was such that Swift would exercise himself in Jovian thunders: sometimes, to be anachronistic about it, he carried on like a kind of Scarlet Pimpernel of the political liberties of the Irish, retrieving them in the face of *force majeure*: in either event, it was essential to his project that he not be driven into any rhetorical corner: and in turn, lest that happen, essential that information and its attendant insights be kept from any potential antagonist. When Ehrenpreis says that, as is certainly true, he 'trusted supremely' the Mrs Johnson who was the real recipient of the *Journal* letters, he might have added that trust was not something which came easily to Swift, or was offered to many — hence, for instance, his dry guess that 'the present ministry' who 'want me', 'may be just as grateful as others'. When Swift gives out information he is like a fisherman paying out the line: you can feel his tenseness as he does so, and he is waiting for any slack to be taken up.

A starker example of this kind of thing is in Letter 17, on 28 February 1710:

> I walked to-day into the city for my health, and there dined, which I always do when the weather is fair, and business permits, that I may be under a necessity of taking a good walk, which is the best thing I can do at present for my health. Some bookseller has raked up everything I writ, and published it t'other day in one volume; but I know nothing of it, 'twas without my knowledge or consent: it makes a four shilling book, and is called *Miscellanies in Prose and Verse*. Took pretends he knows nothing of it, but I doubt he is at the bottom. One must have patience with these things; the best of it is, I shall be plagued no more. However, I'll bring a couple of them over with me for MD, perhaps you may desire to see them. I hear they sell mightily.[5]

Swift in fact, as Harold Williams points out[6] in his edition of the *Journal*, knew perfectly well about the intended publication. Many months before he had drawn up a list of pieces for inclusion. Moreover, it is unlikely that the Esther Johnson who had known Swift since she was a young girl (she was now 29) and to whom he

had for years been in effect guardian and tutor would have been
deceived for a moment.

What he is up to is his old game of pretended deprecation, one
which he could play upon either an object or a person, himself or
another. It is not here a very sophisticated game — the 'I hear they
sell mightily' has the cheerful self-satisfaction which is the proper
reward of saluted authorship. 'One must have patience with these
things', he says: such patience is not hard to find.

But the letters would not be what they are if the rallying and the
flirtation did not take more overt terms. In May 1711, there is the
day's report:

> I dined to-day at lord Shelburn's, where lady Kerry made me a
> present of four India handkerchiefs, which I have in mind to
> keep for little MD, only that I had rather, &c. I have been a
> mighty handkerchief-monger, and have bought abundance of
> snuff ones since I have left off taking snuff. And I am resolved,
> when I come over, MD shall be acquainted with lady Kerry: we
> have struck up a mighty friendship; and she has much better
> sense than any other lady of your country. We are almost in love
> with one another; but she is most gregiously ugly; but perfectly
> well bred, and governable as I please. I am resolved, when I
> come, to keep no company but MD: you know I kept my
> resolution last time; and, except Mr Addison, conversed with
> none but you and your club of deans and Stoytes. 'Tis three
> weeks, young women, since I had a letter from you; and yet,
> methinks, I would not have another for five pound till this is
> gone; and yet I send every day to the Coffee-house, and I would
> fain have a letter, and not have a letter; and I don't know what,
> nor I don't know how, and this goes on very slow; 'tis a week
> to-morrow since I began it. I am a poor country gentleman, and
> don't know how the world passes. Do you know that every
> syllable I write I hold my lips just for all the world as if I were
> talking in our own little language to MD. Faith, I am very silly;
> but I can't help it for my life.[7]

There are, evidently, all sorts of 'slants' in this passage. The Lady
Anne Kerry to whom he refers, Lord Shelburn's sister, has had her
place a number of times before. The previous New Year's Day he
had dined with her and her brother. A month later she was sending
him bottles of bitter medicine such as she herself took — 'and we

are so fond of one another, because our ailments are the same', as Swift tells Stella at the time, contriving in the next sentence to make that too a bond between himself and her.[8] For the present, she is simply the whetstone of Swift's wit as he writes to the woman in Dublin, who knows that *she* is not 'most gregiously ugly', is 'perfectly well bred', and is, variously 'governable' by Swift and herself his governor. That she is this last is obvious from his dependency on the letter from Dublin which he awaits, the while he is finishing his own letter to her — so that, as he had said in the second letter of them all, in September 1710, 'I shall always be in conversation with MD, and, MD with Presto'.[9] His saying that he holds his lips as if he were talking in their private language simply underlines everything already betokened.

What is quite certain, however, is that he is not simply 'a poor country gentleman, and don't know how the world passes'. Not only could he not think himself countrified when in London: the whole bent of his letters, past and present, is that of a man who believes himself in the thick of affairs, even though he might in season pine for the rural life of Laracor. The gesture is a literary one — an Horatian shrug of deprecation, a glancing reference to Don Quixote, much a favourite of Swift's. 'Success in Circuit lies' — if he cannot be with the woman he loves, he can once again 'commence author', and carry through those writerly exercises which have helped bind her to him in the first place: and which will in future so often be turned to celebrate her excellences.

I pointed out earlier that the modern ironising temper can send us with a kind of instinctive alertness to watch at work the Swift who is, in any case, a by-word for self-guarding. This is true, and there will be more to say about it. But it would be a pity, in looking at his special case, to miss the general, and generally interesting point about the familiar letter — that it is inevitably on a 'slant' into the life which it offers to render. In this respect it is like the much more comprehensively studied forms, the novel and the dramatic poem. We look to these for a telling blend of general and particular observation. A Tolstoi or a George Eliot or a Thomas Mann may feel pressed in the direction of the general, and from them we receive summary accounts. A Browning, a Hopkins or a William Carlos Williams may have his attention caught, as it were, on the thorn of the particular, and the poetry will offer its yield accordingly. But neither the generalisation nor the particularisation, try as it will, circumscribes either the processes of consciousness or the objects of allusion. The world, in short, is always being at best darted into, slanted upon: and it is a large part of literary analysis to clarify the manner of the darting, the angle of the slant. A good deal of the *Journal* is in fact given to that interplay between the general and the particular. Swift, so little given to speculation, yet enjoys generalising, but loves to have the generalisation lodged among particular observations. Once again *Gulliver's Travels* is a median case, with the poems running off to the particular end of the scale, and the *Examiner* papers to the generalising. The two dispositions can be seen easily enough in a *Journal* passage like the following:

> I designed a jaunt into the city to-day to be merry, but was disappointed; so one always is in this life; and I could not see lord Dartmouth to-day, with whom I had some business. Business and pleasure both disappointed. You can go to your dean, and for want of him, goody Stoyte, or Walls, or Manley, and meet every where with cards and claret. I dined privately with a friend on a herring and chicken, and half a flask of bad Florence. I begin to have fires now, when the mornings are cold; I have got some loose bricks at the back of my grate for good husbandry. Fine weather. Patrick tells me, my caps are wearing out; I know not how to get others. I want a necessary woman strangely; I am as helpless as an elephant.[10]

This has about it some of the seeming tumble of run-of-the-mill journalism: but a closer look gives us, whether by half-conscious associations or by a more deliberate designing, link upon link. 'Business and pleasure both disappointed' is the précis of the whole, with 'was disappointed; so one always is in this life' as its more general form. Stella is half-consoled, half-accused in that she has acquaintance and entertainment always to hand: Swift, around whom in his triumphs or his miseries the world is always supposed to turn, has 'a herring and chicken, and half a flask of bad Florence'. The last image sparks his reference to fires: things seasonable though the world is persistently unseasonable. And there is, after all, 'fine weather'. Yet as Kafka once said, 'in the battle between the world and yourself, back the world': Swift is in the event as 'helpless as an elephant'. Customarily useless at deduction, and contemptuous of it, Swift induces all the confirmation he likes of whatever sentiment is upon him when he chances to write.

In one sense, this is the registration of mood-play, mood-swing: in another, the designs of the will upon a recurrently recalcitrant world. 'I am as helpless as an elephant', is one of Swift's very frequent essays into animal imagery, a kind of imagery which allows for the looked-down-upon, or at least the domesticated, but also for the bizarre, the self-othering. Australia's present Prime Minister said once, of political involvements, 'If you can't ride two horses at once, you shouldn't be in the bloody circus.' Swift is a great rider of two psychic horses, that of meaninglessness and that of meaning. Orwell did not call him a 'Tory Anarchist' for nothing. Reading a passage like the present one, one regrets even more than usual that none of Stella's letters in reply still exists.

One of the main aspects under which Swift goes about his truth-telling, in the *Journals* as elsewhere, is that of the judge. He is less interested in, or fitted for, alertness to all the evidence, than in giving a verdict and a sentence — separating the sheep from the goats, and punishing the goats for being what they are. It is an activity which lacks charm, but then Swift never set up to be charming. It seems likely that, in writing to Stella, he took it for granted that his commanding manner would be his real attraction. After all, the 'little language' and other scraps of intimate raillery would be an assurance that his powers were not levelled against her — as indeed the very existence of the *Journal* attested. He had little enough time for lawyers, but the actual bringing down of verdicts was as connatural to him as anything could be. Which does not mean that he held judges in any personally high regard, any more than he inevitably respected lords. All had admittedly the sanction of a hierarchical society: but each, being but a man, had all the human vulnerability. It is no surprise then to find a passage like this one:

I was to-day at a trial between lord Lansdown and lord Carteret, two friends of mine. It was in the Queen's-Bench, for about six thousand pounds a year (or nine I think). I sat under lord chief justice Parker, and his pen falling down, I reached it up. He made me a low bow; and I was going to whisper him that *I had done good for evil; for he would have taken mine from me.* I told it to lord treasurer and Bolingbroke. Parker would not have known me, if several lords on the bench, and in the court, bowing, had not turned every body's eyes, and set them a-whispering. I owe the dog a spite, and will pay him in two months at farthest, if I can.[11]

Parker[12] had pronounced a passage in Swift's *The Conduct of the Allies* capable of treasonable interpretation, which would have been enough to make him no good judge in Swift's eyes. Here was politics in a straightforward sense: but Swift was always reluctant at best to acknowledge that he was himself as prone to the selectivities and self-deceits of partisanship. Later in the same letter to Stella he says, 'They say some learned Dutchman has wrote a book, proving, by civil law, that we do them wrong by this peace; but I shall shew, by plain reason, that we have suffered the wrong, and not they.'[13]

There it is, the confidence in personal expertise and the authority which it confers, over against the low arts and mere specialisations of his enemies. There is something positively endearing about the innocence of it all: once again, it would be agreeable to know what the letter's recipient made of it.

It is my impression — I would not put it more strongly — that as the *Journal* progresses, it becomes more scurrying, as Swift becomes more restless. Experience, of course, was thickening about him: his health, always mercurial at best, was a vexation to him: he was angry and lonely even in the midst of applause, when that was to be had. What Yvor Winters once called, memorably, 'the rain of matter upon sense' was probably an affliction to him. Still, less than three months before the *Journal* ends, he is as in command of the processes as he ever was. In the entry for 14 March 1712–13 we find this:

It was a lovely day this, and I took the Advantage of walking a good deal in the Park: before I went to Court. Coll Disney one of our Society is ill of a Feaver; and we fear, in great Danger: We all love him mightily, and he woud be a great Loss. I doubt I shall not buy the Library, for a Roguy bookseller has offered 60 more than I designed to give; so you see I meant to have a good Bargain. I dined with Ld Tr and his Saterday company; but there were but 7 at Table. Ld Peterborow is ill, and spits blood with a Bruise he got before he left Engld; but I believe, an Italian Lady he has brought over, is the Cause that his Illness returns. You know old Ldy Bellesis is dead at last. She has left Ld Berkeley of Stratton one of her Executors, and it will be of great Advantage to him, they say above ten thousd Pounds. I stayd with Ld Tr upon Business after the Company was gone; but I dare not tell you upon wht. My Letters would be good Memoirs, if I durst venture to say a thousd things that pass; but

I hear so much of Letters opening at your Post Office, that I am fearfull &c. and so 'good nite sollahs & rove pdfr Md'.[14]

There is a flurry of persons and circumstances here, and yet, what a sample of Swift's recurrent preoccupations it provides! There is the unaffected savour of the physical — 'It was a lovely day this, and I took the Advantage of walking a good deal in the Park'; there is friendship's celebrant — the one so often loved even in the teeth of his own angers. 'Coll Disney . . . is ill of a Feaver . . . we all love him mightily'; there is the incorrigibly bookish man, out-bidden for a library; there is the courtier of power, dining with the Lord Treasurer; there is the purveyor of sexual gossip, for whom Lord Peterborough comes pat to the case; there is the man who loves to *count*, even if inaccurately, and who etches in Lord Berkeley's 'ten thousand pounds' of advantage. Decisively, though — and let this be the final note — there is the man whose 'letters would be good Memoirs if I durst venture to say a thousand things that pass'. Governed and hobbled by his caution as he was, Swift could not predict that those letters would one day be something better than memoirs — the shadows of a man who, as far as might be, tried to cast no shadow.

Notes and References

1. *The Complete Poems of Emily Dickinson*, Thomas H. Johnson (ed.) (Little, Brown, Boston and Toronto, 1960), pp.506–7.
2. Irvin Ehrenpreis, 'Swift's Letters', in *Focus: Swift*, C.J. Rawson (ed.) (Sphere Books, London, 1971), p.197.
3. Irvin Ehrenpreis, *Swift: The Man, His Works, and The Age. Vol.II: Dr Swift* (Methuen, London, 1967), pp.651–2.
4. Jonathan Swift, *Journal to Stella*, Harold Williams (ed.) (2 vols, Basil Blackwell, Oxford, 1974), vol.1, pp.107–8.
5. Ibid., vol.1, p.203.
6. Ibid., n.8.
7. Ibid;, pp.260–1.
8. Ibid., p.178.
9. Ibid., p.8.
10. Ibid., vol.2, p.407.
11. Ibid., p.568.
12. Ibid., p.478, n.16.
13. Ibid., p.569.
14. Ibid., p.638.

16 'The Harp New-Strung': Nationalism, Culture and the United Irishmen

A.T.Q. Stewart

The Society of United Irishmen had its origins in the volunteer movement and its true significance cannot be perceived outside the context of volunteer politics. Nor can it be fully understood if it is presented, as it so often is, purely in the light of subsequent events. To us it appears to mark the beginning of a new phase of Irish history, but we must never forget that it also marked the end of a phase — it was the last stage of an experiment which failed, an experiment which belonged to the eighteenth century and to no other.

For want of a better term, I would define that experiment as the attempt by Protestants to democratise, and make acceptable to Catholics, the peculiarly eighteenth-century concept of the 'Protestant nation'. That is not a strictly accurate term, though a convenient one, and it is loaded in our own times with implications of prejudice and élitism. What I need is something closer to 'Hiberno-British nation'. For reasons I shall presently explain, I mean by this something quite distinct from 'Anglo-Irish'. And let us recognise that the totality of the definition rests on a multitude of assumptions about society which no longer have any relevance for us.

To begin with, therefore, the United Irishmen were little concerned with what *we* would regard as the Catholic perception of Irish nationality, the perception in fact which has become paramount in the years since, especially outside Ireland. In this country, for example, the United Irishmen forcibly exiled after 1798 appear at least to be predominantly Catholic, and enter the history books as patriots in that tradition, suffering because of their attempt to free their native land. This has coloured all references to 1798 in histories of Australia and it introduces another complication which is not often noticed, that the insurrection is not so closely related to the United Irishmen as is popularly believed. With every year that

258

passes I find myself less able to connect the two, except at the superficial level of transferred ideology. Let me make it clear, then, that I regard the experiment to which I have referred as having failed by 1795, at the latest, with Fitzwilliam's recall and the veto on further progress towards Catholic Emancipation, and that I am here concerned only with the first phase of United Irish history. There are two things which everyone knows about the Society of United Irishmen — that it was founded by Wolfe Tone, and that its primary aim was to separate Ireland from Great Britain as an independent republic. Both are untrue. I have written about the origins of the United Irishmen elsewhere.[1] As to their prime objective it was clearly set out in the United Irish Test:

> I, A.B., in the presence of God, do pledge myself to my country, that I will use all my abilities and influence in the attainment of an impartial and adequate representation of the Irish nation in Parliament, and as a means of absolute and immediate necessity in accomplishing this chief good of Ireland, I shall do whatever lies in my power to forward a brotherhood of affection, an identity of interests, a communion of rights, and an union of power among Irishmen of all religious persuasions without which every reform must be partial, not national, inadequate to the wants, delusive to the wishes and insufficient for the freedom and happiness of this country.[2]

Nothing could be plainer. The reform of Parliament was the end, and an expedient political union or alliance with Catholics was to be the means.

The first Belfast society of United Irishmen, however, chose as their emblem an Irish harp without the crown and the motto: 'It is new-strung, and shall be heard.'[3]

The purpose of this chapter is to examine what they could have meant by this device, that is, to say something about the culture of the original United Irishmen, and their conception of nationality and patriotism. The first society was born where one might least expect, among the Protestant dissenters of Belfast. Every member of it was Presbyterian, and three were sons of ministers. When the second society was formed in Dublin a month later, it had, as might be expected, a more representative mixture of Protestant, Catholic and Dissenter,[4] but even here the Presbyterian influence was strong.

Dr William Drennan, its first president, and Oliver Bond, its secretary, were also sons of the manse.

The process which brought the Presbyterians to the centre of
Irish national politics really began in 1768 with the passing of the
Octennial Act. Henceforth, elections were held every eight years,
and not only on the demise of the Crown, making Parliament more
responsive to popular opinion. In 1776 the Presbyterians succeeded
in electing James Wilson, a half-pay naval officer, to represent their
interests as one of the members for Co. Antrim. He undertook to
submit all his actions in Parliament to the scrutiny of the local
congregations, and in his campaign he had the full support of the
Presbyterian Synod. The Dissenters took the novel step of imposing
on him an elaborate test. He had to agree not to accept any place
or pension under the Crown, to obey his constituents' instructions,
and to work for the reform of Parliament and the repeal of Poynings'
Law, restoring to Ireland her rights as a free country. The adoption
of this form of test was very significant both because of its content,
and because it became the model for those which the volunteers
were later to impose upon their representatives during the campaign
for legislative independence and parliamentary reform.[5] Ultimately,
as we have seen, the United Irish oath of association was called a
'test'.

The American war, the threat of invasion and the popularity of
the volunteer movement caused a wave of patriotic and nationalist
feeling to sweep through the country. In this, the northern Presbyterians enthusiastically participated. Their nationalism was, in fact,
from the government's point of view, of the most dangerous kind,
for it was pro-American and tinged with republicanism. 'Presbyterians in the north', reported Lord Harcourt, 'in their hearts are
Americans.'[6] This was largely to be explained by the massive emigration of Ulster Presbyterians to America between 1718 and 1775,
and it has even been argued that some of the political ideas of the
colonists had their origins in Ulster in the first place, and were
propagated in America by pupils of Francis Hutcheson.[7]

It is perhaps not necessary here to restate in detail the reasons
for the Presbyterians' assumption of an active part in liberal and
opposition politics from the time of the outbreak of the war in
America. Enough to say that in the north they made up the majority
in the Volunteer Corps, and that they provided the whole national
movement with its radical edge.[8] It was the Belfast First Volunteer
Company which responded at once to Flood when he launched the

Renunciation campaign in 1782. Turning aside from the great national achievements of the period between 1778 and 1782, it is interesting to observe that they also succeeded in removing most of the disabilities imposed upon them as a sect, above all the repeal of the famous sacramental test. The attitudes adopted by many of the northern Presbyterians in these years were in marked contrast to the gratitude and loyalty with which their grandfathers had greeted the Hanoverian succession in 1714. 'The Presbyterians in Ulster', declares the author of a pamphlet in the 1720s,

> own themselves to be under very great obligations to Almighty God for their liberty in the exercise of their religion, which they enjoy by the clemency and goodness of the best of governments, and they hope none will be so injurious to them as to construct their steady adherence to those principles which by lawful authority are established in Scotland and tolerated in Ireland as an improper return but to God and our Government for so great a favour.[9]

In 1722 some Ulster students at Glasgow University got into a familiar kind of dispute with the College authorities, over the election of the Principal, and two of them were sent down for lighting a bonfire at the entrance to the University. Eventually they took their case as far as the Court of Session in Edinburgh. The Lord Advocate ruled in the students' favour, but he warned that Irishmen must not be encouraged to think that they could light bonfires in the streets of Glasgow whenever they thought fit. James Arbuckle, objecting to the racialism of this remark, wrote:

> As a reflection on Irishmen, however unmannerly it may have been in itself, it is much more so, when we consider against whom it is levelled, viz., the numerous body of Britons transplanted, who have done and suffered more for the British and Protestant interest than any twenty imperious Ministers of State had ever either the will or capacity of doing.[10]

Nor did Presbyterians complain unduly, until late in the century, about the political disabilities to which they were still subject. As late as 1749, Gilbert Kennedy, the minister of the second Belfast congregation, could write:

We suffer no hardships now on account of religion, expecting such as are negative — I mean, our being put on a level with the notorious and avowed enemies of the constitution; by being legally disqualified from serving His Majesty and the public in any places of trust; for this very reason and no other, because we conscientiously scruple the terms of conformity. For disloyalty and disaffection to the Government is not, cannot *be* alleged, since, when there are public ends to serve which require our assistance, the penal law is superseded as long as the necessity for our service continues.[11]

Thus far the dissenters had a separate sense of identity which was neither Scottish nor Irish. They were the Scots in Ulster, an extension of Scotland, and particularly the Kirk of Scotland, into Ireland, making them, after 1707, part of the British nation in Ireland. They distinguished themselves from the Irish, by which they meant the Gaelic native Irish, and they were certainly not part of the Anglo-Irish Ascendancy. This identity was strongly reinforced by the fact that their ministers were trained at one or other of the Scottish universities, usually Glasgow. There they were entered on the matriculation rolls as a separate nationality, 'Scotus hibernus' while other Irish students were described simply as 'Hibernus'.

After 1775 this simple model of identity was complicated in various ways. As a consequence of their increasing role in national politics, the Presbyterians came to identify more closely with the Protestant Ascendancy's sense of Irishness, without relinquishing any of their grievances against the episcopalians over other matters.

Here a brief digression is necessary. For the episcopalian Protestants the political restringing of the harp began almost as soon as the Revolutionary Wars had secured their ascendancy in 1690. As a minority they were well aware that they depended ultimately on England for support 'and were ever fearful of offending that kingdom, from whose powerful interference, in case of emergency, they hoped for protection.'[12] But as the century progressed, the threat of a Catholic *revanche* receded, and especially after 1745 when Ireland remained quiet during the Jacobite crisis, the Protestant ruling class became bolder and more independent, just as the American colonists were doing. The Irish Parliament was developing a new *esprit de corps* and chafing at the old bonds, above all Poynings' Law and the claim of the English Parliament to legislate for Ireland.[13]

It is too simple, of course, to suggest that it needed the political events of the eighteenth century to make the heirs of the Cromwellian settlers feel Irish. As Bernard Shaw pointed out, 'Eternal is the fact that the human creature born in Ireland and brought up in its air is Irish.'[14] (Unfortunately, however, this intense Irishness has never meant Irish unity.) What *did* happen in the eighteenth century was that the growing sense of security and stability reawakened pride in sense of nation and brought to the surface all the old resentments at the (largely unconscious) English assumption of superiority in every aspect of Anglo-Irish relations. Just as unconscious was the Ascendancy's assumption that they, and they alone, represented 'the Irish nation'. An incidental consequence of the Protestant gentry's increased sense of security was a growing contempt for the Protestant Dissenters, 'so different', as J.C. Beckett writes, 'from the hearty cooperation which had existed during the revolutionary period and from the open confession of community of interest made during the invasion scare of 1715–16'.[15]

Like most emergent nations, this one showed signs of a quest for a cultural identity to underpin its politics, and though in time it was itself to become a recognisably distinct culture, that of the Anglo-Irish, it was then inevitable that it should turn to Ireland's Gaelic past. Gradually, a scholarly interest in the antiquities and ancient culture was created. Contemporary cross-currents of antiquarianism and romanticism throughout the British Isles favoured this development. Studies were produced of the Irish language and new translations made from it.[16] Yet here one must be aware of an important distinction. While the Anglo-Irish wished to reinforce their political claims by emphasising the distinctiveness of Irish culture, they did not attempt to make the Irish language a basis for a national culture *totally* separate from that of England, as was done at the end of the nineteenth century. The Irish nation, like the Scottish nation, could exist comfortably within the wider political framework once its proper rights were restored. Nor did they regard the Gaelic past as 'belonging' in any sense to the Catholic majority of the population, or linked in any way to their political claims.

Thus it is important to see the phenomenon in its contemporary light. The *apparent* contradiction is clearly to be seen in Flood, who left his fortune to Trinity College to endow studies in the Gaelic language and history. Yet, of all the Volunteer leaders, Flood was the most adamantly opposed to Catholic Emancipation. There was one string in the Irish harp which he wished for a long time to be mute. 'I am frightened about the popery business,' he wrote to Lord Charlemont in 1782. 'It ought to be touched only by a master hand. It is a chord of such wondrous potency that I dread the sound of it, and believe with you that the harmony would be better, if, like that of the spheres, it were, at least for a time, inaudible.'[17]

We can trace the process of the Presbyterian identification with the Protestant nation very clearly in the life of William Drennan, the first president of the Dublin Society of United Irishmen. As a student at Edinburgh University during the American war, he wholeheartedly took the side of the colonists, exulting in letters home at Burgoyne's defeat at Saratoga in 1775. He is repelled by the Scottish divines who pray for the success of British arms.[18] From his earliest years his patriotism is of the most ardent kind. He it was who first called Ireland 'the emerald isle' in his best poem *Erin*. (His better lines are often attributed to Moore, in itself a neat illustration of the shift that was soon to occur.)[19]

Drennan had a deep reverence for the memory of his father, the minister of Belfast's first congregation, who had been the friend and colleague of the philosopher Francis Hutcheson, and of James Arbuckle already mentioned. A revealing amount of the ideology of the early United Irishmen stems from Hutcheson's political teaching, but that is another story. The Hutcheson circle regarded themselves as Ulster Scots, yet Drennan indicates in lines written about his father, that his patriotism came from that source, interestingly in a classical disguise. As a child he asks his father why Ithaca was so dear to Ulysses.

'What made a barren rock so dear?'
'My boy, he had a country there,'
And who then dropt a *prescient* tear?[20]

A second complicating factor was that the American and French revolutions widened the definition of patriotism. The United Irishmen were patriots in the Jeffersonian sense, which is almost the opposite of ours. Men of this stamp actually regarded nationalism as uncivilised. To be a patriot was to adopt a wider, more cosmopolitan outlook, supporting the Rights of Man in opposition to the narrow self-interest of national governments. When Wordsworth says in *The Prelude* that he became a patriot, he does not mean that he became a Frenchman. In the Belfast celebrations of the anniversary of the fall of the Bastille the bust of Franklin was carried through the streets with the motto 'where liberty is, there is my country'. Camille Desmoulins talks of the need to support the patriots of Danzig, Cracow and Belfast.[21]

And here we can perceive a tension between the rational political philosophy which Drennan so eloquently propounded and the emotional and very Irish love of home which he and his father had admitted. This tension was of course more widely manifest. The tide of Romanticism was steadily encroaching on the Age of Reason. If the United Irish philosophy owes much to the eighteenth-century rationalist thinkers, much of the revolutionary and nationalist fervour stems from precisely the reaction to all that. Drennan's poem *Glendalloch* has already all the romantic properties, moonlit ruins and mouldering tombs.[22] Order which has become boring is giving way to the sweets of disorder, in society as in literature.

The other contribution of the American and French revolutions was the revival of classical republicanism, and to this the Presbyterians were peculiarly susceptible because of their history. Children are taught in school that the United Irishmen took their republicanism — remember that they were by no means *all* republicans — from the French Revolution. This is only partly true, because long before 1789 we find the Dissenters so described. For example, the Lord Lieutenant, Lord Rutland, on his tour of Ireland in 1784, talks of Lisburn and other centres in the north as being 'full of republicans'.[23]

The Dissenters' republicanism had complex roots — in the doctrines of that Republic on the shores of Lake Geneva where Calvinism began, in the visionary republics of mid-seventeenth-century Levellers, and in the history of republican Rome so admired by the old Real Whigs. Addison's *Cato*, a play I now defy anyone to find readable, owed its extraordinary eighteenth-century fame to that simple fact. Arbuckle and his friends in 1722 further annoyed their professors by performing it at Glasgow, nicely calculating the balance of its popularity against the presbytery's disapproval of play-acting.[24] Some of these students would become the kind of dissenting ministers Hazlitt was still to find objectionable a century later,

(the *Ultima Thule* of the sanguine, visionary temperament in politics) stuffing their pipes with dried currant-leaves, calling it Radical tobacco, lighting it with a lens in the rays of the sun, and at every puff fancying that they undermined the Boroughmongers . . . . Those same Dissenting Ministers throughout the country (I mean the descendants of the old Puritans) are to this hour a sort of Fifth-monarchy men: very turbulent fellows, in my opinion altogether incorrigible, and according to the suggestions of others, should be hanged out of the way without judge or jury for the safety of church and state.[25]

The sudden interest which the Presbyterians of Belfast began to take after 1791 in Gaelic language and culture owed something to the *Zeitgeist*, but it was more solid and businesslike than is sometimes assumed. The festival of blind harpers held in Belfast in 1792 is well known, though it failed to impress Tone ('strum, strum and be hanged').[26] Tone, by the way, is one United Irishman who showed no interest of any kind in Ireland's Gaelic heritage: he was, of course, a southerner and a Church of Ireland Protestant. The *Northern Star*, however, the journal of the northern United Irishmen, made it a plank of its editorial policy. In 1795 it printed the first number of *Bolg an Tsolair* or Gaelic magazine, 120 pages of grammar and vocabulary, Gaelic poetry and translations, and declared that the Irish language would be of value to all who desired the union and improvement of 'this divided and neglected kingdom.'[27]

Surprisingly, the interest of the Belfast Presbyterians in Irish went far beyond the nationalism of the United Irishmen. The city's oldest grammar school, founded in 1785 as the Belfast Academy, was a Presbyterian venture, though it accepted pupils of all denominations. In 1795 Irish was being taught there by one Patrick Lynch, who also gave lessons in private houses. Over 30 years later Irish classes were still being conducted in the Academy by Thomas Feenaghty, author of a standard Irish grammar, and the principal, Dr Reuben John Bryce, a Presbyterian minister, was secretary and founder of the Ulster Gaelic Society.[28]

This reminds us that not all those who were eager to learn Irish shared the ideals of the United Irishmen. Some Presbyterian ministers actually wanted to learn Irish in order to convert Catholics in Irish-speaking areas, and for some it was simply a scholarly interest. The Rev. Moses Neilson of Rademon in Co. Down, one of the original subscribers to the Belfast Academy, was a noted Irish scholar. So too was his son, the Rev. William Neilson of Dundalk. Yet the Neilson family were Loyalists. In 1798 William Neilson was

arrested by the yeomen for preaching in Irish in his church. Since
no one in the court was able to read the evidence, he had to translate
it himself! It was, of course, innocent of political content.[29]

In the first five years between 1795 and 1800, the convergence of
political nationalism with Gaelic culture was abruptly halted. Dr
Marianne Elliott has pointed out that historians have still to explain
to us why the republicanism of the first United Irishmen was so
swiftly transformed by the traditional fears and aspirations of the
Catholic population, and how large sections of 'a non-political and
essentially loyal' peasantry could have acquired in one decade 'many
of the fundamental traits of later separatist movements'. Already
by 1800 popular culture speaks of 'dead rebel heroes, of the English
oppressor and the Protestant enemy'.[30] To put the matter in crudely
simple terms, republicanism went into the 1798 insurrection Protestant and came out Catholic. Republicanism had made no appeal
to Catholics before 1798, rather the reverse. With some notable
exceptions, they took the side of the Crown in the American contest,
though Irish-Americans now refuse to believe this, and they were
indignant at French republicans' treatment of the Church and the
clergy.

When republicanism re-emerged in the second half of the nineteenth century it was firmly attached to Catholic popular culture
and to Gaelic revivalism. It was as if it had to be divested of all its
Protestant and secular content before it could be assimilated into
nationalism and the older Catholic sense of Irish identity. 'It is new
strung and shall be heard.' It was the misfortune of the Presbyterian
United Irishmen to begin to string the harp anew at the very moment
it was to be wrenched from their hands.

Notes and References

1. A.T.Q. Stewart, '"A Stable Unseen Power": William Drennan and the Origins
of the United Irishmen?', in John Bossy and Peter Jupp (eds), *Essays Presented to
Michael Roberts* (Blackstaff Press, Belfast, 1976), pp.80–92.

2. William Drennan to Samuel McTier, 9 November 1791. Public Record Office
of Northern Ireland, Drennan Correspondence, D591/313.

3. R.R. Madden, *The United Irishmen, Their Lives and Times* (7 vols, London,
1842–46) vol.1, p.592.

4. R.B. McDowell, 'The Personnel of the Dublin Society of United Irishmen,
1791–4', *Irish Historical Studies*, vol.2, no.5 (1940), pp.12–53.

5. E.M. Johnston, *Great Britain and Ireland 1760–1800* (Oliver and Boyd, Edinburgh, 1963), pp.182–3.

6. Ibid., p.180.

7. H.F. May, *The Enlightenment in America* (Oxford UP, New York, 1976), pp.19, 38, 293, 343; D.F. Norton, 'Francis Hutcheson in America', *Studies in Voltaire and the Eighteenth Century*, vol.64 (1976), pp.1547–68; J.M. Barkley, 'Francis Hutcheson', *Bulletin of the Presbyterian Historical Society of Ireland* (1985).

8. According to the *Belfast Newsletter*, 17 February 1792, 'nine-tenths' of the volunteer delegates at the Dungannon convention in 1782 were Presbyterian.

9. *An Apology for the Northern Presbyterians in Ireland*, transcript in Edinburgh University Library, La.iii, p.263.

10. [James Arbuckle] *A Short Account of the Late Treatment of the Students of the University of G.....w*, Dublin, 1722.

11. Gilbert Kennedy Jr, *The Great Blessing of Peace and Truth in Our Days*, 1749, in T. Witherow, *Historical and Literary Memorials of Presbyterianism in Ireland 1623–1731*, 2nd series (Aylesbury, London and Belfast, 1879), p.68.

12. Lord Charlemont quoted in E.M. Johnston, *Great Britain and Ireland*, p.3.

13. The Declaratory Act of 1720, which confirmed this claim and that of the English House of Lords to be the supreme appellate jurisdiction, was a particular grievance.

14. G.B. Shaw, *The Matter with Ireland*, David H. Greene and Dan H. Laurence (eds) (Hart-Davies, London, 1962), pp.294–5.

15. J.C. Beckett, *Protestant Dissent in Ireland 1687–1780* (Faber and Faber, London, 1948), p.95.

16. R.B. McDowell, *Irish Public Opinion, 1750–1800* (Faber and Faber, London, 1944), p.23.

17. Flood to Charlemont, 7 January 1782, Charlemont MS, *Historical Manuscripts Commission*, Thirteenth Report, vol.2, p.391.

18. William Drennan to Mrs M. McTier, 14 November 1777; 13 December 1777, PRONI, D591/9a and 17.

19. William Drennan, *Fugitive Pieces in Verse and Prose* (Belfast, 1815), pp.1–3. According to John of Salisbury, Pope Adrian IV gave Henry II an emerald ring when confirming him in his title as lord of Ireland. The relation of Presbyterian radicalism to the Gaelic revival is thoroughly explored in Dr Norman Vance's article, 'Celts, Carthaginians and Constitutions: Anglo-Irish Literary Relations, 1780–1820', *Irish Historical Studies*, vol.22, no.87 (1981).

20. Drennan, *Fugitive Pieces*, 'My Father'.

21. William Wordsworth, *The Prelude*, Book ix, 1–124; McDowell, *Irish Public Opinion*, p.145; William Drennan to Samuel McTier, 22 February 1793, PRONI, D591/391.

22. Vance, 'Celts, Carthaginians and Constitutions', pp.231–2.

23. Rutland MS, *Historical Manuscripts Commission*, Fourteenth Report, vol.3, pp.420–1.

24. [Arbuckle], *Short Account*, p.16. 'The Students have been brow-beaten and abused for acting the tragedies of *Cato* and *Tamerlane*. They have been called wicked and ungodly for endeavouring to raise in their minds the most beautiful sentiments of liberty and vertue, and to adorn their speech and behaviour with a becoming pronunciation and gesture.'

25. William Hazlitt, 'On Coffee-House Politicians', in *Table Talk*, in *The Complete Works of William Hazlitt*, P.P. Howe (ed.) (21 vols, J.M. Dent, London and Toronto, 1930–34), vol.8, pp.191–2, n.

26. Theobald Wolfe Tone, Journal, 13 July 1792, *Autobiography*, R. Barry O'Brien (ed.) (2 vols, Maunsell and Co., Dublin, 1912), vol.1, p.97.

27. *Northern Star*, 4 June 1795; McDowell, *Irish Public Opinion*, p.209.

28. S.O. Casaide, *The Irish Language in Belfast and Co. Down, 1601–1850* (M.H. Gill and Son, Dublin, 1930), pp.35, 40; *Guardian and Constitutional Advocate*, 18 March 1828.

29. O. Casaide, *Irish Language*, pp.22, 40.

30. Marianne Elliott, 'The Origins and Transformation of Early Irish Republican-ism', *International Review of Social History*, vol.23, part 3 (1978), p.405.

17 Maria Edgeworth: The Novelist and the Union

Iain Topliss

I

At the end of Maria Edgeworth's preface to *Castle Rackrent* there occurs a paragraph that has possibly puzzled many readers of a tale commonly taken to offer, in its portrait of the Rackrent family and especially Thady Quirk, a celebration of a distinct, nationally characteristic Irishness: 'Nations as well as individuals', Maria Edgeworth says, 'gradually lose attachment to their identity.' This remark is her cue to look forward to the effects of the legislative Union of January, 1801:

> When Ireland loses her identity by an union with Great Britain, she will look back with a smile of good-humoured complacency on the Sir Kits and Sir Condys of her former existence.[1]

What is surprising here is the equanimity with which the creator of Sir Kit, Sir Condy and Thady Quirk contemplates a severance in the continuity of national identity; the ease with which the past can be forgotten and farewelled.

It is clear that Maria Edgeworth envisages Ireland as about to pass through a decisive break in its history. 1782, the year of the Independence, had been one such break; 1801 is to be yet another. There are 'other times' and there is 'a present age' — both clearly distinguished from one another. There is an old 'identity' to be discarded and replaced by a new one. Underlying these convictions there is the belief that the allegiance of Ireland's true friends ought to be to its future, and that attachment to the past, to tradition, is something to be abandoned and forgotten.

It is possible that Maria Edgeworth and her father, R.L. Edgeworth, had always held opinions like these. If so, we do not find them articulated before late 1798, about nine months before the

Preface I have just quoted from was written. It is reasonable to assume that the events of 1798 and the debates about the proposed legislative Union with England helped crystallise attitudes that had previously remained fluid and indefinite. I take these remarks then to be the first indication of Maria Edgeworth's commitment to Unionist principles. This cast of mind is made more understandable in the Preface to the Edgeworths' *Essay on Irish Bulls*, published in 1802. There the Edgeworths digress at one point to chastise one of the most influential and well-regarded 'native' (that is Roman Catholic and Irish) historians of the 1770s, Sylvester O'Halloran, for the patriotic offence he once took at a passage derogatory to Ireland in Voltaire's *The Age of Louis the Fourteenth*. They dissociate themselves from the kind of patriotism implicit in such over-sensitivity to criticism, and they oppose to this what they see as a more realistic attitude to Ireland. 'We profess', they say, 'to be attached to the country only for its merits.'[2] By 'merits' the Edgeworths meant the potentialities latent in Ireland which the Union might be supposed to bring out, and which, in hastening the improvement of agriculture, the advancement of manufactures and commerce, would ultimately bind Ireland more and more closely with England. It is clear from what the Edgeworths go on to say that the contemporary Irishman has a choice of allegiances — either to the past or to the future — and that these alternatives are mutually exclusive.

For at this point the Edgeworths open up precisely the contrast, central to the Unionist cast of mind, between the Ireland of the historian (past, irrelevant and yet menacing in its reminder of an independent Irish identity), and the Ireland of the true friend (a future Ireland, politically tranquil and the site of indefinite improvement and amelioration). Thus they continue in satiric vein:

> We acknowledge it is a matter of indifference to us whether the Irish derive their origin from the Spaniards, or the Milesians, or the Welsh: we are not so violently anxious as we ought to be whether the language spoken by the Phoenician slave, in Terence's play, was Irish.[3]

These comments might seem fanciful or whimsical in their choice of target, but they are in fact directed at several key speculations of O'Halloran and other historians (or pseudo-historians) of the 1780s, who had pondered upon precisely such matters. They go on to tackle O'Halloran direct:

We moreover candidly confess that we are more interested in the
fate of its present race of inhabitants than the historian (that is,
O'Halloran) of St Patrick, St Facharis, St Cormuc; the renowned
Brian Boru; Tireldach, King of Connaught; McMurrough, King
of Leinster; Diarmod; Righ Damnha; Labra Loing Seach; Tigher-
mas; Ollamha-Foldha; the McGiolla-Phaidraigs; or even the great
William of Ogham; and by this declaration we have no fear of
giving offence to any but rusty antiquaries.[4]

It is a nicely calculated passage, given that O'Halloran traced his
descent from William of Ogham, and given also that it undermines
satirically the dignity and interest of many culture heroes dear to
the eighteenth-century Irish patriot. A frank indifference to a Gaelic,
Catholic past is contrasted with their own interest in Ireland's
'present race of inhabitants' and the new, imagined if as yet uncre-
ated, Ireland of the Union.

Maria Edgeworth's hostility to O'Halloran ought not to be taken
purely on its own terms, however. O'Halloran and other eighteenth-
century Irish historians had used their investigations into Ireland's
past in order to buttress broader arguments about Ireland's unique
pedigree as a nation and distinctive national character. These arguments in turn could be used to support a case for Ireland's political
independence from England. O'Halloran's demonstrations of the
organic coherence of Irish national identity, for example; his insistence that the native Irish, contrary to the common English belief
that they were barbarians, had been a 'polished' and 'learned' race
who had enjoyed one of the great civilisations of the ancient world;
his case that Ireland had never truly been conquered by the English
but had always maintained sovereignty over herself; these were
arguments as relevant in the years before 1801 as they had been in
the years before 1782. We know that the writing of history in Ireland
at the turn of the eighteenth century was an activity charged with
political implication; that contemporary histories of Ireland were,
as Professor Donal McCartney has argued, 'so many political pamphlets illustrating that part of public opinion which is concerned
with what men think about their past'.[5] What men think about their
past is of the utmost relevance to what they think about their future.
Maria Edgeworth's quarrel with O'Halloran has very little to do
with the fact that he was an antiquarian, and a great deal to do
with the fact that even antiquarian interests in 1800 carried a political
charge. Maria Edgeworth's conviction that Ireland's future lay in a

closer identification with England involved a corresponding belief that it was now time for Ireland to relinquish an attachment to its old identity. In 1800 O'Halloran was a somewhat dated figure. But, as Maria Edgeworth's obvious antagonism to him might suggest, his arguments could easily still encourage dangerously patriotic notions of an independent Ireland.

II

Castle Rackrent is a text that is largely untouched by the issues I have just described. It has been known for some time that *Castle Rackrent* was drafted in something like its final form by 1796–97, and that only the glossary and the preface were written under the shadow of the Rebellion. There is little warrant in its textual history for scrutinising *Castle Rackrent* for symptoms of a failure of Ascendancy nerve. Indeed, the reverse is true. As the geniality of its satire suggests, *Castle Rackrent* is an instance of a late-flowering Ascendancy self-confidence, rather than of an anxiety about its social or political role. It is because no such anxiety underlies the tale that Maria Edgeworth could permit herself to write a work that is in a certain sense a celebration of Irishness and Irish national distinctness. In the mid-1790s these notions had not acquired the political colouring they were to gain after the Rebellion. But if *Castle Rackrent* is a celebration of national distinctness, it is only incidentally so, for the author has other far more immediate ends in view.

Castle Rackrent tells the story of the decline of the Rackrent family over three generations, a descent from something like glory to absolute ignominy. By the end of the tale the family estates have been bought out from under them by a sometime factotum and agent, Jason Quirk. The most unusual aspect of the tale is that it is narrated by old Thady Quirk, Jason's father, who is an ancient family retainer. Thady is the half-comprehending witness of the family's decline, a family to which he is unshakably bound in a daze of semi-feudal loyalty.

The Rackrents, then, are landlords, and the tale clearly has something to say about landlordism. The question is, what exactly? A common way of reading *Castle Rackrent* has been to see it as a parable about the decline of the Ascendancy itself — a reading that has often been underpinned by the mistaken assumption that the tale was written during or after the Rebellion. But whether Maria Edgeworth intended the Rackrents to represent the post-1782 Ascendancy is open to doubt. In the first place the events of the tale are represented as taking place beyond a *cordon sanitaire*, a stretch of Irish history separated from the Ireland of the Independency by the magic date of 1782. (This was not only the date of Grattan's Parliament, but also the year in which the Edgeworths returned to take up permanent residence in Ireland.) These are 'tales of other times', as the preface reminds us, 'taken . . . from the manners of the Irish squires before the year 1782'. For Maria Edgeworth no germ of corruption can cross that gap in Irish history, and only because she believes this can she afford to satirise so vigorously a family that might otherwise be taken to represent her own caste, to which, of course, she always remained fiercely loyal.

Nor can we make a simple identification of the Rackrents with the Ascendancy in a more general way. As several critics have noticed, Maria Edgeworth is careful to inform us that the Rackrents are an Irish family. Their name is originally O'Shaughlin, 'related to the Kings of Ireland', as Thady tells us. To take up the Rackrent estates which come to them by inheritance they are obliged 'by Act of Parliament, to take and bear the sirname and arms of Rackrent'.[6] The text is strikingly silent about whether, as seems likely, they are also Roman Catholic. Had they been so, then under the Penal Laws they would also have to convert to the Church of Ireland. On these matters Thomas Flanagan, in his study *The Irish Novelists, 1800–1850*, argues that in making their triple denial of 'name . . . creed . . . blood' the Rackrents take on the sins of Ireland's masters. The misfortunes which subsequently dog the family are, Flanagan seems to imply, the signs of a retribution wrought upon the family by a vengeful God.[7]

If this is meant to describe the author's intention in writing *Castle Rackrent*, the tale would have been a truly remarkable one for Maria Edgeworth to have written. What seems more likely is that in creating the Rackrents, Maria Edgeworth is concentrating upon one strand within the complex social formation of the Ascendancy, and that this strand is Irish rather than English in its affiliations and characteristics. The Rackrents, that is, simply continue and confirm essentially Irish social manners. They show very little sign that they have taken their newly acquired role as Ireland's masters very seriously, or that they have in any way been affected by specifically Anglo-Irish *mores* or values. Their failings do not represent for

Maria Edgeworth the failings of the English element in Irish life, but rather stand as an indictment of typically Irish habits of mind, in particular of a superannuated, irrational, gestural mode of life, especially as it might centre upon notions of honour and hospitality. Indeed, the reverse was thought to be more often the case. This was a mode of life to which, notoriously, the Anglo-Irish tended to capitulate. The spectacle of English settlers becoming 'more Irish than the Irish' was proverbial in Irish history. With the Rackrents Maria Edgeworth satirises the attractions that encouraged that process and it is their unimproved Irishness which the tale exposes.

In what sense are they typically Irish? The portrait of the Rackrents is essentially a portrait of irrationalism, in the special sense in which Maria Edgeworth understood that term: an incapacity to think and act prudently by calculating the long-term consequences of one's actions, an inability to perceive where one's real self-interest might lie. Such irrationality finds expression in the various traits which characterise each of the Rackrents: Sir Patrick's drunken, self-defeating hospitality, Sir Murtagh's obsession with litigation, Sir Kit's gaming and Sir Condy's capitulation to a romanticised sense of the honour of the family. As a brief example, there is the case of Sir Patrick Rackrent. From his first appearance as heir to the estate, to his exit when his dead body is seized as security for certain unpaid debts, Sir Patrick barely takes up two pages of text. These are sufficient to show the world, in Thady's phrase, 'what was *in* Sir Patrick'. Principally, drink, as it turns out. Sir Patrick's irrational trait is his devotion to the honour of the family, which takes the form of a reckless and extravagant conception of proverbial Irish hospitality. His tale opens with one drunken party, to celebrate his inheritance of the estate. It ends with another, his birthday celebrations, in the course of which, after having drunk a bumper of claret, he falls down in a fit and is carried off to die alone in his room, while his guests carouse on, oblivious or indifferent, in the hall below. It goes without saying that his adherence to the traditions of Irish hospitality is not encumbered by an excessive devotion to his duties as the owner of a large estate. His sole contribution to the improvement of Ireland is the invention of raspberry whisky. 'Which is very likely', comments Thady, 'as no one has ever appeared to dispute it with him.'

Traits such as these determine the logic which guides the tale's apparently episodic plot. The logic is that of the Rackrents' self-impelled extinction. At the end of the tale they have effectively erased themselves from the public scene. But this is not for Maria Edgeworth a prophetic metaphor of the extinction of the Ascendancy. Rather, it is a fable about the inevitable self-defeat of irrationality, and of the equally inevitable self-extinction of the retrogressive element in the pre-1782 Ascendancy. In an odd way this story of decline and fall ultimately serves a vision of progress: the disappearance of the Rackrents actually clears the stage for the emergence of genuinely progressive elements in the national culture.

As I have already suggested, the portrait of the Rackrents is an ambivalent one. As well as framing a criticism of the Rackrents, the tale also makes them eccentrically interesting and sympathetic examples of Irish distinctness. They cannot be altogether contained by the satiric intentions of the author. If this is true of the Rackrents, it is even more true of the presentation of the tale's narrator, Thady Quirk. On the one hand, Maria Edgeworth disapproves of Thady. His over-mastering loyalty to the Rackrents and his inability to perceive their faults stand as an exemplification not just of a personal quirkiness, but of a nationally characteristic irrationality. When Sir Kit locks his wife away from the world for seven years, Thady describes the outrage with a laconic neutrality. It is not that he forbears to pass comment, rather that he feels that no comment is necessary in the first place: this is how your masters do things, this is how it is. Thady's idiosyncratic way of looking at life departs completely from the rational and reflective habits of mind that were normative for Maria Edgeworth. On the other hand, it is obvious that Maria Edgeworth loves Thady and that she delights in bringing him to life. She describes the creative process in a telling phrase: 'I could think and speak in [his character] without effort',[8] she once wrote, and it is easy to feel the absence of strain, the pleasure of surrendering to another persona, all through the tale.

As an example of this duality there is Thady's wholly approving account of the chicanery devised by Sir Condy during a general election to help him win a seat in Parliament.

> . . . many of our freeholders were knocked off [the electoral roll] having never had a freehold that they could safely swear to, and Sir Condy not willing to have any man perjure himself for his sake, as was done on the other side, God knows but no matter for that. — Some of our friends were dumb-founded by lawyers asking them — had they been on the ground where their freeholds lay? — Now Sir Condy being tender of the consciences of them

that had not been on the ground, and so could not swear to a freehold when cross-examined by them lawyers, sent out for a couple of cleaves-full of sods of his farm of Gulteeshinnagh: and as soon as the sods came into town he set each man on his sod, and so then ever after, you know, they could fairly swear they had been on the ground.[9]

Thady sums up. 'We won the day by this piece of honesty.' The incident displays habits of mind of which the author disapproves (the Edgeworths were strict upon what they saw as the Irish peasant's willingness to bend the truth).[10] At the same time it is impossible not to feel Thady's distinct charm and likableness.

But Thady is important in another, far more subversive way. What is truly innovative about *Castle Rackrent* is that the narrative is entirely handed over to Thady. In doing this Maria Edgeworth effects a symbolic redistribution of power within her culture. With Thady as narrator, Maria Edgeworth establishes an adversary presence within Anglo-Ireland's official literary culture. It would be naive to deny that Thady as a literary creation is hedged by a dozen literary conventions, and I am not suggesting that with Thady we get a peasant voice unmediated by the consciousness of the Anglo-Irish woman who created him. But in allowing herself to impersonate so freely the voice of the repressed other in the national community, Maria Edgeworth was doing something dangerous. The peasant, as was beginning to be recognised at this time, was the embodiment of a distinctly Irish national identity: Cockery's 'residual legatees of a civilization that was more than a thousand years old'. Michael Hurst, in his study *Maria Edgeworth and the Public Scene*, sums up this notion in a suggestive passage:

> From the time when the old Irish Catholic upper class was either dispossessed and fled as 'Wild Geese' to the continent, or went over to the enemy, lock stock and barrel, the Catholic peasant had become the sole repository of the profound sense of national distinctness felt in Catholic Ireland.[11]

In Thady this hitherto denied Ireland finds, for the first time perhaps, an identity and a voice. A denied Ireland now has the legitimacy which recognising a voice and admitting it into the authorised spaces of an official culture always confers. *Castle Rackrent's* celebration of Thady's distinctiveness, although the object of fairly obvious

authorial satire, takes its place alongside other contemporary stir-
rings of embryonic Gaelic consciousness, and helps inaugurate a
tradition of literary exploration of the other side of Ireland.

The difficulty for Maria Edgeworth with both the Rackrents and
Thady is, we may surmise, that because they are so attractive
they can be read in non-satiric ways, and become an involuntary
celebration of that very national distinctiveness, that old identity,
which, once the tale had been completed, Maria Edgeworth felt the
nation had to abandon. Maria Edgeworth was always conscious of
the difficulty of writing about Ireland. In 1834, for example, after
the Edgeworths' tenants voted against them for the first time, Maria
Edgeworth rejected the consequent political turmoil as a suitable
subject for fiction: 'It is impossible to draw Ireland as she now is in
a book of fiction — realities are too strong, party passions too
violent to bear to see, or care to look at their faces in the looking-
glass.'[12] As a didactic writer she was conscious that her tales
were not just stories about Ireland but interventions in its history,
interventions that had to be circumspectly managed. After the
Rebellion and the Union Ireland demanded a different kind of
fiction from that offered by *Castle Rackrent*, and this is no doubt
why Maria Edgeworth never wrote the continuation of the memoirs
of the Rackrent family she was often asked to write.

III

The Unionist views which Maria Edgeworth and her father came
to adopt after 1798 involved the obliteration of those signs of
national distinctiveness which *Castle Rackrent* betrays, and in the
obliteration of such differences the gradual blending of the Irish
national character with that of England. The words 'blending',
'merging' and 'identifying', form a cluster of key terms for many
analysts of Ireland's relations to England from Burke to Matthew
Arnold. In Burke's view Ireland differed from all other countries
which had a similar history of invasion and conquest in one important particular. In all other countries the passage of time had
'blended and coalited the conquerers with the conquered'.[13] No
such coalition had occurred in Ireland. On the contrary, to take up
Arnold's case, in Ireland

the conquest had again and again to be renewed, the sense of prescription, the true security of property never arose. The angry memory of conquest and confiscation, the ardour for revolt against them, have continued . . . to irritate and inflame men's minds.[14]

The answer was to be found in 'blending' the Irish and English elements in Ireland, to make the Irish (as Arnold put it, a trifle optimistically) 'find in us . . . an attractive force, drawing and binding them to us'.[15]

This same notion is central to the Edgeworths' own Unionism, as we see from R.L. Edgeworth's most explicit statement on the subject. This is the (as yet unpublished) draft of a letter to an unidentified peer on the subject of the Union, dated 26 January 1800. 'The question of the Union', R.L. Edgeworth wrote, 'depends upon the question of identification', adding that it appeared to him that the countries 'must necessarily be identified'. Involved in this hope was the allaying of anxieties that had been reawakened in many Anglo-Irish minds after the Rebellion: 'the hope of establishing the Catholic religion, and Catholic claims to ancient forfeitures must be radically destroyed by melting the people of both nations into one mass'.[16]

With remarks like that we are back to the position adopted by Maria Edgeworth in the preface to *Castle Rackrent*, with its confident expectation that Ireland would soon willingly abandon its old identity and embrace a new one as part of the great imperial family. Ireland, in R.L. Edgeworth's lapidary phrase, should become 'as Yorkshire to Great Britain'. Convictions such as these, which crystallised in the years after the Rebellion, explain why Maria Edgeworth's subsequent Irish tales should be so unlike *Castle Rackrent*, and why there is a break in the continuity of Maria Edgeworth's *oeuvre* analagous to the break in the continuity of Irish history made by 1801.

The Absentee, published in the second series of *Tales of Fashionable Life* in 1812, is Edgeworth's most determinedly Unionist work of fiction. It tells of the incognito return to Ireland of Lord Colambre, whose parents are absentee landlords, and who dissipate their time and income in London. Colambre's journey into Ireland is partly one of discovery. He sees Ireland for the first time in all its diversity and contradictoriness. He also comes to realise its possibilities as a country. The journey also allows him to recover an identity: he finds in Ireland a vocation and a social role. This in turn is offered by the tale as an exemplification of the benevolent and restorative effect upon Ireland of the return of a responsible landowning class.

The Absentee differs from *Castle Rackrent* in a number of important respects. The narrative is now back in the hands of an anonymous, omniscient, third-person narrator whose manner is judicious, rational, dispassionate and authoritative — these 'English' characteristics contrast completely with Thady's Irishness. The Ireland of this tale is one that is located firmly in the present (not set back 20 years), continuous with the time and act of writing of the tale. Although *The Absentee* offers us a diverse and immensely varied representation of Ireland, it is dominated by the essentially English presence of the hero, Lord Colambre. Responsible, concerned, rational, reflective, positive-minded, anxious to improve both himself and his country, Colambre is that ideal representative of a rejuvenated Ascendancy that *Castle Rackrent* so strikingly lacks. Unlike *Castle Rackrent* which concentrates upon a single family and a single locality, creating a sense of almost tribal confinement, *The Absentee* aims to give a panoramic view of the country. The narrative gaze includes peasantry, tenantry and landowners, both urban and rural Ireland. It shows members of the commercial as well as military class. It includes both Catholic and Protestant. It attempts to introduce the reader to both the retrogressive and progressive elements in Ireland. The essential project of the book is to harmonise all these discrepant elements within its narrative embrace. In this way the tale performs a metaphorical act of union of its own, suggesting how through the beneficient influence of someone like Colambre, Ireland might be united and made whole. Finally, whereas the narrative of *Castle Rackrent* enacts a process of decay and disintegration leading to a point of exhaustion and termination in Irish history, the movement of *The Absentee* is one of improvement and amelioration, leading out into an optimistically viewed future.

There are numerous instances in which the process of Union is enacted in the novel. Sir James Brooke gives a careful account of the intricate adjustments to the social life of Dublin that occur after the Union. This results, he tells Colambre, in a blending of hereditary authority and meritocratic ability. After a period of social turmoil marked by the absence of the aristocracy who retreat to their country houses and the preponderance in Dublin society of the *nouveaux riches* who fill their places, there occurs a reconciliation of these and other social groupings. In Dublin, Colambre will now find, Brooke assures him, 'a salutary mixture of birth and education, gentility and knowledge . . . new life and energy, new talent, new ambition, a desire and determination to improve and be improved — a perception that higher distinction can now be obtained . . . by genius and merit, than airs and address'.[17] There is the marriage between Lord Colambre and the heroine, Grace Nugent.

Grace is a symbolic figure in the tale. Her rational attachment to Ireland is pointedly established very early on, when she describes herself not as a partisan for Ireland but as a 'friend'. This is a significant term for the Edgeworths: the 'friend to Ireland', as opposed to the patriot or partisan, they conceive to have a judicious, rational attachment to the country, a clear-sighted understanding of its faults but also an effective grasp of how the country might be improved. (Both Colambre and Sir James Brooke describe themselves at different points as friends to Ireland.) For these reasons Grace is the person in the tale who most assists Colambre's recovery of his social identity. When it appears that he cannot marry her, he reflects that 'since he had forbidden himself to think of an union with Miss Nugent, his mind had lost its object and its spring'.[18] The term 'union' used here hardly seems fortuitous and allows the political implications of the word to play over the marriage of hero and heroine. Grace is, as Flanagan observes, a descendant of the Nugent family 'which had been expropriated, long before, from the lands of Nugentstown, the Colambre holdings'.[19] At the end of the tale Grace returns to Colambre Castle with Colambre and their marriage is foreshadowed. In marrying her, Colambre will heal yet another breach in Irish history. On their return a blind harper plays the old air 'Gracey Nugent' to welcome them. As this suggests, Grace stands as an embodiment of Hibernia herself — a contrary image no doubt to the one mentioned by Maria Edgeworth in a letter to her brother written in 1799, describing a print she had seen of 'a woman meant for Hibernia, dressed in orange and green, and holding a pistol in her hand to oppose the Union'.[20]

One of the most fascinating figures in the tale is, however, Count O'Halloran. His name is surely meant to recall the historian whose arguments Maria Edgeworth had pilloried in *The Essay on Irish Bulls*. Of all the representative figures in a novel populated by representative figures, he is one of the most important. As most commentators have seen, O'Halloran is brought into the novel to represent Ireland's Catholic and Gaelic past. His title and military experience, for instance, are continental, and in this he recalls the Wild Geese. He dresses in the style of 50 years previous — he wears a queue, a gold-laced hat and long skirts to a gold waistcoat. His house is decorated with archaeological finds, for the Count has a Seamus Heaney-like fascination with bogs: skeletons of Irish elk and moose-deer adorn his study. His astonished guests find a menagerie of animals loose in the castle, and Flanagan designates his Irish wolfhound an emblem of Ireland.[21] His library contains volumes on Irish antiquities, and one of his books, *The Burial Places of the Nugents*, will play a part in unravelling the mystery surrounding Grace Nugent's birth. Indeed, O'Halloran plays a major role in bringing Grace and Colambre together. It is worth adding that O'Halloran is a father-substitute for Colambre, making up for many of the qualities that his father lacks, notably an attachment to Ireland.

Much has been made of all this. Flanagan argues in his attempt to recover at least part of the novel for a nationalist reading that it is only through O'Halloran that Edgeworth is able to offer any valid insight into Irish life.

> O'Halloran is Maria Edgeworth's oblique answer to those questions of identity which otherwise the novel poses only to avoid. The old man who spends his days hunting the traditional game of Ireland and spends his nights poring over its great names and monuments represents an ideal past.[22]

'Oblique' is certainly a necessary qualifier when we recall other details of O'Halloran's presentation in the tale. Certainly he stands for an Ireland that is not readily identifiable with the eighteenth-century Ascendancy. But he also embodies the continuity of that past into the present, and suggests the ways in which that Ireland might connect with the Ireland of the Union. In this he too is an instance of the novel's concern with Union. O'Halloran is pointedly made to validate existing political arrangements by, for instance, approving of the presence of the Engish military presence in Ireland: 'he rejoiced in the advantages Ireland, and he hoped he might be permitted to add, England, would probably derive from the exchange of the militia of both countries: habits would be improved, ideas enlarged'.[23] 'The two countries', he thinks, 'have the same interest'. The point is clinched a few pages later when O'Halloran is discovered to have been reading Charles Pasley's *Essay on the Military Policy and Institutions of Great Britain*, a strongly imperialist work in which the author defends the connection between Ireland and England.[24] It is clear that O'Halloran's role in the novel is to be incorporated into the Ascendancy version of the national community, and that he is emphatically not there as an alternative to it: yet another instance of 'union'.

To conclude, I should like to return briefly to the question of the relinquishing of the narrative to an authorial persona. I have suggested that the surrender of the role of the narrator to a previously denied voice is one of the things that makes *Castle Rackrent* a subversive work. *The Absentee* concludes with a pointed allusion to this, and with a strategic reworking of the narrative principle of the earlier work. At the end of *The Absentee* the tale is once again handed over to a denied voice, this time to Larry Brady, the Irish peasant who has acted as Colambre's unofficial guide and companion through Ireland. Larry is obviously meant to remind us of Thady, but it is a measure of the extent to which *The Absentee* strives to revitalise the Ascendancy's claims to own Ireland that he says things we cannot imagine Thady saying.

Larry's is a tamed voice and his task in the tale is all too clear. His letter to his absentee brother in London with which the tale ends, is designed to establish that the process of amelioration has already begun in the Clonbrony's corner of Ireland, and that the benevolent influence of the responsible landlord has begun to flow down and irrigate the lower reaches of Irish society. Larry's celebration of his master's return concludes with an invitation to yet another union and annulment of absence and separation: '. . . so haste to the wedding that is, of Grace and Colambre . . . and another thing Pat, you would not be out of fashion — and you see its growing the fashion not to be an Absentee'.[25]

This leads me to one final observation. Obviously enough we see in Larry's letter a piece of authorial ventriloquism designed to legitimise the owner's tenure upon his land, and his consequent right to social and political privilege. If this is so, then it is clear that Larry's welcoming of Colambre has a dual aspect to it. What this desire on behalf of the author concedes is that Larry is the source of a sovereignty within the native Irish, and that the Ascendancy political authority is not complete unless it can in some way tap that authority. Even as official a version of Anglo-Ireland as *The*

Absentee has its point of self-blindness from which its essential premiss can be dismantled.

Notes and References

1. Maria Edgeworth, *Castle Rackrent*, George Watson (ed.) (Oxford UP, Oxford, 1964), p.5.

2. Maria Edgeworth and R.L. Edgeworth, 'An Essay on Irish Bulls', in Maria Edgeworth, *Tales and Novels* (18 vols, Baldwin and Cradock, London, 1832–33), vol.1, p.278.

3. Ibid., pp.278–9.

4. Ibid., p.279.

5. Donal McCartney, 'The Writing of History in Ireland, 1800–1830', *Irish Historical Studies*, vol.10, no.40 (1957), p.353.

6. Edgeworth, *Castle Rackrent*, p.9.

7. See Thomas Flanagan, *The Irish Novelists, 1800–1850* (Columbia UP, New York, 1958), pp.78–9.

8. Maria Edgeworth to Mrs Stark, 6 September 1834, quoted in Marilyn Butler, *Maria Edgeworth. A Literary Biography* (Oxford UP, Oxford, 1972), p.240.

9. Edgeworth, *Castle Rackrent*, p.56.

10. See, for example, the Edgeworths' remarks on the Irish peasants' instinctive evasiveness in their *Practical Education* (2 vols, Johnson, London, 1798), vol.1, pp.208–10.

11. Michael Hurst, *Maria Edgeworth and the Public Scene* (Macmillan, London, 1962), p.17.

12. Maria Edgeworth to Michael Pakenham Edgeworth, 14 February 1834, quoted in Butler, *Maria Edgeworth*, p.452.

13. Edmund Burke, 'A Letter to Sir H. Langrishe, Bart., MP on the subject of the Roman Catholics of Ireland', in *The Works of the Rt Hon. Edmund Burke*, F.W. Raffety (ed.) (6 vols, Oxford UP, London, 1906–7), vol.5, p.183.

14. Matthew Arnold, 'The Incompatibles', in *The Complete Works of Matthew Arnold*, R.H. Super (ed.) (11 vols, University of Michigan Press, Ann Arbor, 1960–77), vol.9, p.243.

15. Ibid., p.270.

16. R.L. Edgeworth to an unidentified peer, 26 January 1800. National Library of Ireland, Edgeworth Papers, MS 10166–7.

17. Edgeworth, *Tales and Novels*, vol.xi, p.120.

18. Ibid., vol.ix, p.186.

19. Flanagan, *The Irish Novelists*, p.91.

20. Maria Edgeworth to Charlotte Sneyd, 2 April 1799, published in Frances Edgeworth, *A Memoir of Maria Edgeworth* (3 vols, privately printed, London, 1867), vol.i, p.96.

21. Flanagan, *The Irish Novelists*, p.89.

22. Ibid., pp.89–90.

23. Edgeworth, *Tales and Novels*, vol.ix, p.168.

24. Ibid.

25. Ibid., p.54.

Index